NATO and the Defense of the West

NATO and the Defense of the West

An Analysis of America's First Line of Defense

Laurence Martin

Holt, Rinehart and Winston
New York

Copyright © 1985 by Nomad Publishers Ltd.

First published in the United States by Holt, Rinehart
and Winston, 383 Madison Avenue, New York,
New York 10017.

Published simultaneously in Canada by Holt, Rinehart
and Winston of Canada, Limited.

Originally published in Great Britain under the title
Before the Day After: Can NATO Defend Europe?

Library of Congress Cataloging in Publication Data
Martin, Laurence W.
NATO and the Defense of the West

Originally published: Before the day after.

Includes index
1. North Atlantic Treaty Organization — Armed Forces.
2. World War III. 3. Warfare, Conventional. I. Title.
UA646.3.M26   1985   355'.031'091821   85-16355

ISBN 0-03-006018-4

First American Edition

This book was designed by Edward Kinsey

Illustrations by:
Peter Sarson and Tony Bryan, Tony Gibbons,
Phil Jacobs, Simon Roulstone, David Mallott,
Malcolm Porter and Jillian Burgess
Artists/Mike Saunders

Filmset by Pre-Print Photosetting (Leeds) Ltd., UK.

Colour separations by Paramount Litho

Printed and bound in Italy by Grafica Editoriale,
Bologna

Created and produced by Nomad Publishers Ltd.,
The Grange, Grange Yard, London SE1 3AG.

10 9 8 7 6 5 4 3 2 1

CONTENTS

Preface

While a global nuclear war is the ultimate danger facing the world as a result of international tension and the armed camps into which it divides the world, by far the greatest proportion of military expenditure goes to maintain the confrontation between NATO and the Warsaw Pact in Europe. It is here, also, that the spark igniting a global holocaust might find its driest tinder. This book presents some of the facts of this confrontation in its military aspects and briefly discusses their significance. The facts and numerous important and illuminating comparisons between them are very largely shown in graphic form in the hope that this will help the reader supplement or even contradict the author's conclusions with his own.

Professor Laurence Martin
University of Newcastle Upon Tyne
August 1985

Acknowledgements

My thanks are due to **John Pay,** of the Royal Naval College, Greenwich, for his energetic and ingenious contribution to devising and compiling the graphic material, to Shirley Fallaw for her usual impeccable administrative assistance and to Alison Pickard for her patient and perceptive preparation of the manuscript.

The Strategic Significance of Europe

By far the worst catastrophe that today's military machines could bring upon the world would be an all-out nuclear war between the Russian and American Superpowers. So obvious is this danger, however, and so elaborate the system 'of mutual deterrence that stabilizes the so-called "strategic nuclear balance", that it is hard to imagine either side starting such a war with a "bolt from the blue" attack. A much more likely way for the ultimate catastrophe to occur would be a gradual process of "escalation", much of it possibly unintentional, from some limited conflict that initially seemed quite manageable.

For such a conflict to escalate would require high stakes and much the highest stakes at risk in a military confrontation today lie in Europe. It is in Europe, therefore, that the source of the ultimate nuclear catastrophe can most plausibly be imagined and in Europe, for the same reason, that the most powerful array of armed force the world has ever seen is currently assembled.

It is easy to appreciate why Europe has become the leading theatre of potential war. Europe is of immense geopolitical significance to both Superpowers. For the Soviet Union, Europe is the traditional source of military danger and invasion; to occupy Eastern Europe and maintain a permanent military threat over the lands to the West, as the Soviet Union has done since 1945, is the realization of a centuries old Russian design for security. For its part, the United States, despite its early tradition of isolationism, has twice this century felt itself impelled into World Wars to prevent the domination of Europe by a single, militaristic and potentially hostile power. The Cold War between the

Right: Closest geographical neighbours in the Northern Pacific and, significantly in the missile age, across the Arctic, the projection of American military power in NATO places the most important confrontation between the Superpowers in Europe and makes it the strategic centre of the world.
The extensive interests and military reach of the Superpowers ensure, however, that any armed conflict in Europe would inevitably have repercussions in many other areas of the world. Equally, the Superpowers are involved in numerous disputes, tensions and, at least indirectly, wars around the globe, any of which could conceivably bring about a direct confrontation which could feed back into Europe. The European balance thus affects both the course and the consequences of much wider military events. The map also gives some idea of the comparative military power and potential of some of the more important other actors on the strategic scene.

Areas of instability/border disputes

Population in millions

Size of armies
figures in thousands

GNP figure in $ billions

USA
3265 237 7 81

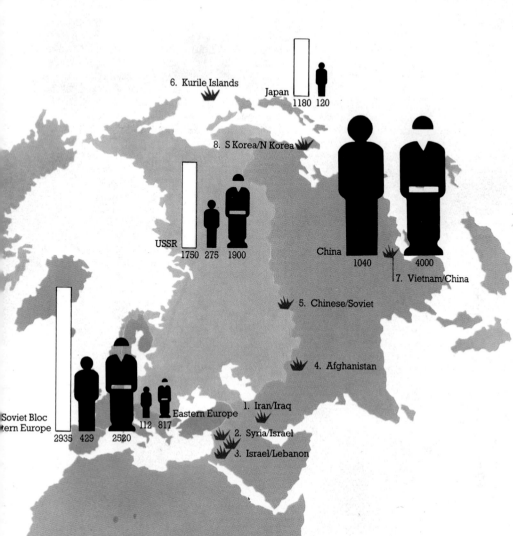

6. Kurile Islands

Japan
1180   120

8. S Korea/N Korea

USSR
1750   275   1900

China
1040   4000

7. Vietnam/China

5. Chinese/Soviet

4. Afghanistan

Soviet Bloc
ern Europe
2935   429   2520   112   817

Eastern Europe

1. Iran/Iraq

2. Syria/Israel

3. Israel/Lebanon

9

United States and the Soviet Union, which still polarizes world politics, quite naturally has its origins in Europe and in the key European geopolitical question of how the great economic and inherent military power of Germany should be disposed. Even today, despite the rise of Japan and the other nations of the Pacific Basin, the greatest aggregation of industrial and strategic power outside the Superpowers resides in Europe; shifted from the American side of the equation to the Soviet, Western Europe would decisively tip the global balance of power.

Europe also has a significance beyond material calculations. Geographically it flanks the energy rich Middle East and the link between Asia and Africa. Culturally it has colonized most of the world. Both Superpowers have their ideological roots in Europe: the United States in English democracy; the Soviet Union in German Marxism. Control of Europe has profound political as well as strategic significance.

For all these reasons it is not surprising that a formidable and well-defined military confrontation has grown up in Europe, organized around two great standing alliances, the Warsaw Pact and the North Atlantic Alliance. These alliances and the military balance established between them, constantly manned and ever alert, have created a sense of stability in this potentially explosive area. The stability is, however, an artificial one, only maintained by constant effort and renewal.

Internally, the alliances are far from quies-cent. In the Warsaw Pact, the Soviet satellites are restless and rebellious. In the North Atlantic Alliance, the European allies of the United States dispute American strategic priorities, grumble under military burdens, and sometimes toy with degrees of neutralism. Meanwhile technology ensures that the military side of the competition is in constant evolution, each side anxiously calculating the shifting balance. The forces which stabilize the situation are also the potential source of disaster, and the local European confrontation that might lead to global nuclear war itself embodies thousands of nuclear weapons, many far more destructive than those that destroyed Hiroshima and Nagasaki.

Below: Manpower is a military resource that can only be produced or substituted for by wealth to a limited degree. Population and gross national product are consequently the two most commonly used crude indicators of military potential. On this basis the preponderant resources of the NATO camp are clearly apparent. Data on the Warsaw Pact economies are uncertain, probably even to the Soviet authorities, as a result of the arbitrary pricing system. Nevertheless it is very obvious that to maintain its effective military competition with the United States and NATO generally, the Soviet Union must tax its population and economy much more severely.

Comparative national resources

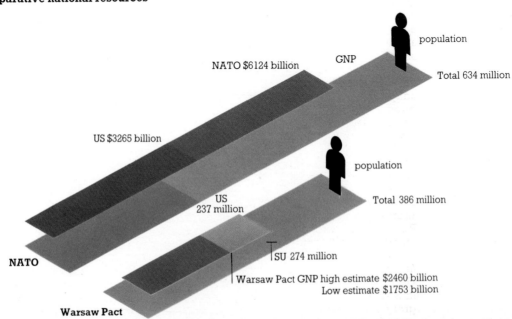

NATO $6124 billion

GNP

population

Total 634 million

US $3265 billion

US 237 million

population

Total 386 million

SU 274 million

NATO

Warsaw Pact GNP high estimate $2460 billion
Low estimate $1753 billion

Warsaw Pact

Origins of NATO and the Warsaw Pact

The origins of the two great alliances were closely linked. Within two or three years of the end of the Second World War relations between the Western democracies and the Soviet Union became sufficiently strained to give rise to the term Cold War and the dividing line between the West and Soviet dominated Eastern Europe earned Winston Churchill's description "Iron Curtain". The Russian engineered coup in Czechoslovakia in 1948 and the blockade of Western communications with Berlin, established in the same year, suggested a Soviet desire to move the Curtain westward and the apparent preponderant military power sustained by the Soviet Union's failure to match the Western pace of postwar demobilization created an overhanging threat of renewed aggression.

Fear that this threat might combine with Communist subversive forces in Western Europe to impede the economic recovery based upon the American Marshall Plan in 1947, led the United States, strongly encouraged by the United Kingdom, to organize the North Atlantic Alliance, which was created by the Treaty signed in April 1949. This Treaty was, in fact, the first formal alliance concluded by the United States since that concluded with France in 1778 during the Revolutionary War and thus marked a major reversal of American traditional isolationism.

The initial intention was that the Alliance, with its contingent promise of American support for the co-operative military efforts already undertaken by Britain, France and other West European nations on the basis of the Brussels Treaty of 1948, would suffice to warn the Soviet Union against aggression and reassure European public opinion. Rightly or wrongly the Soviet inspired invasion of South Korea in June 1950, following the unexpectedly early Soviet test of a nuclear explosive device the previous August, aroused fears that an active military phase in Russian expansion was about to begin. This prompted the conversion of the Alliance into the unprecedented standing military organization we know today. After a major political debate over "Troops to Europe", the United States committed itself to reinforce its garrison in Europe, making what had hitherto been a residual occupation force left over from the defeat of Nazi Germany, into a continuing feature of the postwar world. Perhaps even more important, the United States agreed to provide an American officer of great prestige, General Dwight Eisenhower, as Supreme Allied Commander, Europe (SACEUR), thereby symbolizing the commitment of American military prestige to the defence of Europe. Ever since, this office has been held by an American, a practice which not only reassures Europeans about the commitment of the United States to their defence, but gives Americans ground for confidence that the strategy of the alliance follows lines compatible with American interests. Under and alongside SACEUR has grown up an elaborate machinery for strategic planning, for training, and for military command in war.

When NATO began, it possessed hardly any of the armed forces necessary for effective defence. Few of the forces that nominally existed were organized in operational fighting units and equipment was obsolescent material left over from the recent war. It soon became apparent that adequate forces could only be provided if the numerous and military adept West Germans were rearmed. The Soviet Union was already raising military units in the Eastern Zone. To rearm the Germans so soon after the defeat of Hitler was a highly controversial proposal. French opposition was particularly strong and there was in fact relatively little enthusiasm among the West German public. Nevertheless after much soul-searching, the new Federal Republic of Germany (FRG) became a member of NATO in 1955, Greece and Turkey having already been added in 1952. (Spain signed the Treaty in 1981 but its full membership remained a subject of domestic debate for several years.)

The rearmament of the FRG was taken by the Soviet Union as the cue to formalize the military relationships it had been establishing with its Eastern European satellites by creating the Warsaw Pact. This Pact, signed on May 15, 1955, had an original period of validity of twenty years, and was renewed in 1975 and again in 1985. Being ostensibly a retort to NATO, however, the Pact would theoretically lapse if NATO disbanded.

The Treaty of Friendship, Co-operation and Multinational Assistance, as it is formally designated, is supposed to be a framework for multilateral collaborative efforts between the Soviet Union and Bulgaria, Czechoslovakia, East Germany, Hungary, Poland and Rumania. In practice the organization is wholly dominated by the Soviet Union, which dictates strategy and training, and compels East European participation in the manufacture of weapons standardized on Soviet designs. Possibly in part to provide for any future nominal disbandment of the Warsaw Pact, the Soviet Union has subsequently negotiated a series of bilateral pacts that tie the East Europeans to each other and to the Soviet Union. Moreover "status of forces" agreements authorize a heavy Soviet military presence in East Germany, Poland and Hungary. The role of these forces in disciplining the "host" countries is well-exemplified by the later status agreement of October, 1968, with Czechoslovakia, following the suppression of Czech independence by the invasion of other Pact members. This agreement both established a permanent Soviet military occupation of Czechoslovakia and brought several first-class Soviet divisions that much further forward in their deployment against NATO. The somewhat fictional nature of the Warsaw Pact is also illustrated by the fact that its military command structure came into existence before the ratification of the original Treaty.

Essentially the purpose of the Pact is to facilitate the forward deployment of Soviet forces to defend the Soviet Union and threaten Western Europe, while extracting whatever military assistance possible from the Eastern Europeans. No refusal to participate is tolerated. This is not to say that the Soviet Union gets exactly what it wants. The Eastern Europeans are reluctant to make all the military efforts demanded of them and have from time to time resisted Soviet attemps to extract more resources, and refused to undertake all the exercises demanded or even, on occasions, to lend the Soviet Union full-blooded diplomatic support. Rumania is notoriously recalcitrant. It has the good fortune, however, to lie in an area less strategically crucial than the northern tier countries of Poland, Czechoslovakia and, above all, East Germany. In this area Soviet supervision is close under the watchful eye of Soviet garrisons. Nevertheless the reliability of East European armed forces as Soviet allies in war and crisis is debatable. Much would doubtless depend on what form the East-West crisis took. For historical reasons Soviet problems would be greatly diminished if the blame could plausibly be laid at the door of the FRG.

Command Structure of NATO

The highest authority in NATO is the North Atlantic Council, a forum for political consultation and co-ordination between the allies. At least twice a year the Council meets at ministerial level, with members represented by their Foreign Ministers. Since the departure of France from the integrated military command structure in 1966, in accordance with President de Gaulle's policy of retaining completely independent national decision over the structure and employment of French armed forces, purely military questions are discussed by the remaining allies in the Defence Planning Committee. This also has biannual sessions at the level of Defence Ministers. The Secretary-General of NATO, who controls the international staff of the Alliance, is also permanent Chairman of the North Atlantic Council and Defence Planning Committee. Permanent national representatives (Permreps) at ambassadorial level provide continuity and meet at least once a week.

Under the Defence Planning Committee, the Military Committee, composed of national Chiefs of Staff of the countries that participate in the integrated military structure, constitutes the supreme military authority. It advises the Council and Defence Planning Committee on the one hand, and guides the Major NATO Commanders on the other. On the same pattern as the Council, the Military Committee meets twice a year at Chief of Staff level and continuously through Permanent Military Representatives.

In the early days of NATO a Standing Group of the United States, United Kingdom, and France provided staff to carry out studies and administer policy. When France left the integrated military structure in 1966, the Standing Group dissolved and in 1967 a permanent International Military Staff was established to service the Military Committee. This staff now comprises some 150 officers with associated support services. The staff is directed by a "three star" officer reporting to the Chairman of the Military Committee. This group works in liaison with the permanent political staff that reports to the Secretary-General. Within the Military Staff, six Assistant Directors control divisions for Intelligence, Plans and Policy, Operations, Management and Logistics, Command, Control and Communications (C^3) and Armament Standardization.

The military planning and command structure of the Alliance is shared between three major allied commands, one each for Europe (Allied Command Europe or ACE), the Atlantic area (Allied Command Atlantic or ACLANT), and the Channel area (Allied Command Channel or ACCHAN), the last supposedly a recognition of the importance and special characteristics of the "Western Approaches" but in the eyes of some a sop to British naval pride. Outside these commands there is also a Regional Planning Committee to discuss joint Canadian-American concerns.

Right: The NATO Council exemplifies the large number of political voices that must be coordinated to maintain the cohesion of the alliance and the subordination of the military command to political control. (The figures round the military table are illustrative; all but France, Greece and Iceland participate). The military arm of NATO both depends upon political cohesion for support and tries to provide a sufficiently strong sense of security to permit such cohesion. The dominant role of SACEUR is apparent.

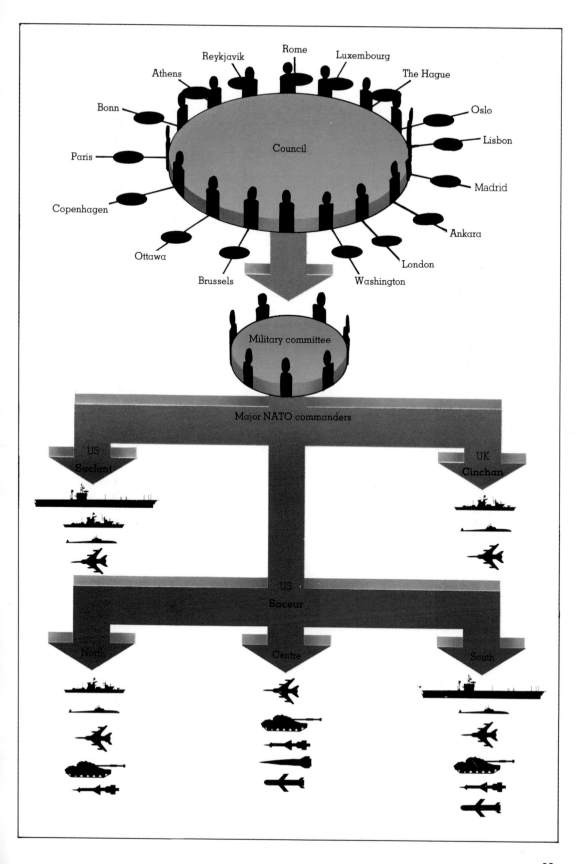

Council

Athens
Reykjavik
Rome
Luxembourg
The Hague
Bonn
Oslo
Paris
Lisbon
Copenhagen
Madrid
Ottawa
Ankara
Brussels
London
Washington

Military committee

Major NATO commanders

US
Saclant

UK
Cinchan

US
Saceur

North

Centre

South

The three Major Commanders are, respectively, Supreme Allied Commander Europe (SACEUR), who has by far the greatest responsibilities and the largest portion of allied forces, based at Casteau, near Mons in Belgium; Supreme Allied Commander, Atlantic (SACLANT), based at Norfolk, Virginia and, like SACEUR, always an American; and Commander in Chief, Channel (CINCCHAN), based at Northwood, near London, and always British. The last two are, of course, always naval officers, while both army and airforce officers have been SACEUR, though the former is much more common.

Member countries assign units to the Major Commanders, who can rely on their availability in crisis and war, while "earmarking" other units that would probably be assigned in war. Some national forces are retained for purely national purposes; as a matter of principle the FRG assigns all its forces.

SACEUR is responsible for defence from the North Cape of Norway to the shore of North Africa, including the Mediterranean Sea, and from the Atlantic to Turkey's border with the Soviet Union in the Caucasus. (The United Kingdom and Portugal as such do not fall within a major NATO command.)

In wartime SACEUR would be the supreme operational commander of all allied operations within his area of responsibility whether by land, sea or air. National armed forces retain responsibility for internal defence of their own territory but this would not override operations SACEUR might carry out as part of the overall defence of the Alliance.

In peacetime SACEUR is responsible for supervising the organization, training and equipment of allied forces. One of his most important tasks is to determine what the force requirements are for a successful defence in the light of his intelligence about Warsaw Pact forces, and pressing allied governments to provide what is necessary. Under SACEUR come three subordinate commands, Northern, based at Kolsaas, near Oslo; Central, based at Brunssum, Netherlands; and Southern, based at Naples. SACEUR also controls the ACE Mobile Force, and is executive commander of the relatively new NATO Airborne Early Warning Force, use of which is shared by all three Major Commanders. The Mobile Force is a small multinational land and air-force intended to be deployed early in crises when desired to symbolize the involvement of the Alliance in local crises as well as to assist in the practical management of crises.

The Allied Command Atlantic stretches from the North Pole to the southern alliance boundary on the Tropic of Cancer, and from the Atlantic sea-board of the United States to the shores of Europe and Africa, excluding CINCCHAN's domain in the Channel and UK territorial waters. SACLANT'S task is to develop plans and to conduct training exercises. His wartime task would be the protection of Atlantic sea-routes and the mounting of offensive operations against Warsaw Pact forces and in support of SACEUR. To facilitate liaison, and provide a ready force symbolic of allied solidarity, SACLANT controls a multinational force of surface ships, the Standing Naval Force Atlantic (STANFORLANT).

SACLANT controls six subordinate commands: Western Atlantic Command, STANFORLANT, Striking Force Atlantic, a carrier strike force, Submarine Allied Command, Iberian Atlantic Command, and Eastern Atlantic Command. The CinC Eastern Atlantic is always CINCCHAN. CINCCHAN, whose responsibilities in his area parallel those of SACLANT in miniature, also has a miniature replica of the STANFORLANT in Standing Naval Force, Channel, a permanent force of small vessels chiefly devoted to "mine counter-measures". The regular contributors are Belgium, Denmark, the FRG, the Netherlands and United Kingdom, with occasional US and Norwegian ships.

Military command of NATO

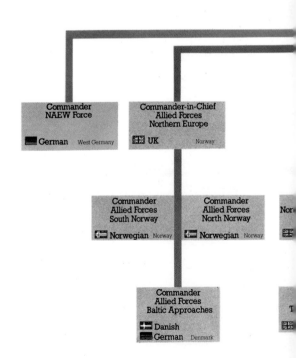

The diagram below shows the immense span of responsibilities born by SACEUR, the NATO major commander in charge of the most likely areas of initial conflict between East and West in the NATO region, and correspondingly the most well provided with military forces. Designation of the subordinate commanders is largely determined by political considerations combining both the sensitivities of the local nations on particular sectors of the front and the need to demonstrate the international solidarity of the Alliance and to involve the major powers directly in the early stages of conflict. French absence from the command structure is noticeable as is the fragmented organizaion in the South-East. Some of the commands change national hands from time to time, but the main pattern is fairly stable. One source of major change over time has been the need to accommodate the increasing weight of Germany in NATO.

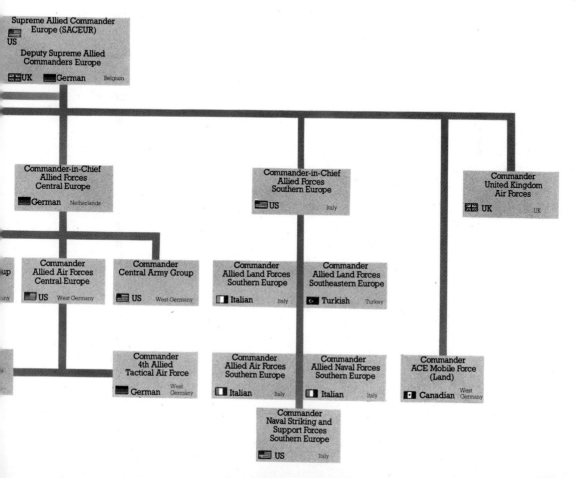

Command Structure of the Warsaw Pact

Nominally at the head of the Warsaw Pact organization is a Political Consultative Committee at ministerial level, which in its fullest form includes heads of member governments, party first secretaries, foreign and defence ministers, the Chief of the Soviet General Staff, and both the Commander-in-Chief and Chief of Staff of the Warsaw Pact Soviet High Command. In practice this body rarely meets and even the so-called Permanent Commission ostensibly designed to provide continuing political guidance meets only irregularly. Political direction actually emanates directly from Soviet authorities, sometimes after bilateral consultations at Soviet initiative with some or all member states. To emphasize Soviet preponderance, the secretariat of the Committee and Commission is directed by a Soviet deputy foreign minister. Like all major organs of the Warsaw Pact, these two bodies are located in Moscow.

In the early years of the Pact, the defence ministers of the Eastern European member states, but not of the Soviet Union, met under the chairmanship of the Commander-in-Chief of the Pact. Since the invasion of Czechoslovakia in 1968, the Soviet Union has made intermittent efforts to make the Pact seem a more egalitarian and genuine alliance. One manifestation of this has been the establishment of a Committee of Defence Ministers, of which the chairman is still the Commander-in-Chief of the Pact, but in which the Soviet defence minister now joins his colleagues. The Committee has not, however, assumed any great importance.

The heart of the Pact and the head of its military organization, is the Joint High Command, charged with the direction and co-ordination of the Joint Armed Forces. Head of the JHC is the Soviet First Deputy Minister of Defence, a Soviet Marshal, under whom serve a Chief of Staff, also a Soviet Marshal, and the Chiefs of Staff of the Eastern European members. At the same time the Soviet Union maintains a military mission in every capital of a European member except Rumania. These missions, which are not to be confused with the familiar military attachés, have representatives attached to many Eastern European military formations, and enable the Soviet Union to observe and to some extent supervise the military policy and activities of its allies. In addition, the Soviet Union possesses for both war and peace, further parallel instruments of control by way of the separate networks of the KGB and the Communist Party Secretariat.

Like the political organs, the JHC is based in Moscow and its staff controls the training and exercises of the Pact's armed forces. The first Deputy Commander in Chief and the Inspector General of Pact Forces as well as the Commander in Chief himself and the Chief of Staff, are always Soviet. The air defence of Eastern Europe is fully integrated with that of the Soviet Union and Pact air defence forces are permanently under direct operational command of the Soviet Air Defence Command. Pact territory in Europe constitutes six air defence districts analogous to the ten such districts in the Soviet Union.

The peacetime work of the Warsaw Pact is organized to support the groups of Soviet forces in Eastern Europe: the Northern Group of Forces in Poland, the Central Group in Hungary, and, by far the most powerful, the Group of Soviet Forces in Germany. In addition there is a Soviet Tactical Air Army. To all these formations are attached various Eastern European units of varying capability and reliability.

The Warsaw Pact, unlike NATO, is not intended to be a structure for command in wartime. If hostilities began, the Eastern European units would be brought under direct Soviet command and used as part of the various Soviet Fronts. It is notable that the joint invasion of Czechoslovakia in 1968 was conducted by the Soviet Military command in Moscow and did not involve the machinery of the Pact. While the Soviet Union has never pressed ahead with schemes sometimes mooted for a fully integrated Pact military force, Soviet models are imposed in training and doctrine as well as equipment, and in recent years specific Eastern European units have been integrated with associated Soviet formations in an increasingly organized way.

Right: The apparently representative structure of the Warsaw Pact with elaborate consultative machinery conceals the threat of Soviet dominance, tacitly enforced by the powerful Soviet forces in Eastern Europe which would also constitute the spearhead of a Warsaw Pact offensive.

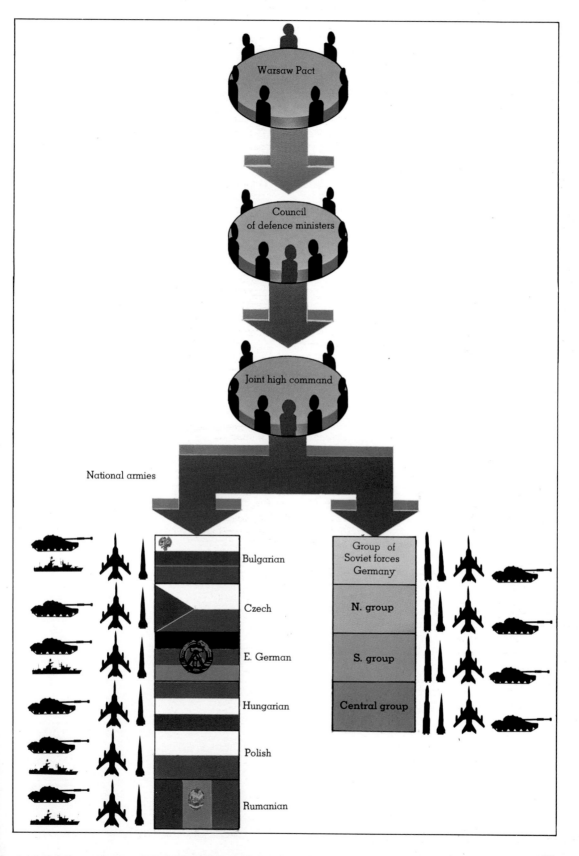

Warsaw Pact

Council of defence ministers

Joint high command

National armies

Bulgarian

Czech

E. German

Hungarian

Polish

Rumanian

Group of Soviet forces Germany

N. group

S. group

Central group

Europe as a Military Problem

The North Atlantic Treaty obliges member states to regard an attack on any other member as an attack on itself and to render assistance by "such action as it deems necessary, including the use of armed force". This is a less than absolute pledge, the tentativeness of which was originally inspired chiefly by sensitivity to the requirements of the United States Constitution, under which it requires the action of Congress to declare war, at a time when there was considerable political opposition in the United States to the proposed break with the American isolationist tradition. The wording of the Treaty also reflects the provisional nature of any pledge of military assistance, a factor that deserves continued consideration in view of indications that the Soviet Union may well hope to divide NATO and manoeuvre some of its members into neutrality during a serious pre-war crisis.

To qualify under the Treaty, the attack must occur within the area covered by the Treaty; that is to say, the sovereign territory of any member or any of its aircraft and naval or merchant vessels in the Mediterranean or in the Atlantic Ocean north of the Tropic of Cancer. The responsibilities of the Alliance thus extend from the Caucasus to Hawaii and from the shores of Africa to the Arctic.

Right: Geo-strategically Europe is a small peninsula extending from Asia. The defeat of Germany and its partition in 1945 destroyed the European balance of power and leave politically fragmented Western Europe vulnerable to the military threat posed by Russia, unified under Soviet Communism. Western Europe is vulnerable both to direct attack along the North European plain and to flanking movements in Scandinavia and the Mediterranean. NATO represents an effort to redress the balance of power by projecting the power of the New World across the Atlantic. This requires safe routes across the ocean which Soviet naval power threatens, particularly from the Northern Seas. This Soviet naval power is in turn severely hampered by geographical constraints.

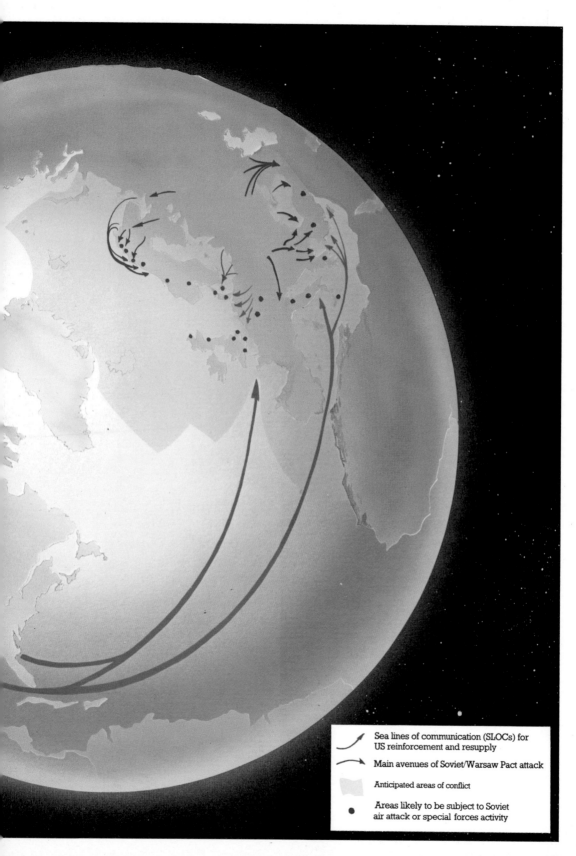

Sea lines of communication (SLOCs) for
US reinforcement and resupply

Main avenues of Soviet/Warsaw Pact attack

Anticipated areas of conflict

Areas likely to be subject to Soviet
air attack or special forces activity

Right: Nuclear weapons for use in direct support of the land battle in Europe were first introduced by the United States in 1953 as an effort to gain advantage from technological superiority. Since then many new types of 'tactical' and 'theatre' nuclear weapons have been placed in Europe. At the same time the Soviet Union has introduced its own weapons in these categories in several of which it has achieved clear superiority.

The first tactical nuclear weapon was an artillery shell of very large 280 mm calibre for firing which a special and very cumbersome cannon was required. Since then nuclear rounds have been developed for standard 155 mm and 203 mm guns, while nuclear warheads have also been made for delivery of missiles of various ranges, both cruise and ballistic, by aircraft, and as land mines. The most recent longer-range theatre missiles, such as the Soviet SS20 can carry accurate multiple independently targettable re-entry vehicles (MIRV).

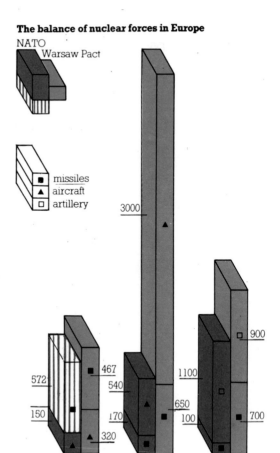

The balance of nuclear forces in Europe

NATO
Warsaw Pact

missiles ■
aircraft ▲
artillery □

3000

572
150
467
540
170
320

longer range

1100
650
100
900
700

1100

shorter range   short range

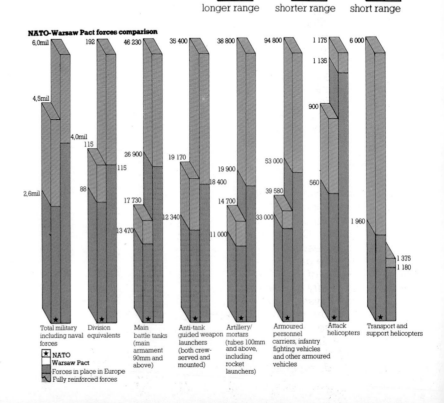

NATO-Warsaw Pact forces comparison

	Total military including naval forces	Division equivalents	Main battle tanks (main armament 90mm and above)	Anti-tank guided weapon launchers (both crew-served and mounted)	Artillery/mortars (tubes 100mm and above, including rocket launchers)	Armoured personnel carriers, infantry fighting vehicles and other armoured vehicles	Attack helicopters	Transport and support helicopters
	6,0mil	192	46 230	35 400	38 800	94 800	1 175	6 000
							1 135	
	4,5mil						900	
	4,0mil	115	26 900	19 170	19 900	53 000	560	
		115			18 400	39 580		
	2,6mil	88	17 730	12 340	14 700	33 000	1 960	
			13 470		11 000			1 375
								1 180

★ NATO
Warsaw Pact
Forces in place in Europe
Fully reinforced forces

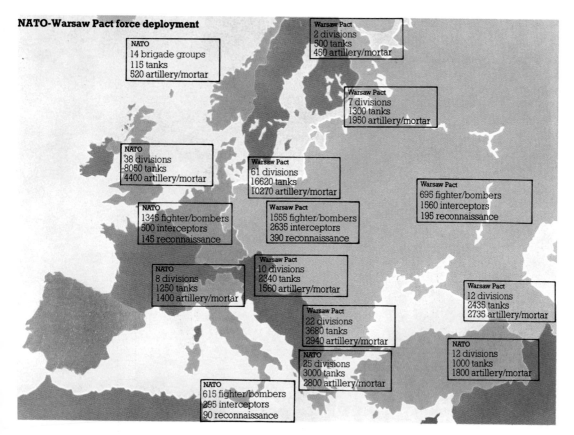

NATO-Warsaw Pact force deployment

NATO
14 brigade groups
115 tanks
520 artillery/mortar

Warsaw Pact
2 divisions
500 tanks
450 artillery/mortar

Warsaw Pact
7 divisions
1300 tanks
1950 artillery/mortar

NATO
38 divisions
8050 tanks
4400 artillery/mortar

Warsaw Pact
61 divisions
16620 tanks
10270 artillery/mortar

Warsaw Pact
695 fighter/bombers
1560 interceptors
195 reconnaissance

NATO
1345 fighter/bombers
500 interceptors
145 reconnaissance

Warsaw Pact
1555 fighter/bombers
2635 interceptors
390 reconnaissance

NATO
8 divisions
1250 tanks
1400 artillery/mortar

Warsaw Pact
10 divisions
2340 tanks
1560 artillery/mortar

Warsaw Pact
12 divisions
2435 tanks
2735 artillery/mortar

Warsaw Pact
22 divisions
3680 tanks
2940 artillery/mortar

NATO
25 divisions
3000 tanks
2800 artillery/mortar

NATO
12 divisions
1000 tanks
1800 artillery/mortar

NATO
615 fighter/bombers
295 interceptors
90 reconnaissance

Above: The map shows the disposition of major air and land forces across all the European fronts with which NATO is concerned. The relative isolation of the Flanks and their internal geographical fragmentation is displayed as well as the advantage the Soviet Union enjoys from its geographical contiguity to the main fronts and the availability of Soviet territory for deployment. The data used is that adopted by NATO; the Warsaw Pact provides no such information publicly.

Left: The overall indices of military power, such as number of men or divisions, need to be interpreted in the light of other indicators of fighting capacity. One such indicator is the number of major weapon systems considered most relevant to the outcome of modern battle. While some of the Warsaw Pact's numerical superiority can be attributed to retention of older systems, for which they have so far found the necessary manpower, these may nevertheless be perfectly adequate for their purpose. In recent years the Warsaw Pact has eroded NATO's traditional technological lead, especially in ground weapons.

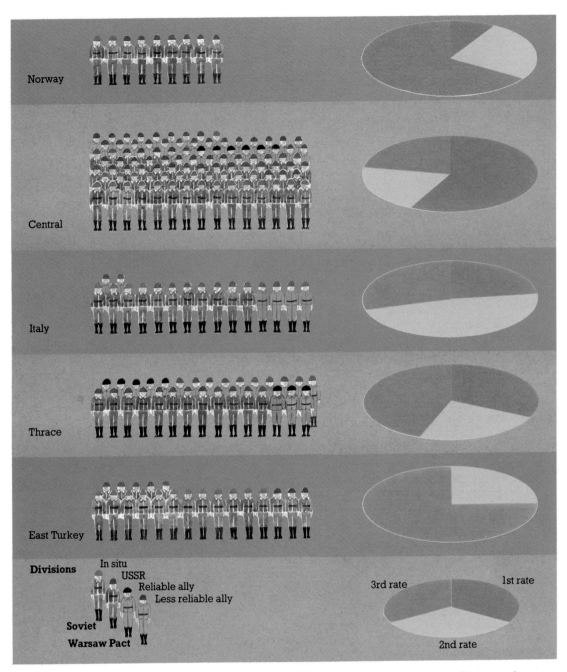

Norway

Central

Italy

Thrace

East Turkey

Divisions

In situ
USSR
Reliable ally
Less reliable ally

Soviet
Warsaw Pact

3rd rate   1st rate

2nd rate

Above: The diagram tries to illustrate the importance of reserves and the variations in readiness on the main potential fronts. Relative significance of ready and reserve forces will depend, of course, on how a conflict begins and how governments respond. There are wide variations of quality within the categories assigned here, while the notion of political 'reliability' is particularly speculative.

Land forces production 1974–83
Annual averages   NATO ■   Warsaw Pact ▨

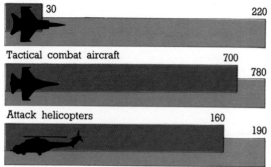

Tanks
1045   2785

Other armoured vehicles
1750   5540

Artillery mortars and rocket launchers
360   2950

Combat aircraft production 1974–83
Annual averages   NATO ■   Warsaw Pact ▨

Strategic defence interceptors
30   220

Tactical combat aircraft
700   780

Attack helicopters
160   190

Above: The Warsaw Pact and particularly the Soviet Union consistently out-produces the NATO powers in heavy armaments, especially those for ground forces. This steady programme of production both explains the quantitative preponderence of Warsaw Pact ground forces and demonstrates that while the high total number of Warsaw Pact weapons is partly explained by retention of old systems, the absolute number of modern systems also heavily out numbers those at NATO's disposal. The larger size of Warsaw Pact ground forces is clearly reflected, as is the relatively greater traditional stress of NATO on airpower, where the discrepancy between the two sides is much smaller. Figures for aircraft production also demonstrate the continued, if reducing, Soviet stress on interceptors for air defence of Soviet territory, a characteristic responding not merely to the traditional NATO provision for tactical and strategic bombing, but also the stress on strategic defence in Soviet military doctrine.

Central Front

By general consent, the heart of NATO's strategic problem lies on the Central Front, on the East-West or "Inner" German border. West Germany is the great geo-political prize located between the two military blocs and the North German Plain is a traditional route for invasions headed either East or West, although the suitability of this terrain as "good tank country" for rapid military advances has been substantially modified in recent years by the vast spread of urbanization.

Deployed on this Central Front for the greatest land-air war imaginable in the modern world is the largest concentration of established combat capability ever assembled. On the side of the Warsaw Pact are nineteen first class Soviet divisions stationed in East Germany (the Group of Soviet Forces, Germany), with two more in Poland, and five which entered Czechoslovakia in 1968, never yet to leave. With these are associated six East German, 15 Polish and 10

Czech divisions, and to the rear lie 38 Soviet divisions in Western Russia. NATO deploys the equivalent of twenty ready divisions in Germany to which the three divisions of the French First Army, stationed at Baden-Baden in the Federal Republic, would probably but by no means certainly join their efforts. Further immediate help would come from six well-prepared West German reserve brigades and some Dutch and Belgian forces deployed to the rear which might or might not get forward in time. To support and harass these forces are the majority of the some three thousand NATO and over seven thousand Warsaw Pact aircraft dedicated to the European theatre.

As this concentration of forces testifies, the Central Front is regarded by both sides as the most crucial and dangerous area. Paradoxically, this formidable balance may also render the area the most stable. That, of course, is what the defensive efforts of NATO are intended to do. The Central Front poses a delicate problem for the Soviet Union if the moment for war ever

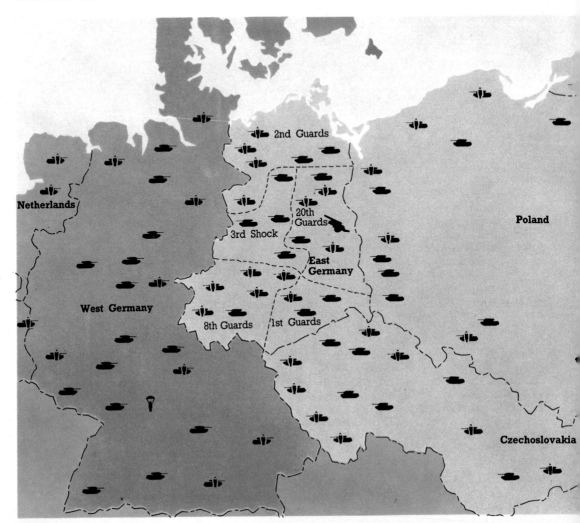

came near. Victory there would yield the greatest prizes but clearly war in this area also entails the greatest risks. Not only are NATO's defences at their best here, but two of the European defenders possess their own nuclear forces. Plausible though many theoretical criticisms of the credibility of those forces may be, their terrifying potential may not be easy to shrug off in practice. For conventional battle, even the North European plain has proved a tougher challenge than numerous armies in history have expected, and today the intense urbanization of the area has created a strategic environment of a kind not yet tested in battle on a large scale.

If the Soviet Union did launch an attack on Western Europe, it would also have to contemplate the problem of terminating the war. Although history is unlikely to repeat itself exactly, Soviet leaders would have to recall the frustration of Hitler's hopes that an advance to the Channel would end his war. Although the Soviet Air Force could bring the United

Kingdom under heavy fire, with the United States already engaged, as it was not in 1940, the Soviet Union would have to reckon with the possibility of a prolonged aftermath, peculiarly dangerous in a nuclear age.

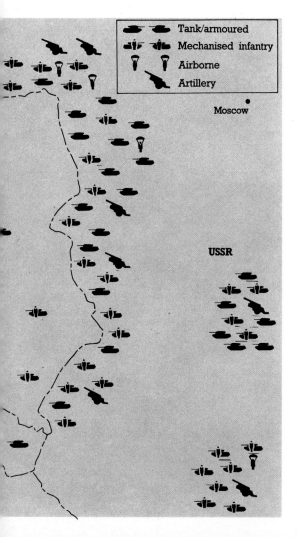

	Tank/armoured
	Mechanised infantry
	Airborne
	Artillery

Moscow

USSR

Left: The map depicts believed peacetime deployment of NATO and Warsaw Pact forces on the crucial Central Front, including Soviet forces in the Western Soviet Union. These deployments have been relatively stable for some years, though organizational structures often change. Excluding Soviet territory, the area depicted is that involved in the Mutual Balanced Force Reduction talks discussed later in this book.

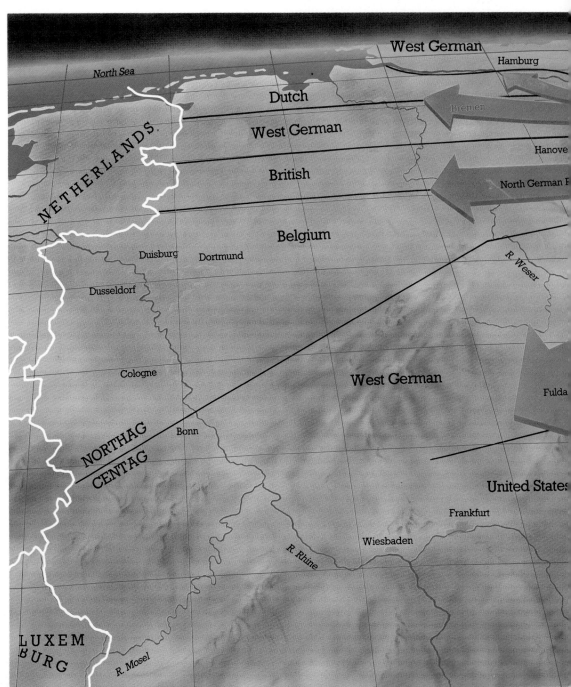

West German

Hamburg

North Sea

Dutch

Bremen

West German

Hanove

British

North German F

Belgium

Duisburg   Dortmund

R. Weser

Dusseldorf

NETHERLANDS

Cologne

West German

Fulda

NORTHAG

CENTAG

Bonn

United States

Frankfurt

Wiesbaden

R. Rhine

LUXEM BURG

R. Mosel

NATO's defensive forces, creating "joints" across which differences of equipment, doctrine and language still constitute obstacles to defensive co-ordination despite considerable efforts to improve interoperability. NATO would attempt to hold a forward line; German interests make such a strategy politically necessary, but as the map shows, the narrowness of the terrain available to NATO makes it impossible even for military reasons to trade too much territory for time and to exhaust the enemy. An obvious line for NATO to try to hold is the River Weser.

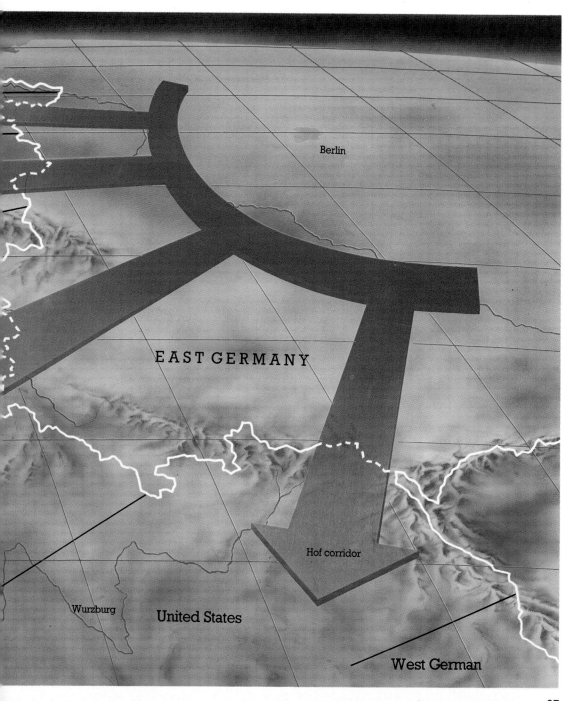

Berlin

EAST GERMANY

Hof corridor

Wurzburg

United States

West German

Below and Right: The tables summarize NATO and Warsaw Pact forces likely to be available in the first two weeks or so of mobilization. Lack of reliable information prevents a full comparison across all categories but in general the tables confirm the general impression of substantial Pact superiority. Although no precise figures for Soviet artillery can be given, the ratio of guns to formations is known to be extremely high by Western standards, capable of providing as many as 100 guns per kilometre of front in an offensive. Similarly the Pact has generous supplies of anti-tank weapons, one category in which NATO is also relatively well supplied as the numbers of launchers shown here confirm. The day when NATO could regard itself as better provided with such weapons has, however, long passed. In the key category of tanks, Pact superiority is patent. Indeed it can be seen that the Soviet units stationed in Eastern Europe in peacetime can alone come close to matching NATO strength. It must be remembered, of course, that the offensive typically needs to amass superiority if it is to prevail and that Soviet doctrine lays particularly heavy stress on this. But it is necessary to amass such strength only at the point of attack and this the Pact could do on several separate axes of advance. One of the great disadvantages of NATO's quantitative inferiority is its lack of a margin of spare capacity with which to mount credible threats of counter-attack into Pact territory. Such threats, by forcing the Pact to retain a stronger defensive line in general, would reduce its ability to concentrate for the offensives. At the present balance, Nato is likely to be confined to counter-attacking the salients created by Pact advances, rather than launching true counter-offences beyond the Pact start line.

Below right: The table gives an estimate of the central front air battle after reinforcement. This is probably the most useful measure given the likely speed of reinforcement — though lack of facilities in Europe may reduce the effectiveness of some U.S. units. It shows NATO's stronger relative position in air power compared to the balance in ground units.

NATO Land forces on Central front M + 10	Brigades	Separate battalions	Home defence brigades	Home defence battalions[3]	Main battle tanks[4]	Artillery	Attack helicopters	Anti tank guided weapons
Belgium	6	9	11[2]	4	330	180	—	370[5]
Canada	1	—	—	—	60	24	—	40
West Germany	36	—	12	45	4230	1290	170	2640
Netherlands	10	4	2	4	925	310	—	620[5]
United Kingdom	12	18	—	—	900	280	60	780[5]
United States[1]	33	—	—	—	5000+	1600+	500+	4500+

1. These figures include war reserve stocks.
All figures are highly provisional given the rate of US re-equipment and expansion of war reserve stocks, and variables such as the scope, timescale and priorities of reinforcement.

2. Regiments.
3. Plus separate company and platoon size units.
4. Includes war reserve stocks.
5. Estimate.

Warsaw Pact Central front forces	Motor rifle/ airborne/ amphibious divisions	Tank divisions	Artillery	Main battle tanks	Men[1]
Czechoslovakia	5	5	N/A	3500	148 000
East Germany	4	2	N/A	3100	120 000
Poland	10	5	N/A	3450	210 000
Soviet forward deployed	12	14	N/A	9000	500 000
Forward deployed total	31	26	8300	19 050[2]	978 000
Western military districts	21	17	7500	10 500	760 000
Strategic reserve	15[3]	3[3]	2000[3]	4000+	320 000

1. The Soviet Army on mobilization might total 4.4 million men, perhaps 2 million might be assigned to the central front. Non Soviet Warsaw Pact countries have 1 million plus reservists, bringing their armies to roughly 1 500 000.
2. Includes 2600+ in reserve.
3. Estimated.

NATO and Warsaw Pact Airforces – Central Front

	NATO*	Warsaw Pact
Long range strike/attack aircraft	210	230
Bombers	—	390
Fighter/bombers	1440	1400
Close air support	600	
Interceptors/air superiority fighters**	440	1930
Total	2690	4050

* Assumes US reinforcements from USA complete. Excludes French forces.
** Excludes Strategic Air Defence aircraft in the Western USSR and British and French Air Defence Forces.

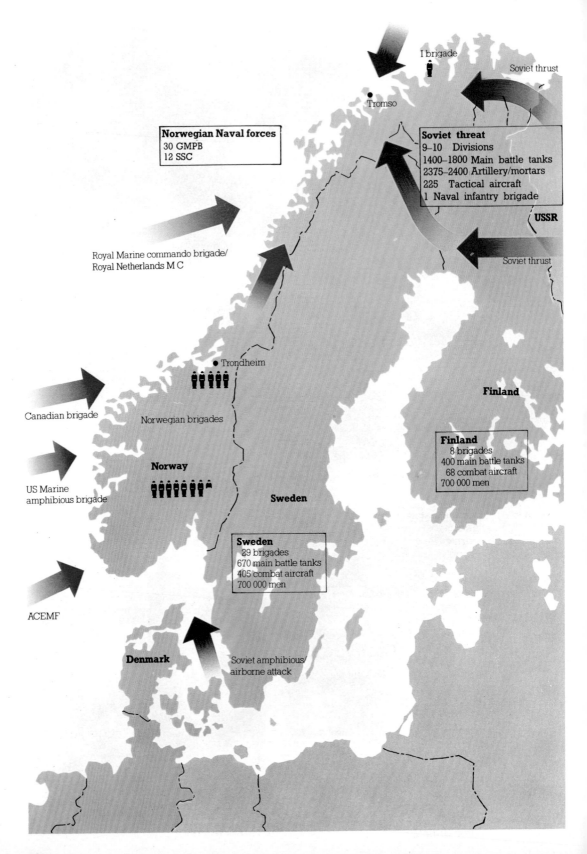

Norwegian Naval forces
30 GMPB
12 SSC

Royal Marine commando brigade/
Royal Netherlands M C

Canadian brigade

Norwegian brigades

Norway

US Marine
amphibious brigade

Sweden

ACEMF

Denmark

Tromso

I brigade

Soviet thrust

Soviet threat
9–10   Divisions
1400–1800 Main battle tanks
2375–2400 Artillery/mortars
225   Tactical aircraft
1 Naval infantry brigade

USSR

Soviet thrust

Trondheim

Finland

Finland
8 brigades
400 main battle tanks
68 combat aircraft
700 000 men

Sweden
29 brigades
670 main battle tanks
405 combat aircraft
700 000 men

Soviet amphibious/
airborne attack

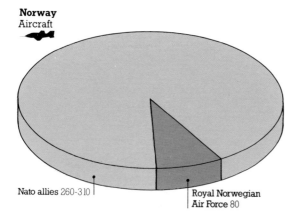

Norway
Aircraft

Nato allies 260-310

Royal Norwegian
Air Force 80

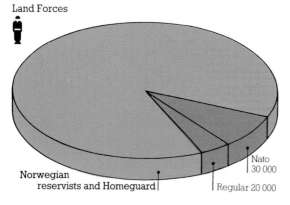

Land Forces

Norwegian
reservists and Homeguard

Nato
30 000

Regular 20 000

Above: The charts show the heavy dependence of Norway on NATO reinforcements and the reliance of its own forces on the mobilization of reserves, a necessity imposed both by the small size of the Norwegian population as a whole and the sparsely inhabited nature of the most vulnerable Northern front near the border with the Soviet Union.

Left: Divided geographically from the rest of Europe, NATO's Northern Flank in Scandinavia could be vital to the outcome of a war in Europe, particularly because of its strategic importance for a maritime battle in the Atlantic. If the Soviet Union seized Norway it would enjoy easy access by land and sea both to the Ocean and for attack on the United Kingdom, a key NATO base for resupply and in the rear of the Central Front. Seizure of the Danish Strait could release the Soviet Baltic Fleet. Possession of Northern Norway would relieve Soviet anxieties about the security of its important bases in the Kola penninsula. The map shows the potential importance of the neutral territory of Sweden and Finland, the former of which maintains especially significant armed forces, though with increasing economic difficulty.

Northern Flank

The NATO forces on the Central Front are not merely the direct defence of the greatest European prizes for a possible Soviet invasion but also the pivot on which the Northern and Southern flanks turn. Should the centre fall, the position on either flank would almost immediately become untenable. Nevertheless the flanks have serious implications for the Centre as well as an intrinsic value of their own and an influence on possible hostilities further afield. Conditions on the two flanks are very different. In the North are Norway and Denmark, themselves flanked by North Germany and the United Kingdom, with Iceland to the rear. These Nordic members of the alliance are politically stable, though permeated to different degrees by quasi-neutralist and pacifist sentiments, partly related to the political task of supporting Swedish and Finnish neutrality. These sentiments have led Norway and Denmark to refuse the permanent peacetime presence of allied forces or of nuclear weapons. Sparse population, especially in Norway, compels heavy reliance on reserve forces, rapid mobilization and swift deployment.

Strategically the significance of the Northern Flank is essentially maritime. Based in Northern Russia, Murmansk and the Kola Peninsula, is the greatest concentration of Soviet naval power, comprising both the forces that might cut NATO's lines of trans-Atlantic reinforcement and many of the submarines that carry the seaborne portion of Soviet nuclear forces. The so-called Greenland-Iceland-United Kingdom (GIUK) gap is therefore a strategic barrier through which Soviet naval forces must penetrate if they are to attack NATO shipping or approach American shores, and which NATO forces must sail through if they are to bring support and reinforcement to Norway or take the war to northern Soviet waters.

Divided though it is geographically from the rest of Europe, Scandinavia, NATO's Northern Flank could therefore be vital to the outcome of the battle on the Central Front. Although much would depend on how the war broke out and hence what degree of mobilization and reinforcement had taken place before the outbreak of hostilities, NATO would certainly be dependent on reinforcement across the Atlantic. If the Soviet Union could seize Norway it would acquire air and naval bases capable of dominating the battle of the Atlantic. Soviet forces could not only threaten NATO's sea lines of communication (SLOCs) but also increase their attacks on the United Kingdom, a key rear base for the Central battle. To the south, seizure of the Danish Straits would both unleash Warsaw Pact naval forces from the Baltic and directly outflank the northern end of the Central Front.

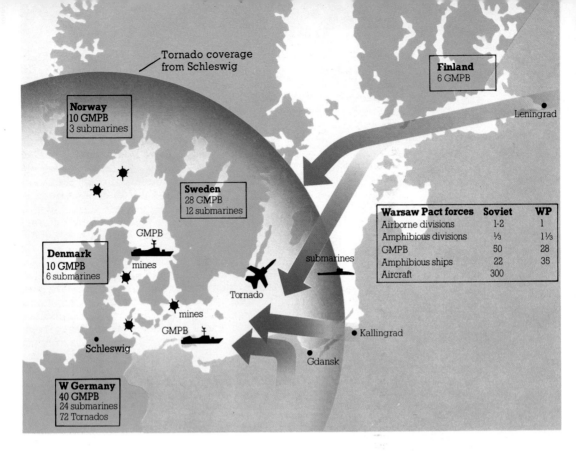

Above: The map depicts the important subtheatre of war around the Baltic. This area is dominated by light naval forces, particularly Guided Missile Patrol Boats and small diesel submarines, aircraft and amphibious forces. The Soviet Navy has a long tradition of supporting land operations in this area and Soviet amphibious and airborne forces pose a serious threat to Danish and Norwegian shores and islands. Full scale invasion or disruptive attacks on and seizure of ports and airfields could seriously outflank the Central Front forces of NATO. If the Danish straits were forced the situation would be even more difficult. A somewhat far-fetched possibility that has nevertheless caused considerable anxiety at times in NATO history is the Soviet seizure of the island of Bornholm in a crisis to test or demonstrate the absence of political solidarity in NATO. Recent Soviet submarine incursions into Swedish waters show Soviet interest in the possible exploitation of neutral territory and waters.

Below: The table shows the balance of land and airforces in the Baltic region, the heavy dependence of the NATO defences on reservists and the key role played by the Federal Republic of Germany, a role not usually emphasized in NATO pronouncements because of Scandinavian political sensitivities.

Denmark

Aircraft

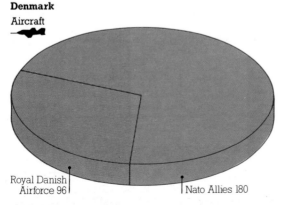

Royal Danish Airforce 96 | Nato Allies 180

Land forces

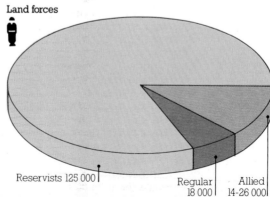

Reservists 125 000 | Regular 18 000 | Allied 14-26 000

32

Seizure of Northern Norway would also relieve the Soviet Union of anxiety about the security of the substantial air and land forces based in the Kola peninsula and, above all, protect its heavy concentration of naval forces both nuclear and conventional also based on the Kola and at Murmansk. Soviet access to Norwegian bases would greatly increase the Soviet threat to the American carrier strike fleet that is one of the means with which the United States might try to attack the Kola.

The Soviet Union could employ several strategies to seize control of Scandinavia. In the north its amphibious forces could undertake landing operations at Tromso and to the South. It would also launch a direct land attack across the Norwegian border in Finnmark or, by violating Swedish neutrality, make a thrust toward Northern Norwegian bases by a shorter route. In the south, the Warsaw Pact could launch amphibious attacks against Southern Norway (or Sweden) and the Danish islands, to take over the Straits and invade the most heavily populated part of Norway.

In the north in particular, Soviet forces heavily outnumber those of Norway, which, like Denmark, does not permit the permanent stationing of other allied forces in peacetime. Norway itself therefore relies on a policy of mobilization of reserves behind a screening force supported by modest but recently modernized air power.

The broader strategy for defending this important factor determining NATO's overall capacity for reinforcement, itself depends on reinforcements. American, British and Canadian amphibious brigades are allocated to reinforce the Norwegians and these units, especially the British, regularly exercise this role, a practice particularly necessary in view of the difficult climate and terrain. Whether these forces actually arrived in time would depend not only on the speed with which the necessary political and military decisions were made, but also on competing demands both for the forces and for the scarce air and sea "lift" available. In recent years NATO has begun to "preposition" equipment in Norway, a device that may have been inhibited previously by Norway's aversion to the peacetime stationing of allied forces. While such prepositioning facilitates reinforcement, it also commits otherwise mobile resources to only one of their possible alternative applications. Naturally such issues are not easy to discuss among allies as they raise sensitive questions of reliability and also may give useful intelligence to the enemy about allied intentions.

The inhibition of the Norwegians and Danes about the stationing of allied forces or nuclear weapons does not arise, as sometimes supposed, from simple neutralist tendencies, though some of these exist, but more importantly from an attempt to stabilize the neutral buffer constituted by Sweden and Finland. Only, it is widely believed, by carefully regulating Norwegian and Danish participation in NATO and depriving it of any conceivable offensive appearance can the Soviet Union be persuaded to moderate its pressures on Swedish and Finnish neutrality. Any such Soviet pressure is deterred in part by the fear that it might drive Norway and Denmark deeper into collaboration with NATO, while a milder Soviet policy, usually accompanied by elements of a "peace offensive", may hope to have the reverse effect of tempting the Scandinavian members of NATO toward neutrality, in war if not in peace. A complicated game of manoeuvre thus goes on in maintaining the "Nordic balance". It remains to be seen whether the greater intrusiveness of Soviet submarines and occasional aircraft into Swedish territorial waters and airspace in the early 'eighties heralded a tougher phase in Soviet policy.

The Southern Flank

NATO's southern flank is also a very maritime affair centred in the Mediterranean, but there, except for a parallel inferiority of available NATO ground and air forces, the similarity ends. The Southern members of NATO, unlike their Nordic partners, have recent histories of domestic political instability. Perhaps more important, they are deeply divided from each other politically as well as geographically. In particular, Greece and Turkey are at daggers drawn over Cyprus, over rights in the Aegean to territorial waters and to oil, and are estranged by the memory of centuries of mutual antagonism. As a result, the command structure of NATO on the Southern flank is fragmented, because the locals will not work together, and it is not much of an exaggeration to regard the area as a series of bilateral alliances between each local ally and the United States. The main arm of the United States in the area is the Sixth Fleet, which depends in part on the Europeans to provide bases. The maintenance of base rights in Greece and in Spain, the most recent and as yet uncertain member of the alliance, involves a sustained and troublesome series of negotiations in which the Greeks and, at least formerly, the Spanish, drive hard bargains under the implicit and sometimes explicit threat not to be allies at all. Greece, indeed, has followed the French example and left the integrated command structure of NATO, though remaining a member of the Alliance.

These weaknesses became, if anything, more serious causes of concern in the 'seventies both as the Greek-Turkish dispute over Cyprus worsened and as the oil crisis of 1973, continued turbulence in the Middle East, and growing Soviet politico-military influence in North

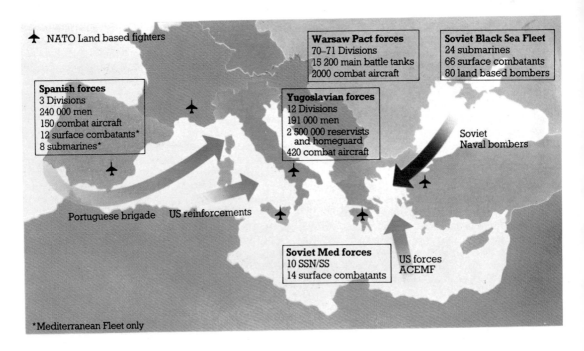

NATO Land based fighters ✈

Warsaw Pact forces
70–71 Divisions
15 200 main battle tanks
2000 combat aircraft

Soviet Black Sea Fleet
24 submarines
66 surface combatants
80 land based bombers

Spanish forces
3 Divisions
240 000 men
150 combat aircraft
12 surface combatants*
8 submarines*

Yugoslavian forces
12 Divisions
191 000 men
2 500 000 reservists
and homeguard
420 combat aircraft

Soviet
Naval bombers

Portuguese brigade   US reinforcements

Soviet Med forces
10 SSN/SS
14 surface combatants

US forces
ACEMF

*Mediterranean Fleet only

Above: The map shows the Mediterranean theatre and illustrates its wide range and variety from Spain to Anatolia. Several somewhat off-centre players could affect this game including Hungary, Turkey, the Soviet Black Sea Fleet, Spain, a major accretion to NATO assets if ever politically related to the alliance in a stable way, and Yugoslavia, whose neutrality could prove tempting to Pact forces intent on access to the Mediterranean.

Below: The balance of maritime forces in the Mediterranean greatly favours NATO, although the European contribution is fragmented. By far the most powerful force in the U.S. Sixth Fleet but this might find the submarine, missile patrol boat and aircraft infested Mediterranean too tight an arena for comfort in full scale war. An invaluable peacetime deterrent and peacekeeping force, the large aircraft carriers might be highly vulnerable in war.

US	France	Italy	Greece	Turkey		
2-4	2					Aircraft carrier
		1				ASW Carrier
12-24	14	21	21	15		Major surface ships
		7	18	14		Guided missile patrol boat
	11	10	10	14		Submarine
4+						Nuclear submarine

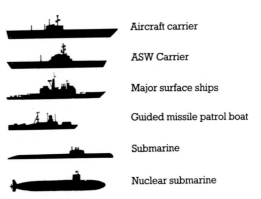

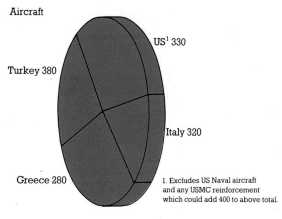

Aircraft

US[1] 330

Turkey 380

Italy 320

Greece 280

1. Excludes US Naval aircraft
and any USMC reinforcement
which could add 400 to above total.

Africa, increased the interests of the NATO powers in those neighbouring areas that fall outside the treaty boundary. The Mediterranean members of NATO have ceased to be merely the Southern Flank of the Central Front and become the front-line for a political and potentially military struggle beyond Europe itself. Yet partly precisely because the dangers have multiplied, Mediterranean members of NATO, while anxious for the protection of the Alliance as a whole and especially of the United States, are reluctant to be dragged automatically into quarrels arising from American policy in the Middle East. Turkey faces a particularly delicate problem because it could be the base from which American forces might threaten the flank of Soviet interventions in such areas as Iran. Equally, Turkish airspace could be valuable to the Soviet Union in such ventures. While the United States is naturally inclined to see Turkish co-operation as its due from an ally, Turkey is far from eager to be the possible point at which a conflict outside NATO becomes a NATO affair. The solidarity of the Southern Flank of NATO in crisis and war must therefore realistically be regarded as problematical, much doubtless depending on the way any such crisis arose.

Italy	Turkey	Greece	
			Modern tanks 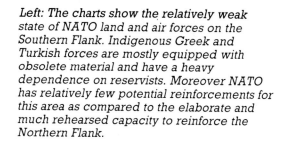
1220	270	530	
			Other tanks
550	3200	1025	
			Divisions*
8	24	15	
			Men*
260 000	470 000	135 000	

*includes brigades

Left: The charts show the relatively weak state of NATO land and air forces on the Southern Flank. Indigenous Greek and Turkish forces are mostly equipped with obsolete material and have a heavy dependence on reservists. Moreover NATO has relatively few potential reinforcements for this area as compared to the elaborate and much rehearsed capacity to reinforce the Northern Flank.

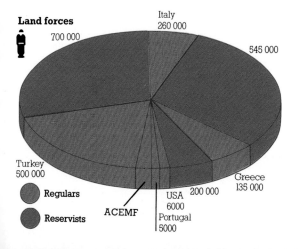

Land forces

700 000

Italy
260 000

545 000

Turkey
500 000

Greece
135 000

USA
6000

USA 200 000

Portugal
5000

ACEMF

● Regulars

● Reservists

Early Evolution of NATO Strategy

From the very beginning of NATO the forces of the Soviet Union and its allies have been superior by most quantitative indices. Soviet propaganda and the scenarios for Warsaw Pact manoeuvres always assume that the task is to repel an attack by NATO. The balance of forces, the pattern of NATO deployment and NATO's military organization and doctrine are such that it is difficult to credit the sincerity of this apparent assumption. In practice it does not make much difference, at least so far as strategic analysis is concerned, because the Soviet scenarios do not credit NATO with much success, so that the Soviet "counter offensive" has the form that an offensive initiated by the Soviet Union would take. Whatever the alleged political "casus belli", Soviet military strategy requires that even a defensive war is fought by an offensive strategy. Soviet strategy therefore calls for a heavy offensive using all available "combined arms", land and air, conventional and chemical and, very probably, ultimately nuclear — to sustain a high rate of advance. In this way the Warsaw Pact could hope to roll up NATO forces before they could mobilize, obtain reinforcements, or deploy and decide to use their own nuclear weapons.

NATO's strategic response to this threat has varied greatly over the years. The Soviet Union's detonation of a nuclear explosive device in August, 1949, just months after the North Atlantic Treaty was signed, before the Korean War began, and before the first SACEUR was appointed and NATO began to create its standing structure of military command, made it clear that soon any war between the United States and the Soviet Union involving nuclear weapons would be a two-way affair. United States military leaders concluded that NATO ought to build up its conventional forces sufficiently to hold the Red Army without using nuclear weapons, so that if Soviet nuclear weapons, neutralized those of the United States, NATO would still be defensible. No doctrine of "no first use" of nuclear weapons was ever formally adopted and there was little if any systematic thought about what such a doctrine would entail. But in this frame of mind the United States pursued a vigorous programme of conventional rearmament and urged similar efforts in its European allies to whom it made available considerable "military assistance" in both money and weapons. The high point of this thinking came in 1952, when a meeting of the North Atlantic Council, at Lisbon, called for the raising within two years of 96 active and reserve divisions — only 25 already existed at the time — and the provision of 9,000 aircraft.

Although a start was made on achieving these goals, the economic and therefore political burden proved too much and contributed in several allied countries, notably in Britain and the United States, to bringing about changes of government. The lapse of the Korean War into a stalemate near the 38th Parallel, with the invasion safely repelled, and the passage of time without further Soviet aggression also contributed to a relaxation of atmosphere. As a result NATO moved toward a radically different strategy, one that in the words of the new American President and former SACEUR, Dwight Eisenhower, could be sustained over the "long haul". This strategy, far from shrinking from dependence on nuclear weapons, placed heavy and explicit reliance upon them in accordance with the thinking becoming dominant in the United States under the description "New Look". British military leaders, by now anticipating the fruits of the United Kingdom's own atomic weapons programme also contributed to this nuclear emphasis.

At the global, Soviet-American level, the United States adopted the nuclear deterrent policy that became known as "Massive Retaliation". According to this doctrine, which was never as clearly or as firmly enunciated as often supposed, the United States would no longer necessarily respond to local aggressions in their own terms but might retaliate "by means and at places of its own choosing". This declaration falls far short of the simple notion of inevitable nuclear attacks on the Soviet Union, which are often supposed to have been implied, but it did reflect impatience with the tedious and costly kind of conventional limited war fought in Korea.

So far as NATO Europe was concerned, although there was again little explicit comment on the point, it had hardly ever been considered that a war could be limited; thus by implication, a war in Europe would be accompanied, as it was in the previous Second World War, by a strategic bombing campaign. Certainly the U.S. Strategic Air Command (SAC) built targets related to "retarding" a Soviet advance into its strategic bombing target plan.

The New Look did, however, make a major difference to NATO strategy. As nuclear materials became more plentiful and warhead designs were miniaturized, nuclear weapons for use on the battlefield began to enter service with American forces in Europe from 1953 onwards and were subsequently distributed for the use of allied forces, with the custody and control of the actual nuclear warheads remaining with the United States. As with so many aspects of nuclear strategy, the rationale for this development was never clearly defined. On the one hand the nuclear weapons represented additional firepower to redress the otherwise unfavourable balance; on the other hand, the introduction of nuclear weapons clearly raised the possibility of what is now called escalation, and consequently might be thought to deter the initiation of aggression. This message was, however, perhaps less significant at a time when scarcely anyone had ever imagined that a major war in Europe could be fought without a strategic bombing campaign between the Superpowers. Whatever the rationale, the number of nuclear weapons based in Europe gradually increased — later, in the 'sixties, it was to multiply very rapidly indeed — and in 1954 the NATO Council formally authorized NATO commanders to plan on the assumption that nuclear weapons would be used in a future European war.

Almost immediately, this strategy began to arouse serious misgivings in both Europe and the United States. As the significance of the Soviet Union having acquired nuclear weapons began to be appreciated, it was realized by many American strategic experts that if NATO used nuclear weapons against Soviet forces they could expect retaliation and that if the war became "strategic", involving Soviet territory, then this retaliation could include nuclear attacks on the United States. For the moment the Soviet Union might lack the necessary delivery systems but their acquisition could be only a matter of time. Indeed Soviet launching of the first man-made satellite, Sputnik, in 1957 dramatized the progress of the Soviet long range missile programme to what later proved to have been an exaggerated degree.

So far as Europe itself was concerned, enthusiasm in NATO for the adoption of nuclear weapons as a leading feature of the defensive strategy had been encouraged by the belief that the American technological lead gave NATO a virtual monopoly of weapons for tactical use. This monopoly, like that at the strategic level, could clearly be only a wasting asset. But even before the erosion of this advantage it came to be realized that NATO's own use of nuclear weapons could have catastrophic consequences for the unfortunate Europeans, chiefly West Germans, who lived on the battlefield. Much publicized exercises held in the mid-'fifties, particularly one significantly code-named Carte Blanche, suggested civilian casualties running into millions.

Consequently strong political resistance to the increasing nuclear emphasis of NATO strategy developed both in Europe and the United States. This did not prevent a substantial relaxation of the original effort to build up NATO's conventional forces now that they were to a large extent officially regarded merely as a "trip wire" to deter aggression by threatening to set off a nuclear war. In the United States the emphasis of defence spending shifted away from the Army and toward the Air Force. But the critique of Massive Retaliation and nuclear emphasis in NATO made rapid political headway and the Kennedy Administration that came

into office as a result of the 1960 election set about reversing the trend both in "declaratory" policy and in the shape of its armed forces.

In NATO, nervousness about nuclear policy was matched by reluctance to contemplate the increased defence expenditure implied by moving to a more robust conventional defence. More significantly, France under President de Gaulle, which had accelerated its own national nuclear weapon programme, remained devoted to a policy based primarily on deterrence by threat of full-scale nuclear retaliation. So long as this attitude persisted, it would not be possible to achieve the unanimity necessary formally to change NATO strategy. By 1966, however, President de Gaulle's refusal to compromise the independence of French action by remaining within the integrated military planning and command structure of NATO led him to withdraw, though remaining a member of the Alliance. This made it possible for the remaining members to revise NATO's fundamental strategic concept and 1967 saw the adoption of a new doctrine, enshrined in a formal document known as "14/3" which still remains the basis of NATO strategy.

Below: In the beginning NATO planned to build conventional forces capable of matching those of the Soviet Union and its allies in conventional terms. Since then the ambition has become a more modest conventional force adequate to defeat and thereby deter an initial Warsaw Pact attack. While the role of nuclear weapons in justifying a reduction in conventional forces has been reduced and the number of such weapons actually deployed has fallen, they still play a central part in NATO strategy.

	Divisions	Aircraft	Tactical nuclear weapons
1952 objective	96	9000	some
1956 objective	26	1400	15000
1967 actual	26	1400	7000
1985	26	1400	4600 +ET?

NATO's Basic Strategic Concept: The Flexible Response

The strategy adopted in 1967 is commonly referred to as the "flexible response". While this term is intended to describe the key characteristic of the strategy as a blend of conventional and nuclear elements, the strategy has also proved flexible in its ability to absorb later modifications without entailing the politically demanding task of explicit radical revision. To a large extent this is because the doctrine is deliberately ambiguous in a way that is thought to enhance deterrence as well as facilitate compromise between conflicting allied strategic preferences.

Flexibile response envisages three stages in NATO's response to aggression: "direct defence", "deliberate escalation" and "general nuclear response".

Direct defence involves defeating an enemy attack at the place it occurs and at approximately the level of warfare chosen by the enemy; in particular, if the enemy does not use nuclear weapons, NATO would try to avoid doing so either. This constitutes the most decisive departure from the previous trip wire strategy embodied in the planning document 14/2.

If the defence mounted on this basis began to crumble to the point at which defeat was imminent or the "integrity" of the territory of an ally was threatened — not easy matters to judge by a coalition under pressure — the flexible response calls for "deliberate escalation". This could mean opening up new fronts or other forms of conventional counter-attack — options sometimes referred to as "horizontal escalation". But it is generally assumed that escalation would entail using nuclear weapons, albeit initially in a limited way. The pace with which nuclear weapons would be introduced and the scale on which they would be used are obviously matters on which both national interest and professional military opinion can differ and it was no mean political feat that in 1969, two years after the adoption of flexible response, NATO formally established "Guidelines" for the initial use of nuclear weapons. This use, it was agreed, should be a "militarily meaningful demonstration of resolve". That is to say, while recognizing that the primary purpose of introducing nuclear weapons was deterrence, hoping to scare the aggressor into calling a halt for fear that this "deliberate escalation" might come to deserve the other common descriptive use of the term escalation, as an unintended and uncontrollable slide towards catastrophe, the guidelines recognized that this gesture would lack credibility if it did not seem to offer NATO some practical military advantage. It was there-

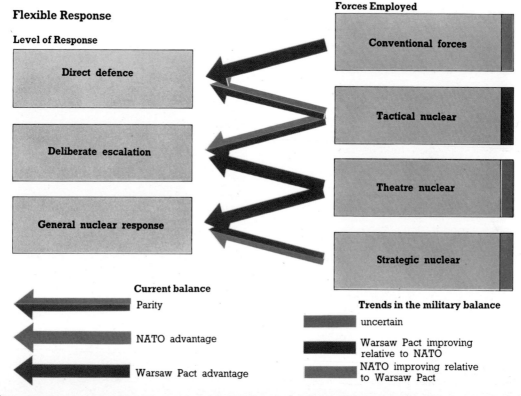

Flexible Response

Level of Response

- Direct defence
- Deliberate escalation
- General nuclear response

Forces Employed

- Conventional forces
- Tactical nuclear
- Theatre nuclear
- Strategic nuclear

Current balance

- Parity
- NATO advantage
- Warsaw Pact advantage

Trends in the military balance

- uncertain
- Warsaw Pact improving relative to NATO
- NATO improving relative to Warsaw Pact

Below, left: The key NATO doctrine of flexible response calls for efforts to defeat an enemy attack with conventional weapons. If this effort begins to fail decisively, NATO plans resort to nuclear weapons both to stiffen resistance and threaten escalation to wider nuclear war. This stage might involve only battlefield nuclear weapons or larger theatre weapons in limited numbers. Failure of this measure could lead to more general nuclear strikes in the European theatre of war, possibly including the use of some "strategic" weapons and perhaps parallel to the outbreak of a strategic nuclear "exchange" involving the United States and Soviet homelands. Because of the severe political and strategic restrictions likely to be imposed on such strikes, the supposed quantitative and qualitative advantages of each side in certain categories of weapon may not be significant.

Below: The diagram shows a purely hypothetical depiction of how escalation might occur and how the target areas might become extended. It also suggests how the initiative might lie with either side. Current

fore not envisaged that initial use of nuclear weapons would be a merely demonstrative detonation as advocated by some strategic theorists.

After the initial use, there might be one or more "follow on" uses of nuclear weapons; relatively little is known publicly about what form such uses might take but the armed forces certainly have elaborate and extensive nuclear fire plans to help them conduct their defence. By this time it must, of course, be expected that Soviet nuclear weapons would have come into play and it is a matter for conjecture how long control could be maintained on such a battle-field.

Should it become clear that this limited nuclear action was not holding the enemy advance or persuading him to call off his attack, the flexible response calls for a move to "general nuclear response". This ultimate step implies the use of strategic nuclear weapons, probably British and perhaps French as well as American, in an attack upon the Soviet Union as well as its forces

doctrine suggests that any "demonstrative" NATO strike would also be intended to secure some useful influence on the battle.

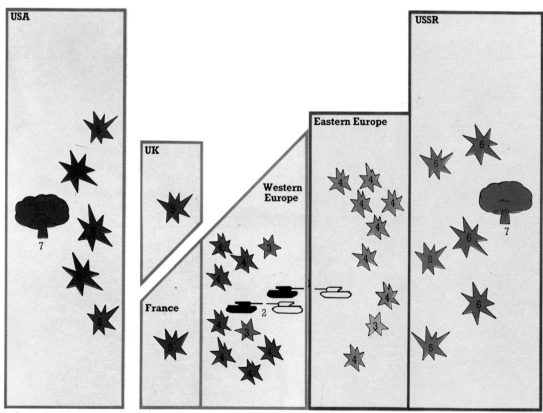

1. Conventional forces clash.
2. NATO falls back. Holds? Unable to force Soviets to retreat? Or faces imminent defeat.
3. NATO escalates to nuclear weapons – demonstrative strike to show risks Soviets run? Or Soviets decide to go nuclear to breakthrough.

4. Tactical nuclear weapons used in large numbers.
5. Selective nuclear strikes extend to USSR, rear areas and USA.
6. Limited nuclear war breaks out between the superpowers.
7. General nuclear war.

in Europe. What the shape of such an attack would be and to what extent it should or could be restrained below the level of a mutual orgy of destroying cities and indiscriminately killing civilians is the subject of constant debate on the wider nuclear scene that transcends the affairs of NATO. If a European war brought the nuclear powers to the point of those decisions it would indeed have proved the trigger for World War III.

While the flexible response was a clear retreat from the primarily nuclear emphasis of the strategy that preceded it, in which NATO's conventional forces were very largely a "trip wire" for nuclear retaliation, the strategy embodied in the new doctrine remains ultimately nuclear. Those who believe nuclear weapons have an inimitable deterrent aura would have resisted any full-fledged effort to "denuclearize" NATO strategy or move to a doctrine of "no first use". This was symbolized at the time the strategy was adopted, by the simultaneous assignment of a number of Polaris submarines to SACEUR to support his fire plan and engage targets of particular significance to the defence of Europe. Allied confidence in the underlying nuclear guarantee extended by the United States to its allies was also bolstered at that time by the establishment of a new Nuclear Planning Group (NPG) in NATO to exchange information and co-ordinate planning with regard to nuclear weapons and to try to develop an agreed and coherent nuclear philosophy. It was in this forum that the Guidelines on initial use were evolved.

Because the actual use of even a few nuclear weapons in Europe would be extremely dangerous, if not immediately very destructive, the flexible response, like the more frankly nuclear policy embraced by NATO before it, remains a strategy designed to deter Soviet attack on Europe rather than to defeat it. Such an approach is inevitable, given the fact that any large scale war in Europe, nuclear or conventional, is an intolerable prospect for the Europeans. In the jargon of strategic theory, the flexible response and the forces NATO maintains to implement it are intended to deter anyone from crossing the line between war and peace and not merely the so-called "nuclear threshold". To achieve this more ambitious goal, the flexible response deliberately retains an element of nuclear risk.

Below: Through all the evolutions of NATO's general strategy it inevitably remains an imperative to maintain a defence of the Central Front. Ever since the Federal Republic of Germany joined NATO and became the major supplier of conventional forces, the task of defending the Centre has been conditioned by the need to protect as much as possible of Germany from invasion. Within the "flexible response" there is therefore a principle of "forward defence". Thus the early expectation, born of necessity, of falling back toward the Rhine was successively replaced by that of holding a screen while nuclear action commenced and, once a conventional phase of defence was emphasized under the flexible response, by "active defence" close to the East-West border — that is, a form of mobile defence and local counter-attack not dependent on major trading of space for time. In the 'eighties, advances in technology for striking enemy forces well behind the front line led to the concept of Follow-on Force Attack (FOFA), which in contrast to falling back, embodies the idea of extending the battlefield into enemy territory.

The evolution of the concept of forward defence

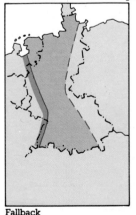

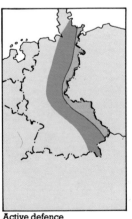

Fallback   Trip wire   Active defence   FOFA

 Delaying zone   ⬤ Main defence line

Contending Strategic Doctrines: NATO

Because the flexible response calls for providing a much more substantial capacity to prolong a conventional defence than the previous nuclear-emphasis or trip wire strategy but still envisages resort to nuclear weapons when necessary, it leaves room for considerable disagreement as to what level of conventional and nuclear forces is necessary to implement the strategy. Moreover since the strategy is one intended to create a deterrent and maintain it for an indefinite period of years, the criteria to be met are not merely military. For not only is deterrence an essentially psycho-political process, so that success or failure depends on the effect wrought on Soviet intentions and not directly upon military effectiveness measured by Western standards, but the military strategy proposed and the forces maintained to carry it out must also win the confidence of public opinion in NATO countries. Only if the Western public believes that the strategy has a reasonable chance of success will the Alliance continue to enjoy political support. The Alliance was, after all, initially founded to create an atmosphere of security in which economic and political life could confidently be carried on in Western Europe.

Fulfilling these military and political criteria is no easy task. Not only is the Warsaw Pact a formidable foe, but the Western situation is full of inherent contradictions: the requirement for military forces competes with the socio-economic welfare policies that NATO is designed to defend; the desire to deter by raising a nuclear threat, conflicts with the need to confine war to conventional means as long as possible if it occurs. In this respect there are also international conflicts of interest between allies. The most widely appreciated instance of this is the obvious tension between Europeans and Americans (and Canadians) as to when the nuclear threshold should be crossed — or, rather, as the policy is one of deterrence, as to the point at which NATO should threaten to cross it. For while on the one hand such a step would open up the first phase in which — at least with existing technology — the war might be visited upon the territory of the United States, on the other hand, by greatly increasing the threat to Soviet territory as well, such escalation might prompt the termination of a battle that had by definition already gone intolerably far for many Europeans.

To ask *which* Europeans indicates yet other conflicts of interest within the Alliance less often aired than those between the United States and Europe. For clearly the West Germans have more to lose from a prolonged conventional war than the French, or even more markedly, the British. The West German requirement that conventional defence be carried out well forward is thus often coupled to the demand — for obvious reasons not always made explicit — that the phase of deliberate escalation be initiated as soon as relatively small losses of territory are suffered. Allies whose homeland is further from the battle are much more inclined to defer escalation and for that reason and for reasons of strategic advantage in the conventional operations themselves, wish to trade ground — German ground — in a "mobile defence".

The peacetime politics of defence on both sides of the East-West confrontation in Europe are therefore concerned not merely to provide and prepare armed forces but to sustain self-confidence and deterrent credibility while sapping that of the other side. At the same time political and technological developments change the qualitative and quantitative nature of the competition and of the war that might ensue.

Ever since 1967 the spirit of flexible response has inspired NATO efforts to increase the capacity of its conventional forces to resist a Soviet attack without escalation. If anything, the misgivings about recourse to nuclear weapons that impelled the shift to flexible response in 1967 have been strengthened both by subsequent strategic thinking and by the conspicuous increase in the Soviet Union's own nuclear capabilities.

At the strategic level, which dictates American fears that a European war might bring devastation to the United States homeland, the Strategic Arms Limitation Talks (SALT), and agreements have explicitly registered Soviet attainment of "parity" or even superiority in some categories of weapons. So far as the balance of theatre weapons is concerned, a level at which the Soviet Union at one time seemed to be neglecting its arsenal or at least to be content with a somewhat crude inventory, the 'seventies saw the rapid deployment of numerous nuclear weapons in all categories, from short-range artillery rounds to the 5000 km range MIRV'd SS20. The idea that once supported NATO theatre or tactical nuclear doctrine, that this was a level of warfare at which NATO enjoyed a clear superiority, if not monopoly, and to which it could therefore have recourse with virtual immunity from retaliation, has thus been discredited. Partly as a consequence, a powerful disarmament movement has grown up in the West to reinforce the anti-nuclear bias in NATO strategy arising from strictly military considerations.

For some years after flexible response was adopted in 1967, the refurbishment of United States forces dedicated to NATO was impeded by the vast diversion of American military resources to Vietnam and by the period of scepticism about military policy that briefly followed the loss of the war. In this interlude the efforts of the European allies to strengthen their conventional forces made more rapid headway than those of the United States. In more recent years this pattern has reversed, as American investment has increased and Europeans have encountered economic recession.

As a result of these exertions, especially since NATO adopted a ten-point Long-Term Defence Plan in 1978, and a commitment to increase real defence expenditure by 3 per cent per annum over a period of years, NATO conventional capabilities have increased considerably, both materially and in training and coherence of doctrine.

Nevertheless the outcome has fallen far short of what the NATO military authorities would like. According to one estimate NATO governments typically provide some 70% of what military commanders claim is the minimum acceptable. In 1984, for instance, when the then SACEUR, General Bernard Rogers, declared that military spending would have to increase by 7% a year in real terms if he was to sustain a conventional defence for more than one or two weeks, most of the European members of NATO were proclaiming their inability to continue any longer with the 3% target, which many had in any case failed to fulfil in the past.

The difficulty of agreeing upon an appropriate level of defence expenditure, never a politically easy task, is compounded by the very nature of the flexible response. One of the characteristics of that strategy which both makes it politically acceptable and, one hopes, effective as a deterrent, is ambiguity about the point at which recourse would be made to nuclear weapons. This inevitably also makes it difficult to determine what the goal of conventional military preparations should be. Are these forces merely to thicken the trip wire, making it a little more credible and a little slower to act, to facilitate the imposition of a substantially longer "pause" before nuclear weapons are used, or to extend that pause indefinitely so that in the ideal outcome the Warsaw Pact would be defeated and forced back to its start line without recourse to nuclear weapons at all? As the persistence of a strong nuclear element in all successful NATO strategies testifies, there are many who fear that too much preparation for conventional war merely suggests lack of will to use nuclear weapons and thereby actually undermines deterrence overall.

These uncertainties are, of course, additional to the difficulty which always attends the establishment of an appropriate military balance and determining what forces are necessary for particular military tasks. The answer to these questions depends very much on the capabilities and intentions of the potential enemy. What is enough for NATO is thus a function of what the Soviet Union might do in crisis and war.

Below: The urbanization of West Germany creates new obstacles to a rapid military advance; at the same time it creates a battlefield on which defending troops would need to be concerned about minimizing damage and casualties from their own operations and to consider the consequences of bringing down intense, possibly nuclear, enemy fire. The map also shows what a large proportion of industrialized West Germany would fall to even a modest advance by the Warsaw Pact.

Population distribution in West Germany

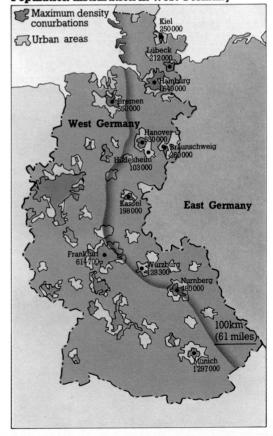

Contending Strategic Doctrines: The Warsaw Pact

How the Soviet Union conducted a Warsaw Pact attack on NATO would be determined by the interaction between the Pact's capabilities and Soviet military thought and doctrine. By tradition Soviet forces — like, indeed, Tsarist Russian forces before them — attempt to secure massive superiority at the point of attack and to prevail by overwhelming the enemy and then establishing a rapid pace of advance. On the modern battlefield such a doctrine leads to a "tank-heavy" configuration.

In numbers of men, Soviet and Warsaw Pact divisions are typically smaller than those of the NATO powers, particularly the United States. Where Western divisions tend to contain logistical and service elements to sustain the unit in combat over an extended period, Soviet divisions emphasize combat troops and are replaced by complete new divisions when exhausted. As a result the smaller Soviet divisions actually deploy as many major weapons as the larger American or West German divisions and considerably more than those possessed by the divisions of other NATO national armies. Soviet higher commanders at Army and Front levels have also in recent years acquired increasing quantities of combat force held outside the divisional structure. Consequently the common comparison of forces between East and West by counting divisions understates the Warsaw Pact's advantage. The outcome of any war in Europe would, indeed, depend very much upon which "philosophy of support" proved to be the wiser one.

For most of the post-war period, Soviet planning and deployment has proceeded on the assumption that a war in Europe would involve nuclear weapons from the first. For much of this period NATO was also superior in nuclear weapons, particularly those for use on the battlefield. This situation clearly posed a serious strategic problem for a military power believing in taking the offensive and in doing so by amassing quantitiative superiority, particularly at the intended points of breakthrough.

To reconcile this predilection for mass attack with the danger of offering lucrative targets for nuclear weapons, the Soviet Union adopted a system of 'echelons' in which its forces could be widely dispersed both laterally across the front and longitudinally right back into the Western Soviet Union. The lead forces would concentrate late at the point of attack and then close as rapidly as possible with NATO troops. In this way Soviet forces might inhibit NATO's nuclear attacks by making it difficult not to harm friendly nuclear forces; as the advance began, NATO would also have to worry about "collateral" damage to West German civilians. Moreover a

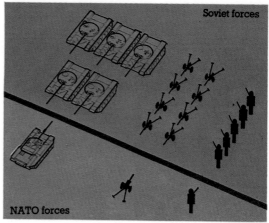

rapid advance might achieve considerable success, including perhaps the overrunning of many NATO nuclear weapons, before the NATO political authorities could take the decision to use them.

Nevertheless, so long as NATO strategy continues to contemplate deliberate escalation

Above: Soviet doctrine calls for amassing at least a 5:1 superiority in major armaments before launching an offensive.

Below: The doctrine also requires the availability of a continuous supply of rear echelons to sustain the momentum set up by the lead waves of the offensive.

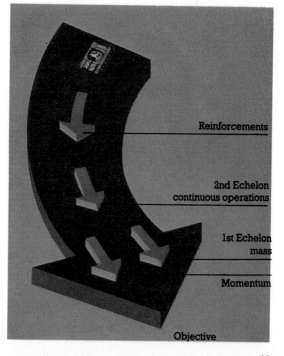

to the use of nuclear weapons rather than accept a conventional defeat, the Soviet Union has no alternative but to assume the war will involve nuclear weapons. Effective Warsaw Pact strategy and tactics may degrade the NATO nuclear capability and reduce its effectiveness, but some nuclear phase to the battle is highly probable. Thus while conventional tactics to counteract NATO nuclear action may be highly successful, just possibly so successful as to compel an advantageous end to the War before NATO crosses the nuclear threshold, the Pact must take care not to let such hopes result in conceding NATO an easy and effective first nuclear blow.

For most of the time NATO and the Warsaw Pact have confronted each other, the Soviet Union has therefore planned to take early nuclear action itself, so that at both conventional and theatre nuclear levels the Soviet belief in the offensive has given its strategy a pre-emptive bias. It would probably be wise to assume that if the Soviet Union starts a major war in Europe it will immediately use nuclear weapons. This assumption is, however, not so safe as it used to be. In very recent years, NATO's obvious uneasiness about the nuclear element in its strategy and its consequent fairly strenuous efforts to improve its capability for the conventional phase of the war, have made the possibility of NATO refraining altogether from nuclear action somewhat more plausible. Simultaneously, the great improvement in the Soviet Union's own theatre nuclear arsenal for war at all levels, has patently made recourse to nuclear weapons less potentially advantageous to NATO.

In this evolving context, Soviet military thought has become more ready to envisage a substantial initial phase of warfare without the use of nuclear weapons and even to speculate about the possibility of local wars between the two great alliances confined wholly to conventional weapons, which in Soviet practice, it should be noted, might well include chemical agents. The equipment, deployment, and exercises of Warsaw Pact troops support the belief that some such trend is at work in Soviet strategy. It would clearly be reassuring to the Soviet Union to reach such conclusions, for if we regard it as the likely initiator of European war, then we must assume that an unmitigated belief that war would be nuclear must be a powerful deterrent. Faith or even substantial hope that a war could be confined to conventional weapons must be welcome to a power possessing the advantages in the conventional military balance enjoyed by the Soviet Union and Warsaw Pact.

Below: The West cannot know with confidence what Soviet military doctrine and intentions are; moreover, as in any military power, doctrine is constantly evolving. The table suggests how some of the underlying assumptions of Soviet military thought may have evolved in the postwar era so far as the place of nuclear weapons in the European theatre are concerned.

Evolution of Soviet military thought on theatre nuclear warfare

	Importance of nuclear weapons	Likelihood of nuclear war	Possibility of theatre nuclear war	Initial phase of war	Main mission for Soviet TNF	TNF use
1945	secondary	inevitable	not applicable	combined arms operations with initial nuclear strikes	disrupt war-making potential	immediate nuclear use
1950						
1955	valuable in combined arms operation				destroy NATO air power	
1960		possible but not inevitable	impossible	pre-empt NATO use of TNF	pre-empt NATO use of TNF	immediate pre-emptive strike
				inter-continental nuclear strikes		
1965	decisive in combined arms context or to deter NATO escalation		possible but likely to lead to general war	possible initial		
				non-nuclear phase or combined arms attack with nuclear strikes	deter NATO from using its TNF in early phase of war	conventional strikes to destroy NATO TNF, nuclear pre-emptive strike on NATO when Soviets see them preparing to escalate to use of nuclear weapons
1985						

The Changing Military Balance

While the outcome of a future war in Europe would depend on many imponderables, which each side will try to evaluate from the perspective of its own strategic theories — a factor greatly complicating the task of deterrence — the material balance between the two alliances is also clearly a fundamental determinant. Moreover, quantitative and technological analysis, or "bean counting" as it is sometimes dismissively described, can yield useful insights not only into capability but intentions, for what a military power provides itself with must give at least some indication of what it expects to do in a war.

A great many details of the material balance between NATO and the Warsaw Pact are presented in the graphic sections of this book. Summed up in a sentence, the overall conclusion so far as the conventional balance is concerned must be that while NATO forces have been considerably modernized and thereby strengthened in the last ten years or so, the Warsaw Pact and particularly Soviet forces have made even more progress, including quantitative reinforcement, and have therefore

improved the balance still further in their favour.

The number of ready divisions in the Central European area has remained fairly steady, at about 25 NATO divisions to 57 for the Warsaw Pact. This figure is, however, very misleading. In the first place it conceals the replacement after the 1968 Warsaw Pact invasion of Czechoslovakia of four weak and disaffected Czech divisions by five first class Soviet divisions stationed on Czech soil. Much more important, the fighting power of the Warsaw Pact and

Below, left: Soviet forces in Central Europe have increased substantially in recent years. The top diagram shows a period of increase in major weapon systems; the lower diagram shows a significant increase in the fighting power of the two main types of Soviet division, increases which have incidentally somewhat reduced the distinction between the two types. The graph at the right shows the approximate trend in the ratio between NATO and Pact forces in several important indices of strength. Note that in all categories the ratio favours the Pact.

Increase in Soviet forces in Central Europe 1968–1976

Tanks	1968	7250	1976	9500
Artillery		3200		4000
Armoured personnel carriers		5300		9450

Increase in size of Soviet Divisions 1973–1985

Tank Division

Men	1973	9000	1985	11000
Main battle tanks	1973	316	1985	335

Motor Rifle Division

Men	1973	10750	1985	14000
Main battle tanks	1973	188	1985	266

The Central European balance of landforces 1975–85

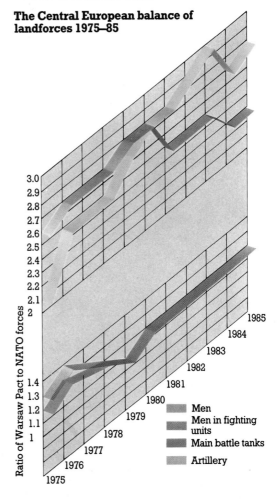

Ratio of Warsaw Pact to NATO forces

3.0, 2.9, 2.8, 2.7, 2.6, 2.5, 2.4, 2.3, 2.2, 2.1, 2, 1.4, 1.3, 1.2, 1.1, 1

1975, 1976, 1977, 1978, 1979, 1980, 1981, 1982, 1983, 1984, 1985

Men
Men in fighting units
Main battle tanks
Artillery

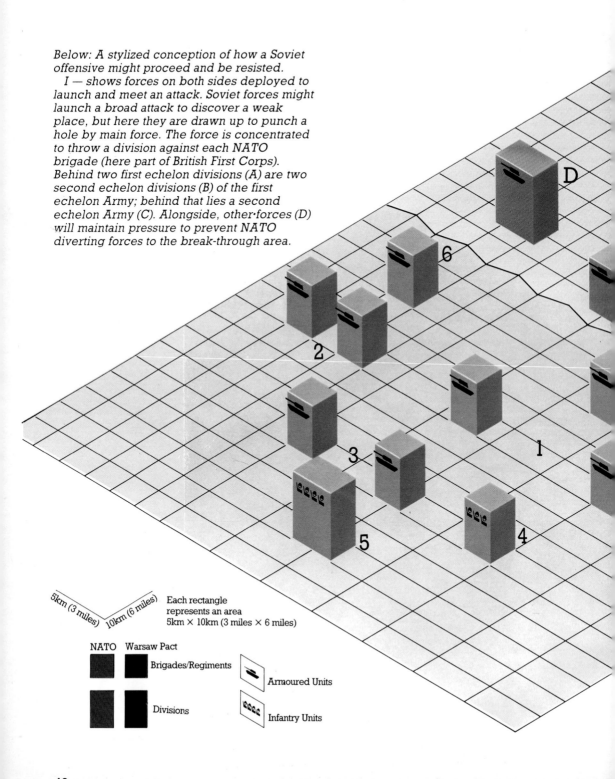

Below: A stylized conception of how a Soviet offensive might proceed and be resisted.

I — shows forces on both sides deployed to launch and meet an attack. Soviet forces might launch a broad attack to discover a weak place, but here they are drawn up to punch a hole by main force. The force is concentrated to throw a division against each NATO brigade (here part of British First Corps). Behind two first echelon divisions (A) are two second echelon divisions (B) of the first echelon Army; behind that lies a second echelon Army (C). Alongside, other·forces (D) will maintain pressure to prevent NATO diverting forces to the break-through area.

5km (3 miles)   10km (6 miles)   Each rectangle represents an area 5km × 10km (3 miles × 6 miles)

NATO   Warsaw Pact
        Brigades/Regiments   Armoured Units

        Divisions   Infantry Units

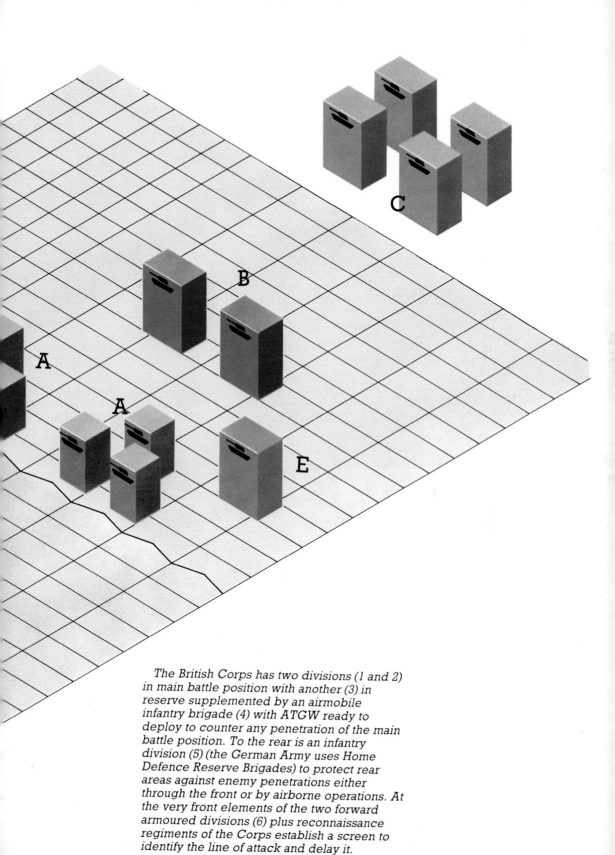

A

A

B

C

A

E

The British Corps has two divisions (1 and 2) in main battle position with another (3) in reserve supplemented by an airmobile infantry brigade (4) with ATGW ready to deploy to counter any penetration of the main battle position. To the rear is an infantry division (5) (the German Army uses Home Defence Reserve Brigades) to protect rear areas against enemy penetrations either through the front or by airborne operations. At the very front elements of the two forward armoured divisions (6) plus reconnaissance regiments of the Corps establish a screen to identify the line of attack and delay it.

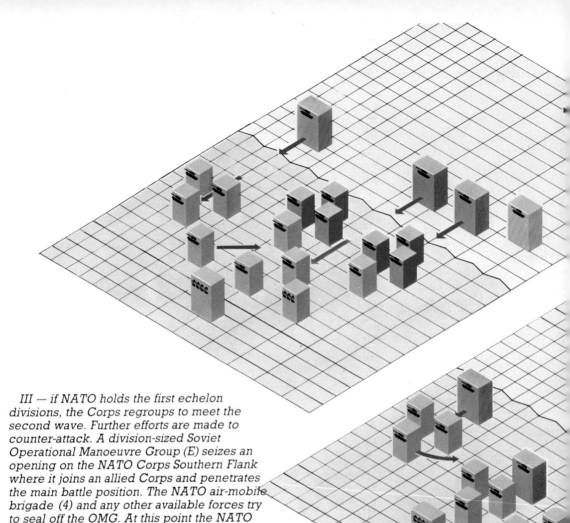

III — if NATO holds the first echelon divisions, the Corps regroups to meet the second wave. Further efforts are made to counter-attack. A division-sized Soviet Operational Manoeuvre Group (E) seizes an opening on the NATO Corps Southern Flank where it joins an allied Corps and penetrates the main battle position. The NATO air-mobile brigade (4) and any other available forces try to seal off the OMG. At this point the NATO Commander faces a difficult choice of priorities between dealing with the OMG and keeping his front intact against the second Soviet echelon. The Corps might call for support from the Army Group reserve but that might not have much to spare. Much would depend on how well NATO had prepared field works and defences in depth during the warning period.

IV — the second echelon army (C) arrives and the NATO Corps has now been hit by some ten Soviet divisions in all. If prepositioned stocks had enabled U.S. reinforcements to give SACEUR a Corps sized reserve the attack might be held. Only two or three days have passed but if the reserves are not forthcoming or the Soviet advance has proceeded faster than suggested here the moment for using nuclear weapons may have arrived. Current NATO efforts to improve capacity to strike deep at the rear echelons and disrupt them are one attempt to postpone this moment as are more traditional efforts to increase the number and power of NATO divisions and other units.

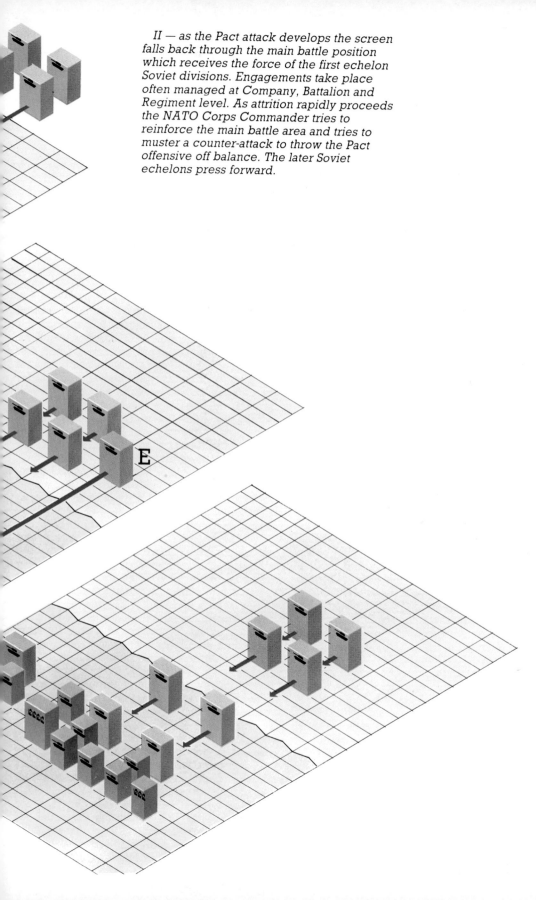

II — as the Pact attack develops the screen falls back through the main battle position which receives the force of the first echelon Soviet divisions. Engagements take place often managed at Company, Battalion and Regiment level. As attrition rapidly proceeds the NATO Corps Commander tries to reinforce the main battle area and tries to muster a counter-attack to throw the Pact offensive off balance. The later Soviet echelons press forward.

E

especially Soviet divisions has been greatly increased by major additions to their combat elements and equipment. Moreover there has been a major growth in the combat units such as artillery regiments held outside the divisional structure at the disposal of the higher Army and Front commands. (A Soviet Army contains some three to six divisions, plus supporting formations; a Front, a command framework only created in time of actual war, contains two or more armies.)

The gross balances also conceal a number of differences between the alliances favourable to the Warsaw Pact: the higher proportion of Soviet forces within the Pact than that which the United States represents within NATO for instance. Between 1965 and 1980 the number of Soviet forces in Central Europe increased as a result of the trends just described from 475,000 to 600,000 men while the number of Americans declined from 435,000 to 300,000. This means that the greater part of Warsaw Pact combat capability is contained within the forces of the leading ally, with consequent minimization of difficulties of language and co-ordination. The Pact also benefits from the standardization of all the members on Soviet designed equipment and the domination of Soviet doctrine and training.

By contrast NATO is fragmented into national armies, each still with strong individual operational styles and a great variety of differing equipment and organization responding both to those styles and to the interests of competing armaments industries. Against this must be set, of course, the major stabilizing role played by the large, well equipped, trained and led West German Bundeswehr, and the doubtful loyalty of the East Europeans to the Soviet Union. Whether this and a probably higher level of flexibility and individual initiative can compensate for the fragmentation of NATO and whether it can successfully co-ordinate land and air operations across the whole front, not offering the Warsaw Pact soft axes of advance along the "joins" in NATO's "layer-cake" of national frontages, would be major factors determining the outcome of European war.

The preponderance of Warsaw Pact rearmament over that of NATO and the dominance of the Soviet Union within the Warsaw Pact effort is palpable. If account is taken of major combat equipment — Tanks, Armoured Fighting Vehicles for Infantry (AFV), Artillery pieces and Rocket launchers, Anti-aircraft guns and Surface-to-Air Missiles (SAM), and Tactical Aircraft and Helicopters, then the Warsaw Pact accounts for more than 80% of the substantial increases in Central Europe between 1965 and 1980. The Soviet Union alone accounts for 46% of this increase while the U.S. share is 7%. Much of the Soviet increase has gone to reinforce the capability of divisions to fight as self-contained

"combined arms teams" on the model long preferred by NATO armies. Thus Soviet tank regiments have added a battalion of AFV and one of self-propelled artillery as well as some 25% more tanks. The Motor Rifle regiments have not only been generously equipped with new AFV but have increased their tank inventory by up to 50%, largely with older tanks displaced in the tank regiments by the newest models. As a result the distinction between the two types of division has diminished. By 1983 the Soviet 3rd Shock Army, with roughly the same number of men as the British Army of the Rhine, had 2.5 times as many tanks, 6 times as many artillery weapons, 1.5 times the number of combat infantry and 1.5 times the logistical "lift" capacity.

All this responds to the lessons of recent wars, as in the Middle East, where anti-tank weapons have made tank units vulnerable without infantry support and artillery to suppress the new threats to the armoured forces on which the Soviet doctrine of rapid penetration and fast advance depends. The advent of airborne anti-armour weapons has posed similar demands for air defence and Soviet forces to a very much greater degree than NATO formations now enjoy a dense series of gun and missile based air defences. Advantage in such air defence weapons is at least two and possibly three to one in favour of the Warsaw Pact.

NATO's strategy for meeting a Soviet conventional attack without recourse to nuclear weapons is based upon the assumption of at least some 96 hours warning to alert and deploy the defensive forces. Placing a screen of forces forward, drawn from the most alert and advanced forces in peacetime, NATO would mobilize, reinforce and fight a battle of 'active defence'. While many of the details of how such a battle could best be fought are continually under debate and lead to frequent changes in plans and force structure, the main purpose remains constant: to take whatever possible advantage from the well-proven methods of "mobile defence" in an armoured battle — that is, yielding space, luring an enemy to where he loses momentum and can be counter-attacked — without abandoning the German political requirement for "forward defence". This latter rigidity in NATO strategy is undoubtedly a serious problem, given the narrowness of the Federal Republic in the East-West dimension and the immense areas which modern armies need for deployment and manoeuvre. In actual war one suspects more departures from forward defence might be made in practice than are admitted in peacetime planning. Nevertheless the constraint is a real one and much NATO strategic thought is directed toward finding ways to make this demanding prescription effective.

Warning, Mobilization and Reinforcement

For large-scale operations both NATO and the Warsaw Pact rely on mobilization of reserves and reinforcement of front-line forces. This is particularly true of NATO both because economic and social preferences restrict military spending in a way that tends to enhance reliance on cheaper reserve forces with fewer fully activated in peacetime, and because the smaller NATO forces have to cover the same frontage as that manned by their foe. Against this must, of course, be offset the margin of at least local superiority the Warsaw Pact requires if it is to implement its offensive strategy. Reinforcement also looms as a more difficult problem for NATO than the Warsaw Pact because of the ocean distance separating the main ally from the battlefield. The distances faced by the Soviet Union from its main source of additional forces for the NATO area, Western Russia, are much less and involve land routes within Pact territory.

Mobilization and reinforcement obviously go together. While there will be completely ready units to bring forward, the typical pattern involves bringing forces up to war strength and then forward. Both processes can be pursued before war breaks out, during the early stages of hostilities and later, if the war continues, to make good casualties and seek to out-last the enemy. For most of the nuclear era, Western nations at least have not paid much attention to the last phase of mobilization, presumably on the assumption that any but a brief war would be nuclear and, as such, over quickly and certainly incompatible with wartime manufacture of arms and training of forces. More recent emphasis on the possibility of belligerents refraining from or severely restricting the use of nuclear weapons has led to renewed interest in "sustainability" — meaning primarily ready supplies for at least a few weeks fighting — and in the "industrial base" for more extended hostilities.

Mobilization and reinforcement can constitute a race with very profound effects on the outcome of initial hostilities and therefore of the war as a whole. If it became clear to an aggressor that he could not win the mobilization race, or if having actually started it he was painfully surprized by the promptness and scale of his opponents response, then he might never launch his attack. Much therefore depends not merely on the effectiveness of the mobilization process but also on when each side begins. Presumably the would-be aggressor begins — though one can imagine a threatening political situation in which NATO, as the weaker side, takes military steps first. Some mobilization and reinforcement can be carried out surreptitiously: ammunition and fuel stocks can be brought up to wartime levels, individual reservists can join units, leave can be stopped, some kinds of training halted and other, more related to the final polishing of combat readiness, begun. But there are tight limits as to how much of this could go on undetected even on the Warsaw Pact side.

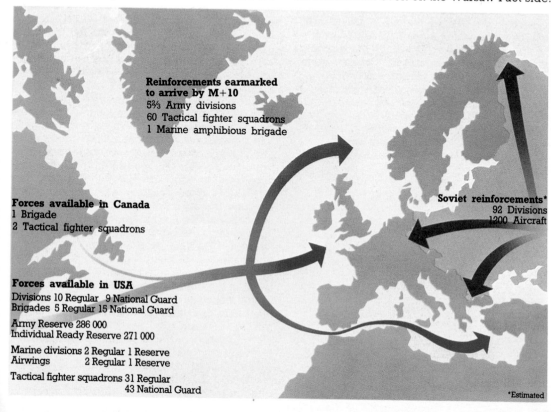

Reinforcements earmarked to arrive by M+10
5⅔ Army divisions
60 Tactical fighter squadrons
1 Marine amphibious brigade

Forces available in Canada
1 Brigade
2 Tactical fighter squadrons

Soviet reinforcements*
92 Divisions
1200 Aircraft

Forces available in USA
Divisions 10 Regular 9 National Guard
Brigades 5 Regular 15 National Guard
Army Reserve 286 000
Individual Ready Reserve 271 000
Marine divisions 2 Regular 1 Reserve
Airwings   2 Regular 1 Reserve
Tactical fighter squadrons 31 Regular
                           43 National Guard

*Estimated

Reinforcement timescales

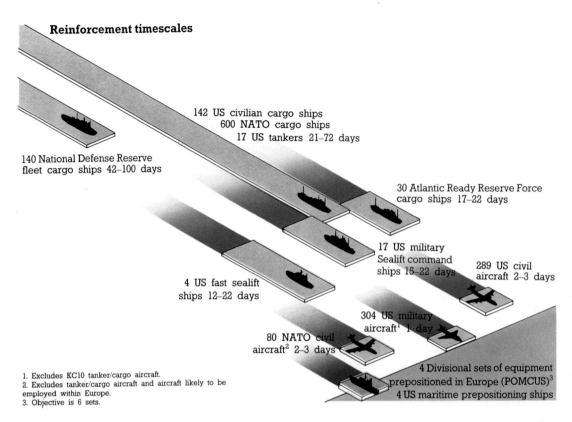

142 US civilian cargo ships
600 NATO cargo ships
17 US tankers 21–72 days

140 National Defense Reserve
fleet cargo ships 42–100 days

30 Atlantic Ready Reserve Force
cargo ships 17–22 days

17 US military
Sealift command
ships 15–22 days

289 US civil
aircraft 2–3 days

4 US fast sealift
ships 12–22 days

304 US military
aircraft[1] 1 day

80 NATO civil
aircraft[2] 2–3 days

4 Divisional sets of equipment
prepositioned in Europe (POMCUS)[3]
4 US maritime prepositioning ships

1. Excludes KC10 tanker/cargo aircraft.
2. Excludes tanker/cargo aircraft and aircraft likely to be employed within Europe.
3. Objective is 6 sets.

Above: The diagram illustrates the speed with which the concept of prepositioning allows airlift to increase U.S. forces in Europe substantially within a few days. It also shows, however, how much more substantial is the lift capability of ships and the much more prompt contribution of dedicated sealift ships compared to civilian or reserve vessels. The U.S. has made heavy investment in recent years to increase both airlift and fast, promptly available sealift, and the position depicted here, though revealing great difficulties, is nevertheless a vast improvement on the situation in previous decades of NATO's existence.

More likely than ignorance of enemy behaviour as a factor delaying NATO mobilization is the difficulty of reaching political decision, especially as sixteen nations have to agree to bring Alliance forces to their full strength. Mobilization can be regarded as a provocative act; 1914 is always cited as a crisis in which the imperatives of mobilization were themselves a major cause of war. In 1973 Israel conceded Egypt many of the advantages of surprize rather than risk the opprobrium of seeming the aggressor. Moreover mobilization is extremely costly, and therefore not a course to take lightly.

It is very clear that these conditions offer opportunities for the Soviet Union to achieve a considerable degree of effective surprize. Military history, much of it very recent suggests that surprize is easier to achieve than one might expect, even in the modern age of electronic surveillance. As Egypt's success in surprizing Israel in 1973 illustrated, strategic preconceptions, as well as political inhibitions about responding to warning, led to serious misinterpretation of what was happening. Because Egypt's policy was misunderstood and viewed through the prism of Israeli strategic thought, what in retrospect seem to have been clear signals were ignored or, more seriously, not ignored but refused credence.

The problem of surprize is made more serious for NATO by the careful attention given to effecting surprize in Soviet doctrine. Perhaps in

Below: The diagram dramatizes the advantages enjoyed by the Soviet Union over the United States in the first stages of mobilization and reinforcement. In the mid-term the United States can come close to redressing the balance of reinforcement (though not of overall available forces). In the long run the United States could significantly reduce its overall disadvantage, but it must be doubted whether a conflict in Europe could be sustained that long without escalation to nuclear war. It would clearly be unwise, however, to have no provision for prolonged mobilization. An element of unrealism in all these estimates is the absence of allowance for the effects of enemy action on the process of mobilization and reinforcement.

part because of the dreadful failure of the Soviet Union to anticipate and respond adequately to Hitler's attack in 1941, Soviet military thought now lays great stress on surprise and believes that the advent of nuclear weapons reinforces the need for it, as a way to achieve quick success before catastrophic consequences ensue. Soviet exercises as well as Soviet theory demonstrate strenuous efforts to achieve surprise. Moreover Soviet writings show that the Soviet Union has realized the difficulty NATO has in reaching collective decisions. This may not only encourage the Soviet Union to hope for success in catching NATO unprepared but also stimulate deliberate efforts of political warfare in a pre-hostilities crisis to increase NATO's inhibitions perhaps even persuade some allies to opt for neutrality.

Even before the intensity of Soviet interest in surprise was widely appreciated in the West and before some of the more remarkable recent instances of successful surprise, most military analysts thought it prudent to assume that the Warsaw Pact would enjoy at least a weeks lead in mobilization.

For the Warsaw Pact the task is to bring up to

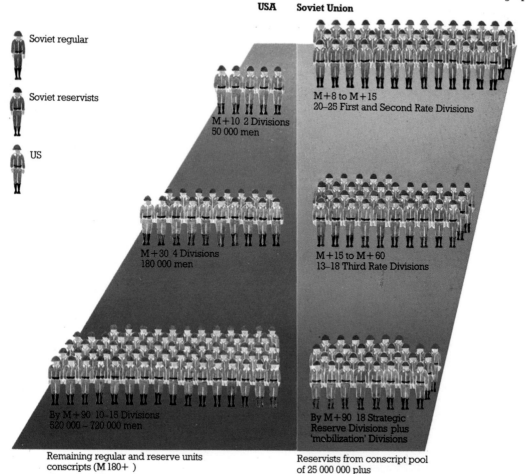

USA   Soviet Union

Soviet regular

Soviet reservists

US

M+10 2 Divisions
50 000 men

M+8 to M+15
20–25 First and Second Rate Divisions

M+30 4 Divisions
180 000 men

M+15 to M+60
13–18 Third Rate Divisions

By M+90 10–15 Divisions
520 000 – 720 000 men

By M+90 18 Strategic
Reserve Divisions plus
'mobilization' Divisions

Remaining regular and reserve units
conscripts (M 180+)

Reservists from conscript pool
of 25 000 000 plus

effectiveness the few Czech and Polish reserve divisions but above all to activate and bring into the order of battle the Soviet divisions in the European Soviet Union; this reserve comprises some 65 divisions, ⅓ tank, ⅔ motor-rifle, of which between ⅓ and ⅔ are Category I and II and the rest needing considerable readying. For the ultimate utility of these units much would depend, as it would for all conceivable mobilization and reinforcement, on whether the process of preparation and movement came under active enemy attack. Moreover for all reserve units, the time taken to get up nominally to wartime strength, whether by addition of individuals or the adding on of whole reserve formations, must be qualified by the anticipated operational capability of such units. In many cases men and command structures will be very rusty and a trade-off must be made between getting performance up to scratch or placing the unit in the line in time to affect the course of the battle, however inefficiently.

On the NATO side a major element in mobilization would be bringing the German Territorial Army into action. This not merely plays a role — which may greatly increase — in rear-area defence but provides many supporting services for the regular armies, allied as well as German. A second task for NATO is to flesh out under-strength active units — the British Army depends on a great deal of this — and bring forward active units from their place of peacetime deployment to their battle station; this process is supposed to take only two or three days. It is particularly crucial for the Dutch forces — nine of whose ten brigades are in the Netherlands in peacetime — and the four Belgian brigades which are stationed back in Belgium.

Below: This diagram gives the alliance-wide potential for mobilization by NATO indicating the relative national contributions in overall manpower at the typical time stages of M + 10 and M + 90, where M is the day at which the decision to mobilize is taken.

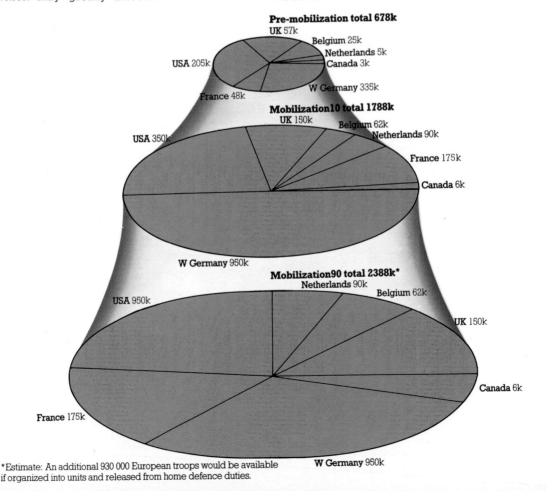

Pre-mobilization total 678k
UK 57k
Belgium 25k
Netherlands 5k
Canada 3k
USA 205k
W Germany 335k
France 48k

Mobilization10 total 1788k
UK 150k
Belgium 62k
Netherlands 90k
USA 350k
France 175k
Canada 6k
W Germany 950k

Mobilization90 total 2388k*
Netherlands 90k
Belgium 62k
UK 150k
USA 950k
Canada 6k
France 175k
W Germany 950k

*Estimate: An additional 930 000 European troops would be available if organized into units and released from home defence duties.

Parallel to this process is the urgent one of bringing over a few British units, a Canadian brigade and, above all, American reinforcements. There is also the imponderable of French forces. While the French conventional army is reorganizing in a way that will reduce its size, it still constitutes one of the few uncommitted potential reserves and its 6–8 small armoured divisions, three of which are stationed in Germany, could be supported by the lightly armed Rapid Deployment Force (Force d'Action Rapide — FAR) being created for an expeditionary role.

The key question is, however, the prompt availability of American reinforcements. The United States is currently committed to bring to Europe within ten days 6 armoured divisions and 60 squadrons of tactical aircraft. This can only be possible by air. Consequently all heavy equipment must be prepositioned in Europe in dehumidified stores. By 1985 sufficient for 4 divisions was so deployed and work was proceeding on the remaining 2 divisions, with the expense of providing the storage facilities funded by the collective NATO "infrastructure" programme. Aircraft can deploy themselves

across the Atlantic with adequate refuelling capacity but they too need facilities at the European end before they can be operational. The shortage of airfields, especially with hardened shelters, was one of the grievances inspiring American congressional critics of European members of NATO in the early 'eighties.

Prepositioning does entail a rigid commitment of a unit to one battlefield. While the Central Front of NATO is perhaps clearly a priority and the only likely place where large numbers of heavy armoured units could be

Below: The diagram illustrates the capacity of NATO powers to reinforce the combat airpower in Central Europe. Almost all the improvement derives from the forward deployment of American aircraft. Providing airfields, hardened hanger protection and other facilities for these aircraft has been one of NATO's most pressing needs. A major contribution to solving the problem has been the idea of "colocating" American aircraft on underutilized airfields of West European air forces.

Central Europe

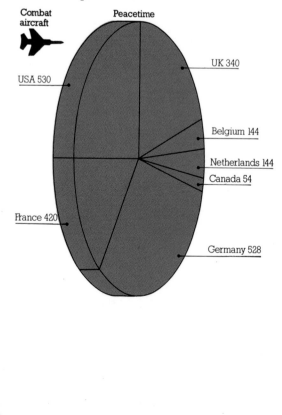

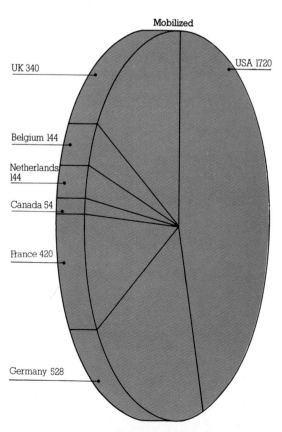

needed, the issue is less clear for the Flanks and the lighter formations destined for them. One solution is prepositioning at sea, an idea long mooted but also long delayed in part because of the U.S. Congress' post-Vietnam distaste for intervention. The Reagan Administration has, however, commissioned Maritime Prepositioning Ships to hold the equipment of three Marine Amphibious Brigades. Troops would be flown to join their equipment at the point of deployment. The first such ship is destined for deployment in the Atlantic.

The later stages of reinforcement in a war would be very dependent on sealift which is immensely cheaper and more efficient than airlift if time permits. Only a few aircraft — the C5 and the proposed C17 — carry such oversize and overweight equipment as tanks and helicopters without dismantling. Aircraft do have the advantage of being often able to fly directly to the point of use. An important distinction exists between inter-theatre and intra-theatre lift; the latter implies a two-segment lift, with consequent delays and vulnerabilities.

NATO faces a problem with shipping for military purposes. Not only is there a severe decline in the number of allied flag ships but many modern merchant ships are ill-suited to military lift. In particular container ships cannot easily carry mixed cargoes and require specialized port facilities. In the Falklands the British found most useful "break-bulk" ships with their own cranes. The scale of the problem is suggested by the fact that European members of NATO have earmarked 600 ships to supplement U.S. lift. Work is proceeding on adaptation tests to convert container ships to carry military cargo, by, for instance, constructing slide-in decks.

Right: The pattern of quantitative NATO inferiority to the Warsaw Pact is more or less reversed in the naval field where NATO forces are formidable, particularly where the larger vessels are concerned. This reflects NATO's overriding concern with the security of the Atlantic and maritime approaches to Europe for reinforcement and the role of naval forces in supporting NATO operations on the Northern and Southern Flanks. Hidden in this chart is the powerful presence of several large U.S. aircraft carriers which far outmatch those of other nations. The emphasis of the Warsaw Pact on submarines and mine warfare reflects the Pact's need to break through NATO naval barriers and its effort to keep NATO amphibious forces at bay and to impede NATO martime transport.

The Maritime Battle

It is no more than to be expected that an alliance actually named after a major ocean should face a problem of maritime reinforcement, especially as by far the single most powerful member is on a different continent from the battlefields. The success of the reinforcement effort would clearly depend not merely on the availability of the necessary logistical equipment but also on the outcome of the war at sea.

Several members of the North Atlantic Alliance have been major naval powers for centuries and since its inception NATO has always maintained large naval forces dedicated to a prospective third Battle of the Atlantic. The Soviet Union is also a major naval power. Contrary to common belief, this is not a new development but until relatively recently the Soviet Navy was confined chiefly to a role in the direct support of operations on land, including amphibious landings. Over the last thirty years or so the Soviet Navy has substantially extended its capabilities. In the early part of the Cold War a force heavily dependent on submarines as an appropriate counter to the surface power of NATO, especially the aircraft carriers which then had a significant role in the United States strategic nuclear strike plan, the Soviet Navy now possesses a much more balanced fleet, having added powerful surface units to its order

of battle, including helicopter carriers soon likely to be supplemented by a significant component of seaborne fixed-wing aircraft.

The Soviet Navy has adopted an increasingly forward pattern of peacetime deployment, establishing in the NATO area a permanent presence in the Mediterranean and conducting regular exercises far out into the Atlantic Ocean. At the same time, of course, Soviet ballistic missile carrying submarines (SSBNs) have become a major element in Soviet strategic nuclear striking power.

Despite all this, the role of naval forces in NATO strategy has long been and still remains a controversial one. While NATO clung to the early "Lisbon goals" for a full fledged conventional rearmament, it was possible to think of a future European war as a rerun of World War II and thus to envisage a third Battle of the Atlantic with the Soviet submarines cast in the role of Nazi U-boats. But once NATO strategy took on a nuclear flavour, particularly that of Massive Retaliation, it was hard to see how a land war in Europe could go on long enough to make resupply across the Atlantic relevant. Moreover it was unlikely that a port structure would survive on either side of the Atlantic to send or receive supplies. West European ports were, indeed, commonly assumed to be one of the

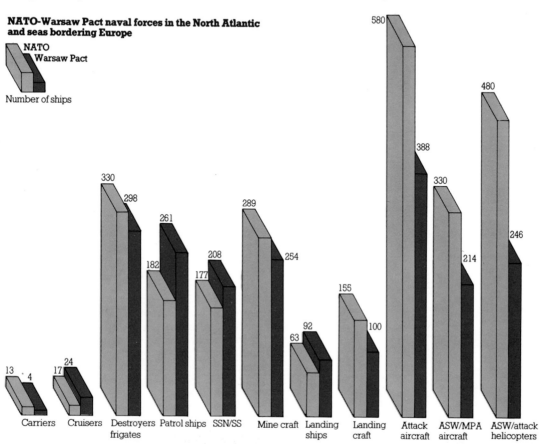

NATO-Warsaw Pact naval forces in the North Atlantic and seas bordering Europe

NATO
Warsaw Pact

Number of ships

	NATO	Warsaw Pact
Carriers	13	4
Cruisers	17	24
Destroyers frigates	330	298
Patrol ships	182	261
SSN/SS	177	208
Mine craft	289	254
Landing ships	63	92
Landing craft	155	100
Attack aircraft	580	388
ASW/MPA aircraft	330	214
ASW/attack helicopters	480	246

North Atlantic maritime balance	Strike a/c carrier	Anti-sub a/c carrier	Nuclear submarine	Submarine	Major surface combatants	Fighter *	Strike/reconn-aissance*	ASW *
USA	2–5		49		90	84–156	68–170	255-285
Belgium					4			
Canada				3	12			14
France				9	24			16
West Germany					13			?
Netherlands				6	18			11
Norway				12 (coastal)	8			7
Portugal				3	17			
Spain					11	24		
UK		3	12	14	46	30	24	31
NATO total	5	3	61	47	243	138–210	92–194	334-364
Soviet Northern Fleet	0	2	71	54	85	28	120/70	60

ASW = Anti submarine warfare

* Carrier and land based, excludes helicopters

Above: A breakdown of NATO naval forces in the Atlantic shows the widespread contributions of many members of the alliance and the major role played by the United Kingdom. French aircraft carriers are normally deployed in the Mediterranean. Several of the smaller allies such as Belgium make major contributions to mine and anti-mine warfare with vessels not shown on the chart.

prime target sets envisaged for the earlier Soviet theatre nuclear weapons.

This logic never led NATO to abandon its naval efforts, but the anti-submarine component was for a long time only imperfectly welded to the logic of the prospective war in Europe. The advent of the flexible response clearly made it necessary to reopen this question but it by no means answered it. A maritime battle to facilitate resupply was more plausible under flexible response than massive retaliation, but the general ambiguity of flexible response left the duration of the war and of its conventional phase so uncertain as to offer no clear cut guideline for what would be an appropriate maritime posture. So long as NATO did not provide itself with the

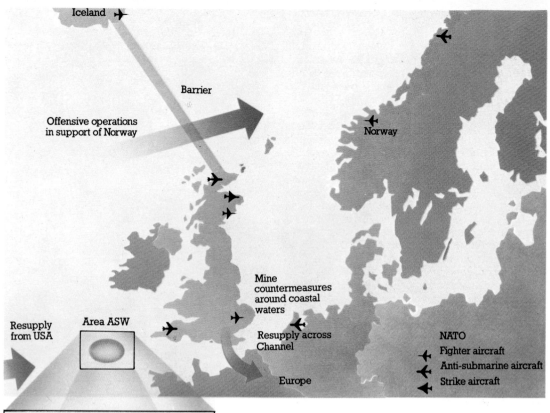

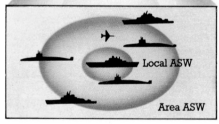

Above: The map characterizes several of the primary operations likely to be conducted by NATO naval forces in a future full scale war. These include anti-submarine operations conducted by convoying supply ships, area ASW and the maintenance of an ASW barrier in the Greenland-Iceland-United Kingdom gap; mine counter-measures in European waters; and offensive strikes by carrier forces in support of Norway. A wide variety of ships and aircraft contribute to these operations.

forces or military stocks for even thirty days of war, it seemed unlikely that there would be time before defeat or nuclear escalation to deliver substantial seaborne supplies, even if there were any to be delivered.

On the other hand flexible response does not rule out a prolonged war or the possibility that even if some nuclear weapons were used the war might be limited and kept under control. It would indeed be very destructive of the credibility of flexible response to abandon all pretensions to extended operations or to resupply. It would also be psychologically very damaging to the morale of an Atlantic alliance if control of that ocean were conceded to the Warsaw Pact. Indeed to do so might offer the Soviet Union various ways of squeezing NATO by operations of limited liability. Thus in the maritime sphere, as in other aspects of its strategy, NATO provides a substantial though far from unquestionably adequate capacity to fight, without ever being completely explicit about how it would fight or under what circumstances.

Maritime warfare has altered its character greatly since World War II. That war had already taken far the multi-dimensional character of maritime war that had had its origins even in World War I. The aircraft and the submarine provided new challenges to the surface ship that monopolized naval warfare until this century. Now ballistic and cruise missiles take this revolution much further, so that the maritime battle is no longer merely a matter for naval forces and navies are no longer confined to effectiveness at sea but can strike far inland. Indeed land-based aircraft pose one of the Soviet Union's major threats against NATO shipping.

The traditional problem in the battle of the Atlantic has been the protection of merchant shipping and twice the answer has proved to be convoy. There is, however, an irrepressible urge for navies to find some less defensive, more offensive answer. In World War II one such was found in "hunter-killer groups" which sought out submarines rather than await them near the convoys. Today the speed of merchant ships and greatly increased size are factors' placing convoy in question and NATO may try to establish protected lanes and areas rather than escort convoys.

Two new possibilities also arise. One is to take advantage of the Soviet Union's severe geographical difficulties and try to bottle-up Soviet surface and submarine forces behind the Greenland-Iceland-United Kingdom gap. Such efforts are greatly assisted by the modern capacity to implant detective devices on the seabed, linked to information processing computers and to automated mine and moored torpedo systems as well as to friendly vessels and aircraft. This system can hope to impede and destroy not merely submarines intent on attacking NATO shipping but also Soviet SSBNs. Such a NATO capacity is a serious threat to Soviet nuclear power. One Soviet response has been the deployment of submarine launched ballistic missiles (SLBMs) with sufficient range to hit targets from behind the barrier, probably in the Barents Sea. But in fact SSBNs also pose a difficult problem for NATO, for it may be considered dangerously escalatory in a pre-nuclear war to attack elements of the Soviet strategic force. It would remain to be seen which side, if any, exercised self-restraint to prevent this situation arising.

The Soviet Union possesses numerous options for waging war in the Atlantic. To its surface fleet, now deploying increasing organic airpower, are added nuclear and conventional submarines in large numbers, maritime reconnaissance and attack aircraft, equipped with a variety of stand-off missiles, and a highly developed capability for mine warfare.

In recent years the U.S. Navy has increasingly espoused a second novel approach to the maritime problem by adopting an offensive strategy to deal with this multiple threat, by launching powerful attacks on Soviet forces in their northern bases from the American strike carrier fleet deployed forward into the Norwegian Sea. Critics of this policy argue that it is expensive, tending to distract resources from the less glamorous escort and hunter-killer submarine forces, and that the carrier forces would be

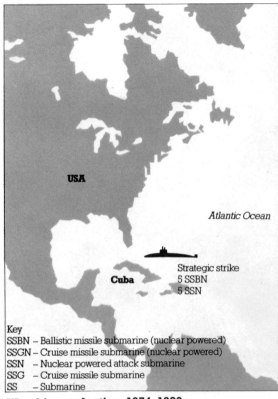

Atlantic Ocean

USA

Cuba

Strategic strike
5 SSBN
5 SSN

Key
SSBN – Ballistic missile submarine (nuclear powered)
SSGN – Cruise missile submarine (nuclear powered)
SSN – Nuclear powered attack submarine
SSG – Cruise missile submarine
SS – Submarine

Warship production 1974–1983

Major surface combatants – 900 tons and over

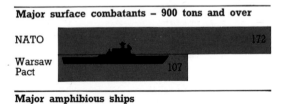

NATO — 172

Warsaw Pact — 107

Major amphibious ships

NATO — 9

Warsaw Pact — 33

Ballistic missile submarines

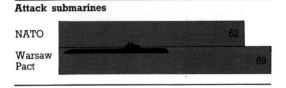

NATO — 6

Warsaw Pact — 34

Attack submarines

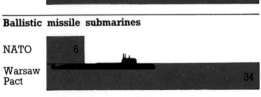

NATO — 62

Warsaw Pact — 69

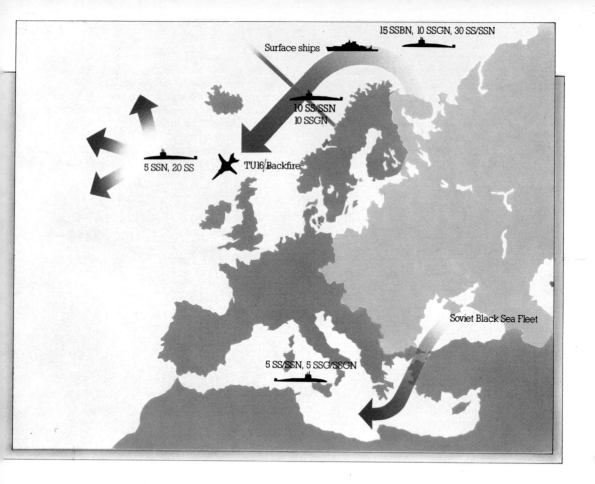

15 SSBN, 10 SSGN, 30 SS/SSN

Surface ships

10 SS/SSN
10 SSGN

5 SSN, 20 SS

TU16/Backfire

Soviet Black Sea Fleet

5 SS/SSN, 5 SSG/SSGN

Left: In recent years the Warsaw Pact has outstripped NATO in building warships but NATO holds a decisive lead in the procurement of major surface combitants. The record in attack submarines is relatively balanced. NATO amphibious ships tend to be larger than those of the Pact. The Soviet lead in ballistic missile submarines is large over this period but here the record should be read with caution as the cycle of procurement for strategic nuclear weapons follows major policy trends and other periods would show comparisons much more favourable to NATO. Moreover these weapons, mostly not directly relevant to the theatre balance, have to be studied in relation to other arms of the major deterrent forces, such as ICBMs, rather than naval forces. Nevertheless in all-out war attacking SSBNs could be a major naval task.

Above: The map illustrates operations that might be conducted by Soviet naval forces, including breakout through the GIUK gap to attack NATO forces, primarily by aircraft and submarines, and possibly deployment of additional SSBNs forward, perhaps with the aid of Cuban bases. If the Turkish Straits could be forced, units of the Black Sea Fleet could join those deployed forward in peacetime to operate in the Mediterranean, especially against the U.S. Sixth Fleet.

Below: The map depicts the areas of NATO barrier operations and the task of the Soviet Northern Fleet in Breaking out. The pictures illustrate the variety of weapons employed in such operations. In the smaller illustration is a Soviet helicopter carrier with one of its aircraft, together with a supporting land-based ASW aircraft. In the larger illustration an RAF Nimrod ASW aircraft drops sonar buoys while a Royal Naval Sea King uses a sonar to penetrate to sound layers below the surface. This is desirable because variations in temperature and salinity create barriers that reflect and sound channels that convey sonar signals. An attack submarine trails a sonar detecting device below a Royal Naval 'through deck cruiser' or light aircraft carrier, accompanied by an ASW frigate. Moored on

NATO submarine patrol areas
USSR submarine routes
NATO maritime aircraft patrol

the seabed in support of barrier operations are fixed sonar arrays, probably linked to land-based computers, and mines including some containing guided torpedoes which can be activated by the target to home on it. Interceptor aircraft both land-based and seaborne would doubtless harrass maritime patrol aircraft and ASW helicopters, while attack aircraft would threaten surface ships.

Most of the attack systems could employ either conventional or nuclear warheads. While the use of nuclear weapons at sea would have serious implications, the relative lack of collateral damage and the good command and control systems employed by naval forces lead many to believe that maritime use would be the safest and least 'escalatory' way to employ nuclear weapons.

unlikely to survive Soviet air, submarine and possibly long-range ballistic and cruise missile attacks if they ventured as deeply into hostile waters as the range of their attack capability would require. At the very least, it is argued, defending the carriers would absorb a disproportionate amount of NATO's maritime strength.

This debate continued unresolved in the mid-'eighties, although the offensive carrier strategy enjoyed support at the highest levels of the U.S. Navy. The aircraft carrier is certainly a very vulnerable as well as powerful system and although harder to attack than many of its critics claim, represents an immensely valuable single package of losable military force.

The Atlantic is not, of course, NATO's only theatre of naval operations. American naval power built around the carrier forces of the Sixth Fleet is one of NATO's major military assets in the Mediterranean. To a large extent the Sixth Fleet must be regarded, however, as a Cold and limited war-force related to American policy in the Middle East. In a war with the Soviet Union, the Sixth Fleet and associated French and Italian fleets would find the Mediterranean, especially its Eastern end, a very confined space in which to face a threat that has greatly increased in recent years as the Soviet Union has extended the range of its airpower. This would be particularly deadly if it had access, as it may, to North African bases, perhaps in Libya. Such a threat is greater than that posed by the substantial but still weak and isolated Soviet Mediterranean naval squadron, though as always much would depend on the degree to which NATO forces were fully alert and politically authorized to act in the early stages of crisis and war.

In the remaining NATO maritime areas, the Baltic and Black Seas, NATO is at something of a disadvantage and naval operations on both sides are likely to be confined to support of land operations, including the possibility of major Soviet amphibious operations.

U.S. Carrier Battle Groups and the Norwegian Sea

One of the most controversial questions in U.S. and NATO maritime strategy concerns the role of aircraft carrier battle groups in the battle for maritime supremacy around the Northern Flank and in the Atlantic generally. Closing the Greenland-Iceland-United Kingdom (GIUK) gap against Soviet air, surface and sub-surface maritime forces and facilitating the penetration of NATO forces in the opposite direction is an undisputed priority for NATO. Much more debateable is the role of large U.S. carrier forces both to strike at Soviet bases and to assist in the maritime battle proper.

Proponents of carriers argue that they would project an unrivalled striking power; critics suggest to sail carriers into the Norwegian Sea would entail the almost certain destruction of immensely costly assets. Moreover as this role is argued as one of the main reasons for sustaining U.S. carrier forces at fifteen groups, it must also be viewed as a diversion of U.S. resources from other naval and military tasks.

The cost of a modern carrier group is immense. At 1984 prices a typical task force would have a capital cost of some $17 billion.

This would be made up of a nuclear powered carrier, at $3.4 billion, three anti-aircraft and anti-missile cruisers equipped with Aegis radar, at $700 million-$1 billion each, eight destroyers at $600-$700 million each, two or three nuclear attack submarines at $700 million, plus assorted supply ships. To these must be added the aircraft, which on one carrier might comprise 24 F14 air defence aircraft each costing $37 million, 24 F18 shorter range defence and attack aircraft at $21 million, 14 A6 strike and tanker aircraft at $29 million, 4 EA6B electronic warfare aircraft at $34 million, 4 E2C early warning aircraft at $39 million, 10 S3A anti-submarine aircraft at $43 million, and six anti-submarine helicopters at $24 million respectively.

It can be seen that much of this investment is to defend the carrier rather than to strike. Proponents of the carrier argue, however, that the escort ships and others in the area would be very vulnerable without the close-by air cover of a carrier group. British losses at the hands of rather simple Argentinian air forces during the Falklands war are cited as evidence. Thus it is suggested that the relationship between the carrier's defensive needs and offensive naval capability is a complex one rebutting any condemnation based on simplistic cost analysis.

The threat against a carrier force in the Norwegian Sea would come chiefly from Soviet aircraft and submarines. Of the former probably the most formidable is the long range Backfire, equipped with the AS4 missile provided with both a cruise and ballistic capability; in the latter

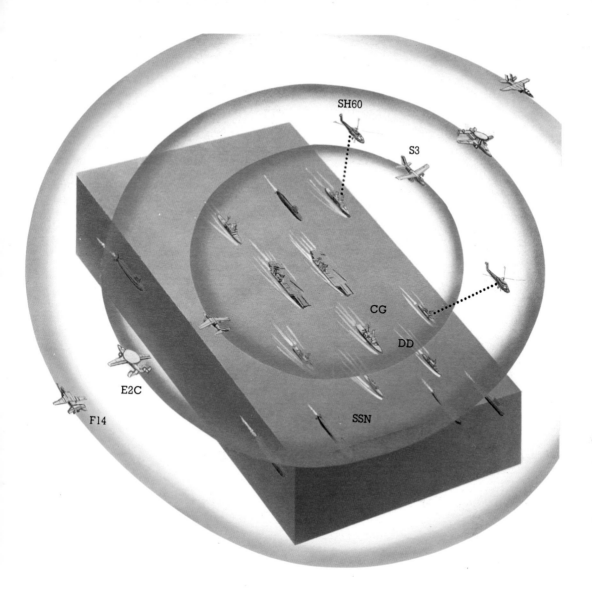

Above: The diagram illustrates the pattern of deployment of the vast and expensive array of forces required to defend the several billion dollars worth of naval assets represented by a pair of modern nuclear aircraft carriers. Attack nuclear submarines (SSN) provide sub-surface escort, surface escorts (DD) search on the surface for enemy submarines as do fixed and rotary wing ASW aircraft, while electronic surveillance and interceptor aircraft combine with guided missile cruisers (CG) to deal with the threat from the air.

mode its speed of Mach 2.5 creates a difficult defensive problem. The best defence is attack on the mother aircraft before missile launch which requires interception at least 200 miles from the target. To effect this the carrier uses its early warning aircraft backed up by a pattern of F 14s on airborne "cap" patrol. Closer-in the missiles of the Aegis equipped cruisers have an intercept range out to 60 miles. A carrier group in the Norwegian Sea might also benefit from the coverage of land based AWACS aircraft and F 15 interceptors. If so, then of course the attributable costs of the operation need to be revised upwards and the task force becomes dependent on bases in Norway, the United Kingdom and Iceland, the last not the most politically reliable participant in NATO. Soviet forces would doubtless try to swamp these defences by one or both of two tactics; "stream", sequential attacks to wear out the defences, or massed "saturation" assaults to

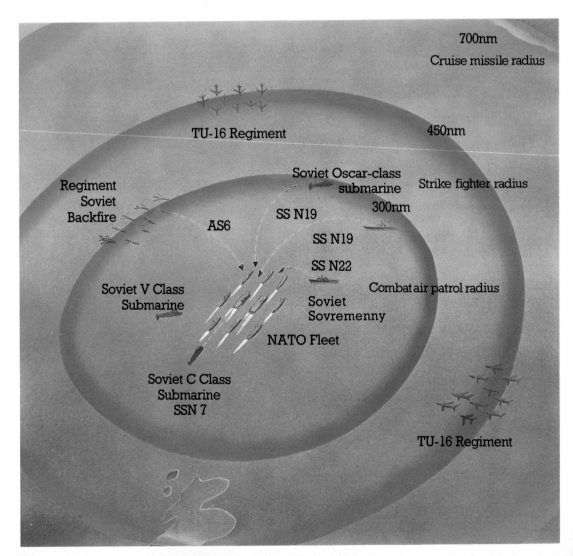

700nm

Cruise missile radius

450nm

TU-16 Regiment

Soviet Oscar-class
submarine

Strike fighter radius

Regiment
Soviet
Backfire

AS6

SS N19

300nm

SS N19

SS N22

Soviet V Class
Submarine

Soviet
Sovremenny

Combat air patrol radius

NATO Fleet

Soviet C Class
Submarine
SSN 7

TU-16 Regiment

overwhelm them.

The carrier group's defences against the submarine threat are derived from P 3 land based anti-submarine aircraft ($33 million), towed sonar arrays (SURTASS) and the sonars and other detection devices of individual ships, submarines, aircraft and helicopters. A major component in the ASW network is the escorting nuclear submarines.

Left: A Soviet attack on U.S. aircraft carriers would be mounted by submarines and aircraft. The former would employ both torpedoes and guided-missiles, possibly nuclear armed. Two regiments of TU16 and one of Backfire attack with air to surface AS6 missiles with a range of 175 miles. An escort 'cap' of F14 patrolling at 300 miles radius could keep this threat at bay. A Kirov cruiser attacks with 270 mile range surface to surface SSN19 missiles; against this threat and that from the Sovremenny destroyer F18 attack aircraft could engage out to 450 miles. Oscar and Charlie class nuclear submarines might launch SSN19 and SSN7 missiles while an older Victor class submarine could close with torpedoes. Given adequate warning the carrier thus has a defence against current Soviet threats but it would require high vigilence and training not to be worn down by such a varied attack. The trend is for naval missiles to have longer and longer ranges with the U.S. deploying anti-ship Cruise missiles of 450 miles range and land attack missiles with ranges of 700 miles (conventional warhead) or 1500 miles (nuclear) and the Soviets building similar systems.

The Land Battle

Of all the forms of modern warfare, that on the ground is almost certainly the most complex. While even today's sophisticated armies may not dispose of the most technologically advanced weapons of all, which may be in the hands of naval and air forces, the variety of weapons and equipment in army hands is by far the greatest, while the influence of terrain adds a further immensely variable and idiosyncratic element. Moreover the individual role of large numbers of soldiers gives a special importance to such intangibles as morale and leadership.

World War II saw a proliferation of specialized equipment like mechanized mine clearing and bridge laying vehicles, and the intensification of the third dimension to land warfare in the form of aerial and counter-aerial operations. Such tendencies have now gone much further and major weapons of all kinds have become more powerful and more numerous, while a large new family of technologically advanced aids for the foot soldier has appeared. The management of this array of forces has consequently become a much more complicated task which, because of these added capabilities for combat, must be discharged more rapidly than ever before.

The tank, centrepiece of ground warfare since, 1918, is today much faster, heavier, better armoured and more powerfully armed than its ancestors. To counter it, infantry now possess not merely much more effective anti-tank weapons but also many more of them. A battalion that had perhaps eight recoiless rifles in the 'sixties today may have more than seventy anti-tank guided missile launchers. Artillery has progressed from the towed 25 pounder to standardization on the 155 mm calibre or thereabouts, a gun that in 1945 would have been regarded as a specialized heavy piece. All of the heavy weaponry is now also associated with a wide range of mechanized logistic and engineering equipment.

One result of all this has been to put a premium on training, to make much greater demands on soldiers of all ranks, and to put a higher and higher proportion into supporting rather than immediately weapon-firing roles. Another consequence is to intensify the "combined arms" nature of modern ground warfare. Not only do the various forms of land force have to be closely co-ordinated on a faster moving battlefield, but the third air dimension must be built in both defensively and offensively. This demands not merely careful co-ordination to avoid simple error — like bombing friendly troops or shooting down friendly aircraft — but at a more fundamental level the design of operations to maximize the mutually supportive effect of various arms. Ground forces, for instance, may concentrate on harrassing and destroying enemy air defences so as to enable friendly

Above: NATO forces facing a major Warsaw Pact armoured attack would find a massive force of vehicles bearing down on them, doubtless after a heavy artillery bombardment. Overhead would appear M124, "Hind" ground attack helicopters. At present among the tanks would be the 1960s generation mainstay, the T62, 37 tons with 115 mm guns and a speed of 50 km/h, the newer T72, 41 tons with 125 mm guns and a speed of 60 km/h, and some of a new T80 with improved chemical/nuclear/biological protection. Lighter PT 76 tanks suited to reconnaissance duties, are being replaced by tanks. SU122 (M1974/2-S1) assault guns follow the tanks. Infantry support rides in the BMP with a 73 mm gun, a Sagger anti-tank missile launcher, a 7.62 mm machine gun, a crew of three and eight infantry men who can use their personal weapons from the vehicle while on the move. Highly useful in concept, the BMP has proved vulnerable to ATW in the Middle East and it may be inadequate for the European battlefield. A formidable enemy for it would be the U.S. A10 tank-busting aircraft flying overhead.

MIL MI-24

SU 122

A 10

T 62A

BMPI

aircraft to destroy the rest.

Modern technology enables an increasing number of all types of operation to be carried out at night. This is yet another contribution to a faster moving battle. Such a battle, conducted with such weapons consumes stocks at an increasing pace. Yet the expense is such that only limited numbers can be afforded. While the number of launchers is high, for example, and although Warsaw Pact stocks of ammunition tend to be higher than those of NATO, a typical anti-tank launcher may have only 20-40 missiles and each anti-tank helicopter — itself a major innovation — some 5-10 reloads. Since the

helicopter, if it survived, might hope to fly four or five sorties a day, the limitation is obvious. On the other hand if even a modest proportion of the anti-tank weapons available killed a tank, the attrition of those vehicles would also be very great. An intense modern ground war might, therefore, be a short affair before it either reached a decisive conclusion or bogged down into an exhausted stalemate. The possiblity that the latter might occur may perhaps constitute something of a deterrent to anyone contemplating the launch of such a war.

Below: The tank was invented in World War I as an answer to barbed wire, field fortifications and the machine gun which had virtually destroyed the ability of infantry to advance. Essentially the tank is a piece of firepower enabled to move in a hostile environment by its armour and to cross rough terrain by its tracks. Often regarded as the queen of the battlefield, the tank now faces a variety of sophisticated enemies, all armed with projectiles or mines designed to penetrate the tanks protective shell or to break its tracks. Aircraft like the U.S. A10 shown deploy powerful anti-tank guns; those like the Tornado dispense clusters of mines or anti-tank bomblets many times more effective than old-fashioned "iron" bombs. Anti-tank missiles carrying shaped-charges of various sizes are fired by infantry men while anti-tank helicopters also carry a variety of guns and missiles. Kinetic armour piercing ammunition is fired from guns, including those on other

Aquilla RPV (remotely piloted vehicle) for reconnaissance

A10 anti-tank aircraft

Challenger

Soldier with Dragon anti-tank guided missile

anti-tank mines

tanks, still one of the most effective tank-killing combinations, especially given the high rate of fire and rapid engagement capacity of modern laser aimed tank guns. Indirect fire from longer range artillery, very effective against tanks with traditional H.E. shells, is now given new potential by guided projectiles, possibly dispensing cluster weapons. The tank is also rendered vulnerable by a variety of sensors which may detect it where previously it would have enjoyed cover behind terrain, in trees or at night. Such sensors may be on distant aircraft or on cheap remotely piloted vehicles which penetrate to the rear of the enemy.

An ultimate anti-tank weapon exists in ordinary and enhanced radiation nuclear weapons, but wider strategic considerations prevent commanders relying on permission to use them.

Tornado dispensing anti-tank submunitions

AH 64 attack helicopter armed with anti-tank guided missile and gun

15km (9 miles)

precision-guided anti-tank artillery shell (Copperhead)

Below: Anti-tank weapons may have made great strides but the tank itself is evolving rapidly in an effort to survive on the battlefield. In 1945 the U.S. Sherman tank had a 75 or 88 mm gun, a weight of 31.5 tonnes and a 500 hp engine. By 1985 the standard NATO tank like the German Leopard II depicted here had a gun of 120 mm, weighed 50.5 tonnes and had an engine of 1500 hp. One result is a much greater cross-country speed, now of some 35 mph. The consequence is much greater manoeuverability, with new tactical possibilities, and less time for hostile weapons to acquire their target. Better armour and such devices as smoke dispensers further reduce vulnerability, while the 120 mm guns with laser rangefinders, computerized aiming, and night vision equipment provides a weapon for killing tanks and other targets very competitive with the new missiles. At a cost of some £1.5 to 2 million the newest Western tanks are expensive but remain the dominant element in the land battle.

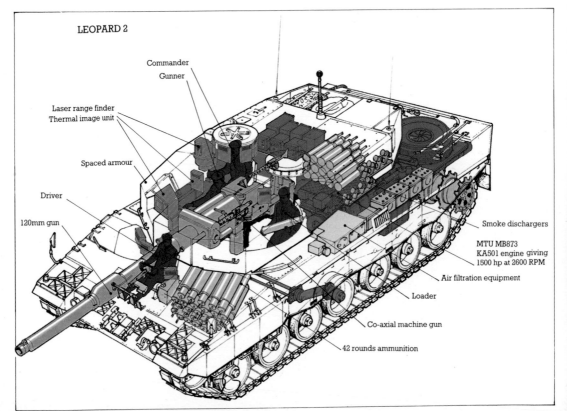

LEOPARD 2

Commander
Gunner

Laser range finder
Thermal image unit

Spaced armour

Driver

120mm gun

Smoke dischargers

MTU MB873
KA501 engine giving
1500 hp at 2600 RPM

Air filtration equipment

Loader

Co-axial machine gun

42 rounds ammunition

Below: Sheer explosive energy released near a tank is relatively ineffective; consequently the two main approaches to destroying it are either a solid shot penetrating by kinetic energy or the chemical energy of a shaped charge directly applied to the armour. Kinetic weapons, usually fired with a "discarding sabot" use heavy metals — typically tungsten, now often replaced by depleted uranium, fired at increasing velocities. Guns using such projectiles have much higher rates of fire than guided missiles.

The missile is able to break armour by use of the shaped charge, by which a jet of hot gas forms a projectile from a shaped liner of copper or other material which if exploded an optimum distance — some inches — from the armour by means of a projecting probe, can penetrate considerable thickness of hardened material. The power of the charge is proportionate to its diameter. Such charges can be rendered ineffective by spaced armour, whereby the explosion is prevented from occurring at optimum distance from the main armour; such armour is, however, proportionately more vulnerable to kinetic energy. Chobham armour, invented in Britain, seeks to provide better protection against both types of threat by creating a sandwich of various metallic and ceramic materials.

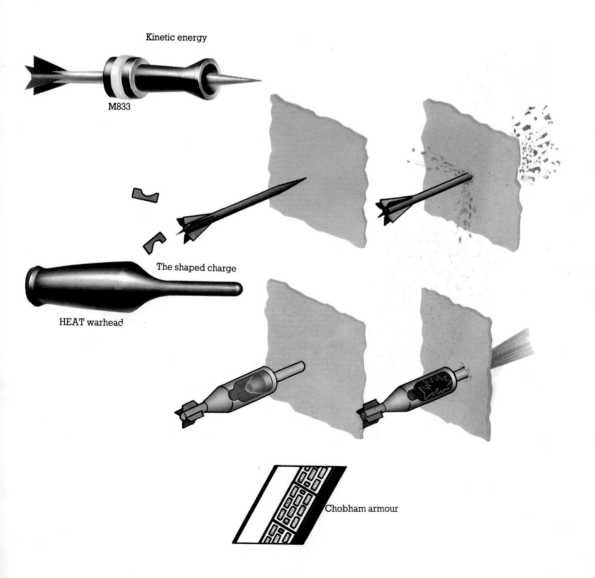

Kinetic energy

M833

The shaped charge

HEAT warhead

Chobham armour

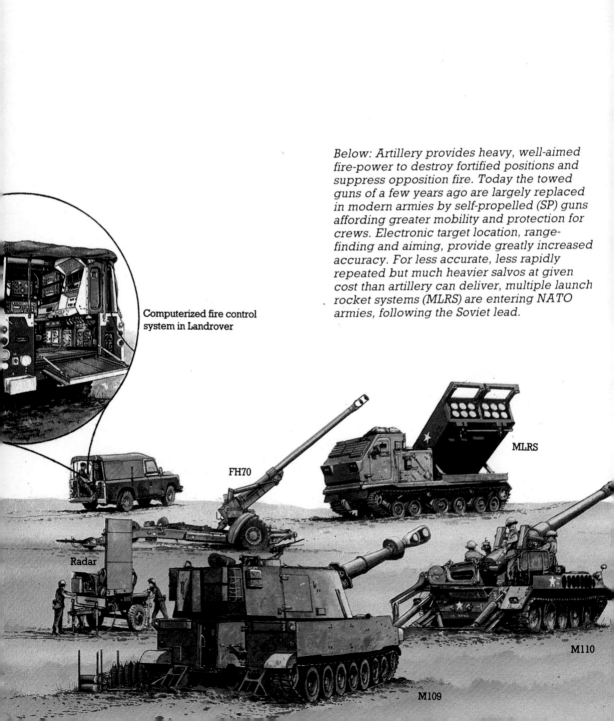

Below: Artillery provides heavy, well-aimed fire-power to destroy fortified positions and suppress opposition fire. Today the towed guns of a few years ago are largely replaced in modern armies by self-propelled (SP) guns affording greater mobility and protection for crews. Electronic target location, range-finding and aiming, provide greatly increased accuracy. For less accurate, less rapidly repeated but much heavier salvos at given cost than artillery can deliver, multiple launch rocket systems (MLRS) are entering NATO armies, following the Soviet lead.

Computerized fire control system in Landrover

MLRS

FH70

Radar

M109

M110

BM21

M1973

M46

M1974

Above: The Soviet Army has always laid great stress on artillery and has developed an elaborate doctrine to establish appropriate fire plans for all tactical situations. Heavy artillery preparation is a feature of most Soviet offensive tactics and this is especially valued today to suppress the NATO anti-tank systems that threaten to impede the Pact's armoured advance. Self-propulsion is being rapidly introduced, giving mobility that accords with redoubled emphasis on the importance of a rapid rate of advance in the face of new NATO defensive capabilities and the danger of escalation to nuclear war. Several types of new 122 mm and 152 mm guns and howitzers have been introduced since 1978, together with a 203 mm SP gun and a 240 mm self-propelled mortar; most are capable of firing nuclear rounds. A new 220 mm rocket launcher has 16 tubes capable of delivering chemical as well as HE rounds. The amount of artillery provided to most artillery units has been substantially increased.

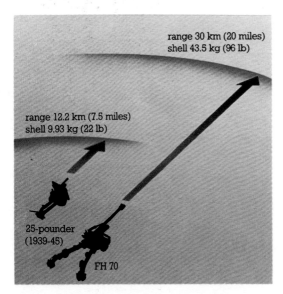

range 30 km (20 miles)
shell 43.5 kg (96 lb)

range 12.2 km (7.5 miles)
shell 9.93 kg (22 lb)

25-pounder
(1939-45)

FH 70

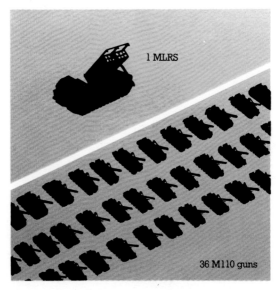

1 MLRS

36 M110 guns

Above: An illustration of the extension of artillery ranges since World War II: the comparative range of the classic British 25 pounder (left) with a modern 155 mm gun, the FH70. Even larger increases in range derive from the introduction of rocket assisted shells. Effectiveness of ammunition has also greatly increased as have rates of fire; the latter bring with them the logistical problem of supplying enough ammunition, transporting it to, and safeguarding it on, the battlefield.

Below: Until after World War II artillery disposed almost solely of H.E. shrapnel, smoke and, if used, chemical rounds. Now this selection has been vastly widened, including nuclear shells, guided projectiles, electronic warfare and cluster weapons, the variety of which is illustrated above.

Above: The Multiple Launch Rocket System can place 7728 anti-personnel or anti-armour charges on target in one salvo, equivalent to that of 36 M110 artillery pieces.

Right: Despite the power of the modern tank and artillery, infantry remain indispensable for occupying ground and completing the clearance of enemy infantry from their positions. Traditional devices of concealment and fortification, facilitated in Europe today by urbanization, combine with a vast array of new improved weapons to keep the infantryman a formidable foe.

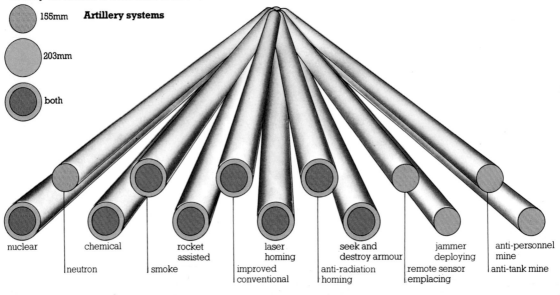

155mm **Artillery systems**

203mm

both

| nuclear | chemical | rocket assisted | laser homing | seek and destroy armour | jammer deploying | anti-personnel mine |
| neutron | smoke | improved conventional | anti-radiation homing | remote sensor emplacing | anti-tank mine |

Marder

M113

Radio (Clansman)

L7A2 machine gun

7.62 sniper rifle (L42A1)

Carl Gustav

Laser Rangefinder

81mm mortar

LAW 80
(shown stowed for carrying)

Infantryman with 7.62 FN FAL rifle

Milan (anti-tank guided missile launcher)

Passive night sight

Air Power in the Land Battle

As the nature of modern maritime war well illustrates, the advent of the aircraft as well as the submarine has made the battle a three-dimensional affair. What was once a wholly naval matter may well be decided by airpower. This is no less so on land; indeed, as the historically more advanced technological alliance, NATO has throughout its existence hoped to use air power to help redress the unfavourable balance of ground forces. NATO air forces have therefore long laid great stress on attacking ground targets both close to the battlefield and further to the rear in "interdiction" missions. Until the 'seventies the Warsaw Pact air forces emphasised air defence even though the Soviet Union had a successful record in the use of ground attack aircraft in World War II. More recently the Soviet Union has redressed the balance of effort and introduced increasing numbers of attack aircraft.

There has been much experience in the use of air power since World War II. Israeli attacks on Egyptian air bases in 1967 showed the dramatic potential of surprize air attack, while in 1973 the Israelis suffered an equal surprize in the initial stages of the war at the hands of the Soviet supplied Egyptian air defence combination of surface to air missiles (SAM) and guns. Over North Vietnam the U.S. Air Force both executed highly effective missions and experienced the hazards of a modern air defence based on missiles, guns and interceptors. In Afghanistan the Soviet Union has exploited the potential of ground attack by rotary and fixed-wing aircraft relatively free of opposition.

The lessons of all this experience are mixed. Air power has been confirmed as a military instrument given great flexibility by its range and speed in both deployment and actual combat. It has been shown to be both highly effective and highly vulnerable according to circumstances both in the air and on the ground. It is also a form of power in which technological and tactical innovation proceeds at a great pace.

Airframe and engine design are producing aircraft that can carry heavier and heavier loads, faster if need be, at lower altitudes and from less and less elaborate bases. Diagnosis of faults and their repair can be hastened and handled in a more dispersed way, though these attributes are only secured at a price. Manned aircraft continue to offer great advantages in flexibility of mission and in capability to mount technological or tactical counter measures. The manned aircraft is, however, increasingly expensive and now faces unmanned alternatives for many airborne missions which can be executed by remotely piloted vehicles (RPV), drones, or cruise and ballistic missiles, devices largely made possible by modern electronic data-links and surveillance devices. Such systems may seek out targets for manned aircraft or actually engage the targets, perhaps creating a less dangerous environment for the manned vehicle to exploit.

The battle between airborne systems and their foes, whether other aircraft or on the ground, is one very much permeated by deception. Aircraft can use chaff, flares, smoke, decoys and electronic counter measures, as well as their speed and capacity to reduce radar images or fly below radar lines of sight. Ground forces can use concealment, camouflage, mobility, hardening, and active defences to repel air attack.

Defence against air attack can also take the offensive form of "counter air" operations as well as "air defence". The former entails seeking out hostile air forces on their bases. Once a task for other aircraft, today various forms of missile promise to carry out such operations more cheaply and more certainly, taking advantage of the fact that the location of most air bases is well known. One of the leading elements in recent proposals for "Deep Strike" involves using large ballistic missiles akin to the Pershing II to deliver modern conventional munitions to airfields.

Runways are not an easy target to destroy and are one mission for which it is difficult to devise a conventional alternative nearly as effective as a tactical nuclear weapon which, with residual radiation, would put an airfield out of business "for the duration". Modern conventional weapons to penetrate and heave up the concrete of runways now offer some anti-airfield capability, but to keep an airfield out of operation would require repeated attacks. If the main operating bases are out of action even for a while, however, their aircraft are forced to operate from less effective secondary bases where they may also be more vulnerable to attack by hostile aircraft for lack of shelters and active defences. Trends in aircraft design and investment in alternative airfields of a simple nature can, of course, do a lot to minimize these dangers. The counter air mission is thus likely to be one of the most active areas for tactical and technological innovation in the next few years.

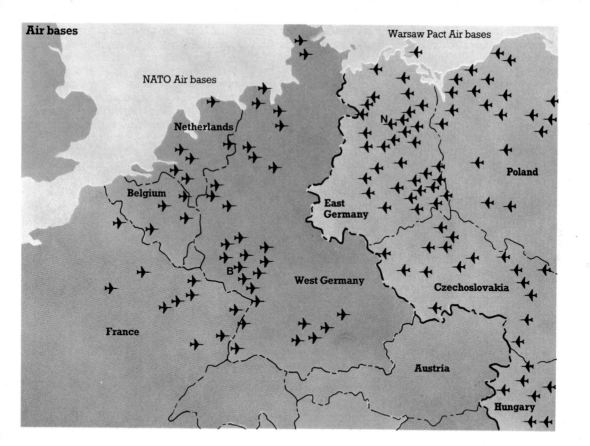

Air bases

NATO Air bases

Warsaw Pact Air bases

Netherlands

Belgium

East Germany

Poland

West Germany

Czechoslovakia

France

Austria

Hungary

Above: The map indicates major NATO and Warsaw Pact air bases. These, together with other secondary, and civil airports, and, in emergency, some sections of motorway, provide considerable scope for redeployment and dispersal. Many Western airfields might be overrun by Pact ground forces but as NATO plans to fight forward the war might well be lost already if overrunning occurred. The area depicted, about the size of Oregon, could be the scene for some 3000 NATO sorties a day. These combined with Pact sorties and battlefield helicopter operations suggest an intensely crowded air environment with consequent severe problems of identification and reaction. From Neuruppin (N on the map) to the U.S. F15 base at Bitburg (B) is 30 minutes flight for a Mig 27 at low level. Speed of response would clearly be vitally important.

Below: If vulnerable to air attack, modern armies cannot conduct their own operations and are likely to be rapidly destroyed. Although counter-air strikes to destroy aircraft on the ground are important, an army needs assistance from friendly defensive aircraft as well as its own methods of defeating air attack. War in Europe would involve an intense defensive battle fought by NATO F4, F16 and F15 aircraft against numerically superior Pact Mig 21, Mig 23, SU27 and Mig 29 aircraft. Airborne warning and control for the defence would come from NATO E3A AWACs and soon the Pact will have a similar facility in the IL76. From the ground, layered defences range from long range anti-aircraft missiles like Patriot and the medium-ranged Hawk, through shorter range missiles such as Roland and Rapier, to sophisticated anti-

aircraft guns like the German Gepard and shoulder fired anti-aircraft missiles like Stinger and Redeye, all co-ordinated so far as possible by sophisticated radar and automated command posts. A similar, more numerous if less sophisticated, network exists on the side of the Pact. High kill rates are predicted and the fight for air superiority over the battlefield might well be decided in three or four days with NATO technologial sophistication and training pitted against Pact members.

E-3A AWACS (NATO)

F16 (Dutch)

F15 (US)

F4 (German)

AN/TPS-43 search radar

Hawk (US)

Patriot (US)

Roland 2 on Marder chassis (German)

Gepard (Dutch)

Mig 29

SU24

SU25

SU27

Stinger (US)
Battle front

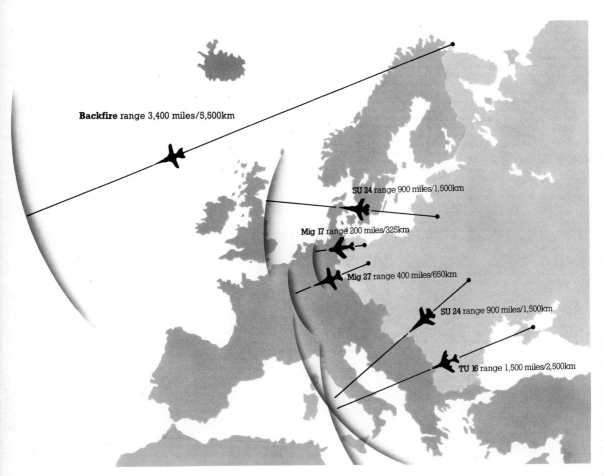

Backfire range 3,400 miles/5,500km

SU 24 range 900 miles/1,500km

Mig 17 range 200 miles/325km

Mig 27 range 400 miles/650km

SU 24 range 900 miles/1,500km

TU 16 range 1,500 miles/2,500km

Above: The map shows the combat radius of various Soviet strike aircraft from bases comfortably within Pact territory. It can be seen that much of NATO is within range of most of these aircraft with the SU24, TU16 and Backfire providing sufficient range to cover all European NATO if necessary. In practice range varies greatly according to payload and mission profile. The change from the 1960s when the Soviet Union relied upon the short-range and low payload of the Mig 17 is particularly remarkable.

Right: In the post-World War II era nothing did more to dramatize the potential of attacking enemy airforces on their bases, preferably by surprise, than the devastation of Arab air forces achieved by the Israelis at the start of the 1967 war. The tactic has, however, been a recognized success for much longer; it played a prominent part in inter-war strategic debate and the Germans secured significant successes at the start of their 1940 offensive in France and in their July 1941 attack on Russia.

Three possible lines of defence are distant destruction of attack aircraft by interceptors or ground-based air defences, dispersal of aircraft, or sheltering aircraft in protective hangarettes and affording close air defence to the airfields. Runways are difficult to destroy with conventional weapons; neither shelters nor runways can survive the successful use of nuclear weapons and only dispersal would suffice. V/STOL aircraft like the Harrier afford special opportunities for such action.

TU 16

MIG23

MIG29

MIG27

hardened aircraft shelters

SU24

Rapier surface to air mi.siles

83

Above: Stand-off weapons are increasingly important to enable costly aircraft to evade rapidly improving air defences. Other improvements in munitions can also reduce the sorties required to achieve intended effects.

In the picture a NATO aircraft uses a GBU 15 glide bomb from up to 10 km from the target, the bomb (red) being guided by infra-red or TV seekers employed either from the launch aircraft or, in this case, a friendly F4 (green). The launch aircraft (blue) escapes at low level. This attack on enemy airfield defences assists a Tornado which drops anti-runway submunitions from its two JP 233 dispensers. Each JP 233 contains 30 SG 357 bombs to break up runway concrete and 215 HP 876 shaped charge mines to impede repairs.

Right: The "interdiction" of communications behind enemy lines can greatly impede the enemy's operations. Soviet offensive tactics, based on bringing forward supporting echelons in a tightly time-tabled mass advance should be especially vulnerable to such operations. Because aircraft engaged in interdiction must penetrate deep into enemy airspace, running the gauntlet of hostile fighters and anti-aircraft weapons, attrition can be high.

In the picture an RAF Tornado uses a laser guided bomb against a bridge illuminated by a co-operating Buccaneer. Pact anti-aircraft guns and missiles are supplemented by prowling Mig 23s. The RAF aircraft are escorted by defence suppression F4Gs. Night and bad weather operation may alter the terms of engagement.

The central front air battle: targets and defence

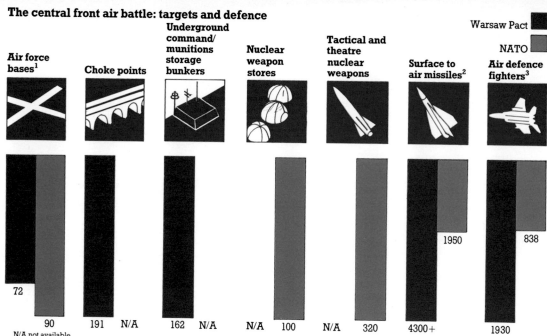

	Warsaw Pact	NATO

Air force bases[1]	Choke points	Underground command/ munitions storage bunkers	Nuclear weapon stores	Tactical and theatre nuclear weapons	Surface to air missiles[2]	Air defence fighters[3]
72 / 90	191 / N/A	162 / N/A	N/A / 100	N/A / 320	4300+ / 1950	1930 / 838

N/A not available.
1. Excludes France, and numerous dispersal strips available to both alliances.
2. Excludes manheld weapons.
3. Excludes Soviet strategic air defence aircraft and UK based air defence aircraft. Includes NATO F16 aircraft assumed to be deployed in air defence role.

Above: Beyond the immediate battlefield lie many targets for attack by deeply penetrating ground-attack aircraft or guided and ballistic missiles. Some of the key types of target are shown on the chart with rough estimates of the number presented by each side. The numbers are large, many of the targets are hardened, at least against conventional weapons, and attrition of attack aircraft may be high.

Right: Success in air war will depend in large part on an electronic contest, with electronic measures, counter-measures, and counter-counter measures. The techniques for this contest change rapidly with new devices and tactics being introduced even day-by-day within an intense campaign. This picture shows the possible shape of the contest on the European front with smaller numbers of highly sophisticated NATO systems pitted against less developed but more numerous Soviet counterparts. Each aircraft will have its own internal or pod-mounted electronic weapons and counter-measures, while specialized aircraft like the U.S. F4G will seek out and destroy Pact radars on the ground with weapons like the High Speed Anti-Radiation Missile (HARM). Aircraft like the NATO EF111, EC13OH and Soviet TU16 and AN12 and helicopters like the Mi14, will jam radar/communications. Agility in frequency changes, advantages in power and other technological capabilities will be thrown into the competition. The great prize is to secure information and deny it to the enemy.

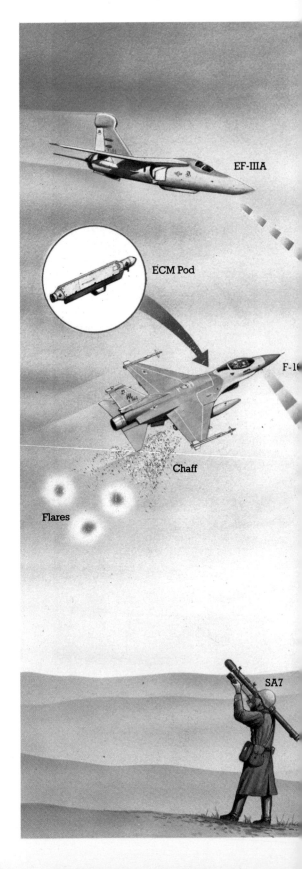

EF-IIIA

ECM Pod

F-1

Chaff

Flares

SA7

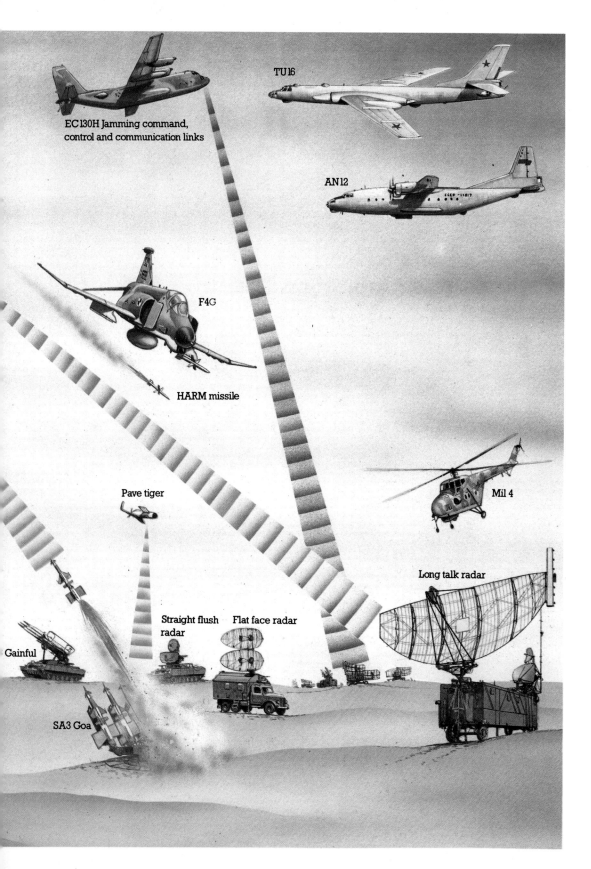

EC130H Jamming command,
control and communication links

TU 16

AN12

F4G

HARM missile

Mil 4

Pave tiger

Long talk radar

Straight flush
radar

Flat face radar

Gainful

SA3 Goa

The Technological Challenge to Soviet Strategy

In the 'seventies and 'eighties a technological revolution in military affairs entered an advanced phase that posed serious problems for a Soviet strategy based on a traditional quantitative preponderance coupled with steady but not spectacular qualitative improvement. This revolution, dominated, but by no means exclusively, by electronics, is best characterized by the concept of "precision guidance", made possible by staggering advances in the capability of sensors and computers available at progressively falling cost.

Despite considerable Soviet success in military technology, the West and especially the United States, still hold a lead in most of the more advanced areas and nowhere is this more so than in the electronic elements of the "new weapon" or "emerging" technology. While it is true that NATO has all too frequently seized on a technological lead — tactical nuclear weapons or the nuclear weapon itself being prime examples — to offset Soviet numerical advantages, only to see the Soviet Union even more promptly exploit the same technology, even temporary advantages may unsettle Soviet strategy, buy time, and impose on the Warsaw Pact a burdensome and costly catching-up exercise.

As we shall see in more detail later, the present technological changes may be altering the balance not only temporarily, perhaps, between NATO and the Warsaw Pact, but also permanently between conventional and nuclear weapons.

The essence of the revolution in precision guidance is the ability to give the weapon information about how to hit the target after launch, whether by providing the weapon with on-board sensors and computing capacity or by feeding it data acquired by sensors elsewhere. This technology gives weapons an immensely greater probability of scoring a hit — some define precision-guidance as achieving a better than fifty-fifty chance. This at once permits the economical use of more complex and effective weapons and in many applications permits the use of conventional warheads to achieve effects that could previously only have been produced by using a large nuclear explosion to compensate for inaccuracy.

While this great advance in guidance is probably the supreme element in the new weapon technology, one capable of application in different ways over a wide range of weapons from the intercontinental missile to the anti-tank gun or hand-held anti-aircraft missile, it has been accompanied by many other technological advances. In particular, there have been great improvements in conventional warheads.

One of the oldest and best known is the "shaped-charge", which by attacking armour and other hard targets not by kinetic energy but by the power of focussed gases, permitted the substitution of missiles for high-velocity gun-fired projectiles, a change only now coming fully into its own as the new accuracies ensure the warhead achieves a hit.

Yet another important advance is the cluster-weapon, perhaps of bomblets or minelets, each embodying a lethal charge and capable of dispersal by such varied means as dispensers on aircraft, artillery shells or free-flying rockets. In the eighties, such "sub-munitions" depend simply on a pre-set distribution pattern once the cluster is accurately delivered, but there are hopes of achieving individual terminal guidance for the bomblets at tolerable cost.

All of this remarkable military technology has many varied actual and potential applications. For the NATO-Warsaw Pact confrontation, however, its most immediate significance is a possible NATO answer to the tank-heavy Soviet strategy. Particularly after the initial Egyptian success in holding off armoured Israeli counter-attacks in 1973, followed by less convincing successes of air-launched PGM against Egyptian tanks, great and almost certainly exaggerated expectations were aroused about the impending demise of the tank.

Even in 1973, counter measures to help the tank were devised. Infantry using anti-tank missiles can be suppressed by artillery fire or attacked by infantry mechanized to accompany the tanks. If, in turn, the PGM are mounted on armoured vehicles, as they now often are, they cease to be the cheap panacea they were once believed to be. New types of composite armour are also much more effective against shaped charges. Moreover, vulnerable or not, there is no obvious, less vulnerable substitute for the tank as armoured, mobile firepower, a combination invented in World War I as an answer to the machine gun and defensive field fortifications, embodied in decisive new "blitzkrieg" tactics for independent use in rapid penetrations, above all by the German Wehrmacht of World War II, and still the centrepiece of modern offensive warfare. Furthermore, unless the defence is to be wholly static in the discredited "Maginot" mould, then even the defender needs tanks for his counter-attacks and then he, on the local offensive, will come up against the new anti-tank weapons and tactics.

Nor is the new technology confined to the land battle. An even more vulnerable target than the tank is the offensive aircraft, and the modern SAM, coupled with the air-to-air missile (AAM) mounted on an interceptor, poses new hazards for aircraft operating over hostile territory. If the 1973 Middle Eastern War showed a possible inclement future for the tank, American experiences over North Vietnam demonstrated the dangers awaiting ground-attack aircraft in a hostile environment of SAMs and interceptors.

This aerial aspect of the revolution has very different implications in the European theatre from that in anti-tank weapons, for throughout the earlier history of the confrontation NATO relied, as it still does to a large extent, on qualitatively superior airpower to strike Warsaw Pact forces not only on the battlefield but more importantly by "interdiction" to the rear, seeking to cut-off the reinforcing rear echelons. This threat was a major reason for the large force of Soviet interceptors. By modernizing that force, by building an elaborate SAM network all over Eastern Europe, and by providing its armies with an integrated mobile air defence exploiting so far as they were able the new technologies for guidance and target acquisition, the Soviet Union made the task of the NATO airforces much more difficult.

For all that, the possibility that NATO forces, substantially improved if still quantitatively in-ferior, and equipped with increasing numbers of the new anti-tank weapons, might thwart the Soviet strategy of rapid advance and early success, has compelled the Soviet military to undertake a radical reappraisal in recent years.

Below: As explained in the text, Soviet strategy envisages maintaining the weight of attack by a series of echelons at every level of army organization, coming forward successively in support as the units ahead achieve their objectives and become exhausted. The map indicates the goals likely to be assigned to various formations in an advance to the Channel: first echelon Divisions of the first echelon Army break through to 70 km, their comrades in the Army carry on to 150 km, at which point a second echelon Army takes over to win forward to the 300 km line before being overtaken by the units of a second echelon Front.

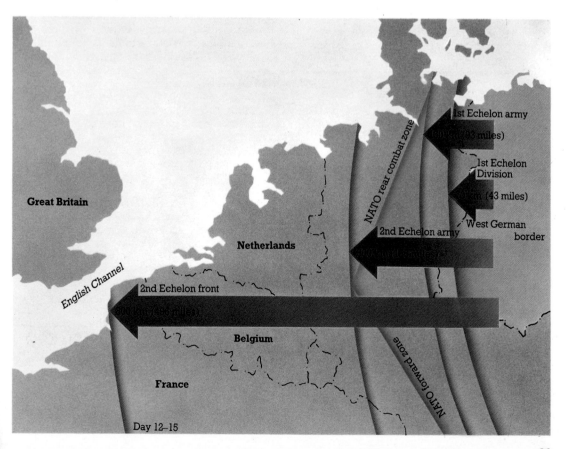

Soviet Responses to the Technological Revolution

The Soviet strategy was always a highly demanding one. Whether the Soviet Union used its nuclear weapons from the start or not, the strategy called for making NATO realize it had lost the war in Europe before it had time to decide on and implement any extensive use of its own nuclear arsenal. Added to this over-arching time factor, was the fact that the Soviet strategy of rapid advance supported by advancing rear echelons itself calls for extremely accurate timing. Any possibility that this time-table might be upset by the failure of Soviet armour to breakthrough on schedule would have a daunting deterrent effect on Soviet commanders. The thought that new technology might enable NATO to administer such a set-back required serious consideration by Soviet strategists.

A major reconsideration of Warsaw Pact strategy apparently began in the late 'seventies and was still proceeding in the 'eighties. It seems unlikely that the Soviet military authorities have yet hit on a complete and coherent new strategic doctrine, and, because massive armed forces are not quickly redesigned, re-equipped and retrained, even the results of provisional reappraisal are slow to appear in the field. Nevertheless Soviet military writings and trends in their organization and practice suggest that the Soviet formula is to retain the essence of the former strategy while consider-

Below: The Operational Manoeuvre Group heavily supported from the air and by surface to surface missiles rushes armoured forces forward through NATO lines, perhaps accompanied by parachute landings and helicopter borne assault teams.
Its objectives are the disruption of NATO's rear and the seizure or destruction of key targets dangerous to the Pact's advance, including airfields, nuclear delivery systems and stockpiles, bridges and other choke points and perhaps important industrial facilities.

ably modifying their method of implementing it.

The most important characteristic of Soviet strategy has long been an imperative to launch overwhelming attacks, setting up a pace of advance rapid enough to preclude NATO nuclear action, confining the war so far as possible to the battlefields and thereby escaping the penalties of escalation. Today more emphasis than ever is placed on surprise and speed of advance. To effect this Soviet army and airforce units are provided with greatly increased hitting power and with much better facilities for logistics and movement by night as well as day. A greater proportion of fighting power has been brought forward in peacetime by building up the divisions and other formations deployed in Poland, Czechoslovakia and Germany, the last reorganized fairly recently as the Group of Soviet Forces, Germany.

As always Soviet forces are organized at all levels in echelons, so that second echelon regiments follow those of the first echelon within divisions, second echelon divisions support first echelon divisions within armies and so on. It may be, however, that on the broader view, with more Soviet fighting power brought forward and even greater emphasis on shattering NATO defences quickly, that the rearward forces advancing through Eastern Europe are becoming less critical determinants of success or failure for Soviet strategy. This would clearly have implications for the balance of NATO effort between holding the main battle-line and interdicting Warsaw Pact reinforcements. Holding a much higher proportion of combat power forward also enhances Soviet chances of launching an attack with minimum warning — the so-called standing start attack.

There may also be a change afoot in Soviet conception of a breakthrough. To succeed at all Soviet doctrine ideally requires an overall superiority of three to one in ground and air forces making possible concentration of much greater superiority in breakthrough sectors: ideally 4-5:1 in manpower, 3-5:1 in armour and as much as 6-8:1 in the traditionally favoured element of artillery. This might mean some 80-100 major artillery tubes per kilometer.

While in the past the Warsaw Pact style called for concentrating on a few main axes of attack, carefully predetermined though only revealed to NATO if possible by last-minute concentration, recent thinking and exercises suggest the possibility of a broader attack with forces sufficiently flexible to exploit breakthroughs as they occur, rather in the manner called the "expanding torrent" by the inter-war British strategist, Liddell-Hart. Such a plan calls for a pool of reserves kept well forward to facilitate prompt seizing of opportunities.

To support this approach the Soviet Union has revived a device from its practice in World War II, the Mobile Group, now designated the Operational Manoeuvre Group. Originally this was a concept rather than a formation, the idea being the creation *ad hoc,* as necessary and in varying sizes and combinations, according to circumstances, of military units of up to divisional size or even larger, to plunge through holes in NATO's front and fan out in the rear in order to, in the words of one Soviet officer: "destroy groupings of nuclear missiles, command posts, radio electronic warfare equipment and anti-aircraft defence weapons . . . also . . . *inter alia,* to prevent the withdrawal of enemy troops; to hinder the advance of his reserves from the depth; to paralyse his system of logistics; to capture major important areas and objectives; and to hold these until the approach of the main forces". NATO's political imperative to forward defence could clearly render it more vulnerable to such tactics. More recently it appears that large, corps sized units may have been established and trained for the OMG role.

Soviet tactical air forces are similarly being reshaped to support the revised strategy. From an interceptor force chiefly designed to keep NATO offensive air at bay, the Soviet Air Force is now itself increasingly equipped for operations against ground targets. More and more Soviet aircraft are designed for ground attack both on the battlefield and as deep in the rear as the United Kingdom, while the armed helicopter, once the characteristic of NATO and particularly American forces, is now much more numerous on the Soviet side. Coupled with Soviet preparations to land raiding forces (DESANT forces) in the rear of NATO by air, these Soviet redispositions and investments have gone far to transfer the initial stages of the air war from East to West, so that NATO air forces may be seriously distracted from their priority of attacking Warsaw Pact air bases, in the "counter-air" mission, and from impeding the advance of Warsaw Pact ground forces, to the defence of their own bases and attempting to keep Pact air power off the back of NATO armies. In recent exercises it has in fact been the difficulty of conducting the battle for air supremacy over the battlefield that has most often driven NATO commanders to request the use of nuclear weapons.

By the mid-'eighties it seemed that this was to be the Soviet response to the new technological environment. It was not yet clear that the evolution of Soviet thought had reached a resting place, still less that Soviet forces had attained the capacity actually to do what the new doctrine required of them. Assuming, however, that this was the Soviet recipe for the next decade or so — and there are severe limits to how rapidly an army can change its ways — the question for NATO in the middle 'eighties became how to respond.

NATO's Options: (1) Nuclear

One possible NATO reply to the new Soviet strategy of rapid offensive conventional operations would be to reverse the trend of recent thought and revert to a more frankly nuclear strategy. If even the flexible response has always retained an ultimately nuclear element for the last resort and if the Soviet Union was now expending so much effort to win without incurring the penalties of such a nuclear outcome, why not make the prospect more stark and less avoidable?

The so-called tactical and theatre nuclear arsenals — roughly speaking the former directed toward the immediate battlefield, the latter to longer range nuclear action short of attacks on the Soviet or American homelands — have evolved dramatically since the first crude artillery shells and missiles were introduced in the 'fifties. By the 'eighties, both sides possess nuclear systems for artillery, ballistic and cruise missiles, aircraft and land mines. From Hiroshima-sized yields of some 20 kilotons (KT) equivalent of TNT and much more, warheads now range down to the sub-kiloton size. At the same time, the methods of delivering nuclear weapons have, like those for conventional weapons, enjoyed the benefits of modern guidance technology. The resultant accuracy, permitting the use of much smaller yields to achieve intended effects, has also made possible a degree of precision that could in theory greatly reduce the old problem of collateral unintended damage to friendly forces or civilians. Moreover, as tit for tat escalation could provide one of the more obvious routes to a wider and wider nuclear war, the capacity to avoid unintentional damage to enemy forces is also a valuable contribution to controlling the battle.

Possibilities of this kind led by the late 'sixties to proposals for the much earlier use of nuclear weapons, probably small "mini-nukes", as a prime method of defence, rather than an escalatory signal. The design of "enhanced radiation weapons" the so-called neutron bombs, which could emit much more instantly effective, armour-penetrating radiation in proportion to heat and blast, seemed to some to offer the ideal answer to Soviet superiority in tanks.

In the event, such proposals have not found favour. The reluctance to base NATO strategy on early use of nuclear weapons that occasion-

	US Forces	NATO Forces
Medium range: aerial bombs	1415	320
Pershing I SSM	195	100
Short range: 8in artillery	505	430
155mm artillery	595	140
Lance SSM	325	370
Honest John SSM	—	200
Nike Hercules SAM	300	390
Atomic land mines	370	—
ASW depth bombs	—	190
totals	3705	2140

Above: The chart indicates the major tactical nuclear systems that have become common within NATO by way of dual-key operation of U.S. owned warheads. These numbers are not precise and are changing rapidly as modernization proceeds, usually resulting in a reduction of overall inventories.

Below: The diagram shows the approximate relationship between the two primary "killing" effects of nuclear weapons, blast and radiation, and in particular the wider radiation affect of the Enhanced Radiation Weapon (ERW) or "neutron bomb", a prompt and relatively precisely calculable effect, achieved without the greater radius of blast that achieving the same radiation effect with a larger "conventional" nuclear warhead would entail. This effect is thought by many to offer a "kill" mechanism against enemy troops, particularly in tanks which do little to shield crews from radiation, while minimizing wide and often unpredictable collateral damage from blast.

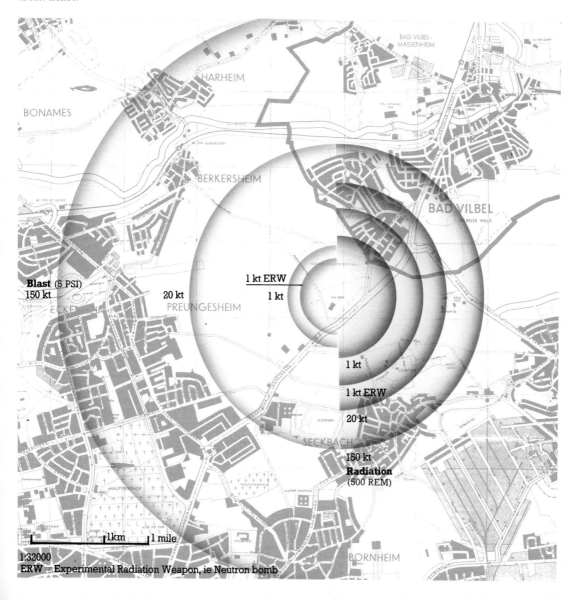

Blast (5 PSI)
150 kt

20 kt

1 kt ERW
1 kt

1 kt

1 kt ERW

20 kt

150 kt
Radiation
(500 REM)

1 km 1 mile

1:32000
ERW = Experimental Radiation Weapon, ie Neutron bomb

93

Below: The map shows planned deployment of U.S. operated GLCM and Pershing II in Western European NATO countries; the chart gives an impression of the difficulty the Soviet Union would have in blanketing the GLCM force with a SS20 strike if the GLCMs had achieved full planned dispersal. The wide selection of countries chosen for GLCM deployment is the result not merely of strategic concern for dispersed deployment but also a political desire to associate a large number of NATO countries with the programme so as to minimize the exposure of West Germany both as a target and as the location of nuclear "proliferation". The map also indicates Soviet SS20 and ICBM sites in Western Russia.

ed abandonment of the nuclear emphasis of the 'fifties and adoption of flexible response, still prevails. While the new technology might make a local nuclear war less destructive and more controllable, great scepticism still prevails as to how reliable such limits might be. Besides the fears that crossing the nuclear threshold would have dangerous psychological and political effects, perhaps leading to the abandonment of restraints, there are anxieties that nuclear war would rapidly get out of control for technical reasons as widespread devastation and the deleterious effects of the electromagnetic pulse (EMP) emitted by nuclear explosions on electronic equipment and communications destroyed the machinery of intelligence and command.

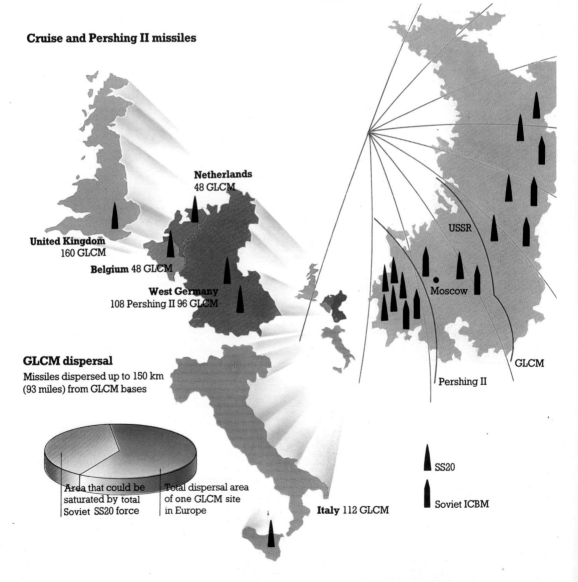

Cruise and Pershing II missiles

Netherlands
48 GLCM

United Kingdom
160 GLCM

Belgium 48 GLCM

West Germany
108 Pershing II 96 GLCM

USSR

Moscow

GLCM

Pershing II

GLCM dispersal
Missiles dispersed up to 150 km
(93 miles) from GLCM bases

Area that could be saturated by total Soviet SS20 force | Total dispersal area of one GLCM site in Europe

SS20

Soviet ICBM

Italy 112 GLCM

Such fears have multiplied within NATO as the Soviet Union has improved and diversified its theatre nuclear forces to the point at which NATO's original monopoly has been replaced by at best parity and more probably by inferiority. NATO's original nuclear emphasis was founded not only on superiority at the strategic level, so that all-out retaliation was an unattractive option for the Soviet Union, but also on monopoly or superiority at various tactical levels. Thus NATO could hope to take the war to a stage at which NATO prevailed and the Soviet Union had no reply.

Step by step over the past twenty years or so, the Soviet Union has matched or surpassed NATO capability from the artillery weapons of the battlefield, through the nuclear capable aircraft, to the intermediate range missiles exemplified by the notorious SS20. Thus for NATO to have recourse to nuclear weapons would entail the danger not merely of escalation to inter-continental nuclear war but defeat in the immediate military engagement.

In the light of these developments, it becomes a cause for concern that, by promising an ultimate resort to nuclear weapons rather than accept defeat, NATO's strategy of flexible response provides a strong incentive for the Soviet Union to use its own nuclear weapons from the outset, if it ever decides to go to war in Europe. Otherwise NATO would enjoy the benefit of striking the first blow at a moment of

The expansion in the size of deployment zones

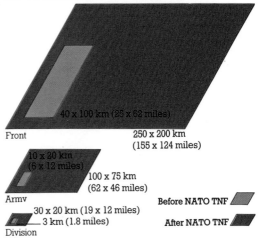

Front — 40 x 100 km (25 x 62 miles) / 250 x 200 km (155 x 124 miles)

Army — 10 x 20 km (6 x 12 miles) / 100 x 75 km (62 x 46 miles)

Division — 30 x 20 km (19 x 12 miles) / 3 km (1.8 miles)

Before NATO TNF

After NATO TNF

Above: A major bonus NATO derives from its tactical nuclear weapons is to compel Warsaw Pact forces to deploy in dispersed fashion inconvenient for conventional operations. The diagram shows how typical pre-offensive deployment areas of major formations have expanded since nuclear weapons were deployed. Below: Deployment of cruise missile flight prior to camouflage operations, showing links between erector launchers, missile programming and control centres. Other vehicles provide logistic support and local protection.

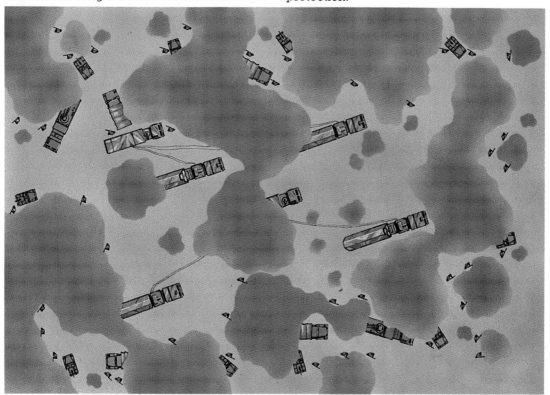

its own choosing. This consideration has given rise in some Western quarters to the demand that NATO, should issue a pledge of "No First Use" of nuclear weapons; a policy that would repudiate the central element in the flexible response. More extreme versions of this line of thought would entail removing many of NATO's theatre nuclear weapons so as to make the sincerity of the pledge credible to the Soviet Union.

Orthodox opinion in NATO rejects the idea of a No First Use declaration and any accompanying large scale dismantling of NATO's apparatus for nuclear war. This would, it is argued, actually reduce Soviet incentive to refrain from first use of its own nuclear weapons, NATO having greatly weakened its capacity to retaliate by the reduction in forces and diminished the credibility of such retaliation by showing infirmity of purpose with regard to nuclear weapons. Insofar as doubts about the nuclear element in the flexible response arise from American reluctance to incur the risks of nuclear action on behalf of Europeans, it is hard to see why those risks should be significantly more acceptable after Europe — but only Europe — had suffered a nuclear attack.

Moreover a No First Use declaration and the force modifications required to make it credible to the Soviet Union, would imply NATO defending itself with conventional weapons alone. Yet from the early days of NATO it has been clear that a large scale conventional war is almost as unpleasant a prospect for Europeans as a nuclear conflict. History also suggests that conventional deterrence has repeatedly failed. Why then, it is argued, abandon the peculiarly effective deterrent fear generated by nuclear weapons? The flexible response involves the possibility of nuclear action, but does not compel it. The hope that nuclear conflict can be avoided would provide a Soviet aggressor with a powerful incentive not to force the issue, and if NATO shows its own reluctance to cross the line — though does not promise not to do so — by refurbishing its conventional forces and designing its nuclear forces to be clearly under good control and not so vulnerable as to tempt a Soviet pre-emptive strike, whether by nuclear or the new, accurate conventional means, then the best deterrent balance against both war and escalation to nuclear weapons will have been established. In this vein NATO in the 'eighties began both to modernize its theatre nuclear force, most conspicuously with the Pershing II and Ground Launched Cruise Missile (GLCM), and to reduce its numbers, particularly in the most numerous, vulnerable and hard to control categories such as land mines, air defence weapons and artillery shells.

Command and Control of Theatre Nuclear Weapons

The problem of keeping nuclear weapons under control in both peace and war constitutes one of the major obstacles to making them the centrepiece of NATO strategy for fighting as distinct from deterring a war. This issue not only presents severe technical problems but also arouses divisive political issues between allies.

Nuclear weapons for use in support of the land battle were first deployed to U.S. forces in Europe in 1953 in the form of a cumbersome 280 mm shell for a special cannon. Other shells, mines, bombs and missiles followed, including some for use against aircraft and others for use at sea. In December 1957 the North Atlantic Council formally approved the establishment of "stocks of nuclear warheads which will be readily available for the defence of the Alliance in case of need". A meeting of the North Atlantic Council at Athens in 1962 adopted guidelines for consultation about the use of these weapons, if "time and circumstances" permitted. These guidelines have been refined from time to time, laying particular stress on the right of up to three parties to a voice; the owner of the weapons, the party from whose soil they would be used and the ally, if any, on whose soil they would explode.

Keeping nuclear weapons under close control from the highest possible political and military levels of command is obviously a matter of great importance not merely because of the immense damage any particular nuclear weapons can do but also because of the signals any such use would send in the process of potential escalation to a wider and more intense nuclear war. Control takes several forms: within the forces of a nuclear power nuclear weapons will be subject to specially stringent forms of political and military discipline, with authority clearly designated and with most actions requiring simultaneous co-operative action between at least two individuals. Where, as in NATO, nuclear warheads are provided by one nuclear power for use in delivery systems manned by a non-nuclear member of the alliance, the owner of the warhead retains custody or at least physical control over the warhead until the moment of agreed use arrives. In the early days of such systems, the warheads for the intermediate range Thor missiles made available to the Royal Air Force, for instance, the control took the literal form of a "two key" lock and the phrase two or dual key has persisted to describe a physically ensured veto by two or more allies over the use of nuclear weapons, even though today the control is more likely to take the form of sole access to electronic codes needed to arm the system. Safeguards against unauthorized use of nuclear weapons include devices

Below: The procedure for release of nuclear weapons within NATO is so complex as to be possibly unworkable in the heat of battle. It can be seen how the national U.S. chain of command could be used to cut through the maze so far as U.S. forces are concerned. The full international procedure could scarcely take less than 24 hours. In theory requests for use feed up and lead to consultations prior to the passing downwards of authority to fire. In practice the decision might come from the top. Parallel to NATO and, it is to be hoped, carefully if informally co-ordinated is the French control system. NATO guidelines call for special attention to the views of the ally, if any, upon whose territory the weapons would be detonated.

Nuclear release

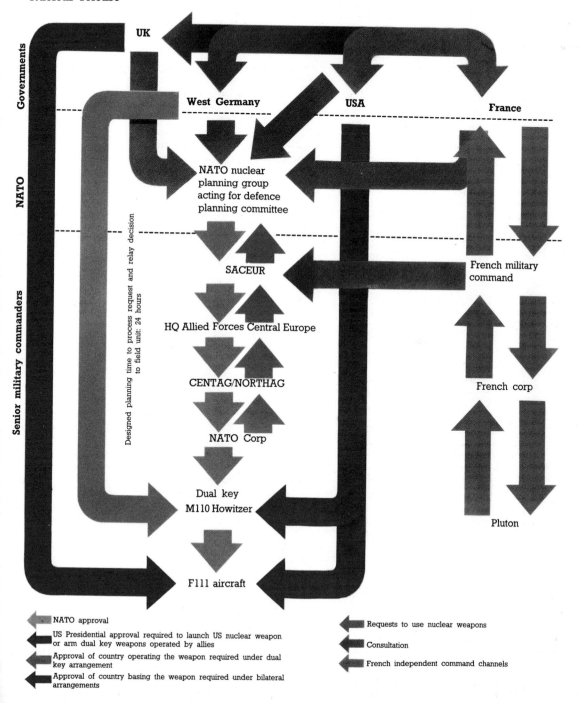

Governments — UK — West Germany — USA — France

NATO

NATO nuclear planning group acting for defence planning committee

SACEUR

HQ Allied Forces Central Europe

CENTAG/NORTHAG

NATO Corp

Dual key M110 Howitzer

F111 aircraft

French military command

French corp

Pluton

Senior military commanders

Designed planning time to process request and relay decision to field unit: 24 hours

NATO approval

US Presidential approval required to launch US nuclear weapon or arm dual key weapons operated by allies

Approval of country operating the weapon required under dual key arrangement

Approval of country basing the weapon required under bilateral arrangements

Requests to use nuclear weapons

Consultation

French independent command channels

whereby the warhead is disabled if the controls are tampered with and allied mechanisms provide against efforts to penetrate the weapon itself so as to bypass controls or secure access to the fissile material. There are also multiple provisions against the accidental detonation of weapons, including features of the fundamental design that make the perfect functioning of the fusing system necessary for a nuclear reaction to take place.

In peacetime most nuclear warheads are kept in a small number of storage silos — less than a hundred in NATO Europe — heavily guarded by "custodial" troops. Considerable concern has been expressed in recent years about the vulnerability of such sites to enemy action. Some warheads are permanently married to the delivery system where the force in question is on quick reaction alert (QRA). The storage silos and the QRA system exemplify an inescapable dilemma in weapon custody: that there is an inevitable conflict between safety and control on the one hand and reliable availability for prompt use when needed.

The control of nuclear weapons is the most politically sensitive issue within NATO. In recent years the deployment of Soviet nuclear weapons further forward in Eastern Europe has revealed some parallel tensions in the Warsaw Pact, although so far as is known Soviet control is absolute and no consultative mechanisms comparable to those of NATO exist. In NATO the European members have typically vacillated between fear that the United States would use nuclear weapons rashly and anxiety that is willingness to use them at all was too uncertain to deter Soviet aggression in the first place or resort to nuclear weapons later. Reassurance against such fears has taken the form both of the control mechanisms just described and an increasing degree of interallied consultation on the philosophy of nuclear strategy and on the guidelines within which use would take place.

Following the adoption of flexible response in 1967, in part a retreat from nuclear weapons, NATO established a Nuclear Defence Affairs Committee for all members (except France and Iceland) and a Nuclear Planning Group (NPG). The latter, originally composed of four permanent and three rotating members now includes all members who choose to participate. The NPG has proved to be the forerunner of a number of "special groups" set up to develop policy, primarily on nuclear and related arms control issues.

The special characteristic of the NPG is that it combines high level representation at Ministerial level capable politically of committing allied countries at least to some degree, with detailed staff work on complex technical issues. It's first and perhaps most important achievement was to draft the "Guidelines for Initial Defensive

Tactical Use of Nuclear Weapons by NATO" in 1969. These have been followed by models of selective employment packages from which leaders could choose in emergency.

It is not the business of the NPG to draw up operational plans for the use of nuclear weapons but to establish guidelines for such plans which are the responsibility of the military authorities. If and when a military commander wished to use nuclear weapons he would make a request to higher military authority which would pass it up the chain through SACEUR from where it would become the subject of consultation in the Defence Planning Committee. At the same time there would of course be debate in national commands and governments. If the NATO authorities decided affirmatively they would request a nuclear member of NATO, in all probability the United States, to release the appropriate weapons. These would be released to SACEUR and so on down the chain doubtless subject to restrictions as to the actual time and place of use. Release packages have been designated in an effort to clarify to higher authorities the scope and implication of what they are being asked to do. The criteria for deciding upon release would include such considerations as the probable military effect of the proposed use of nuclear weapons, the political consequences, the collateral damage, and likely Soviet response.

All of this communication and decision making must be carried out by secure means. There is indeed a danger that the activation of the relevant communications and procedures would let the enemy know what was about to happen. It has therefore been estimated that twenty-four hours might be the very fastest that a request from the battlefield could be granted. In practice the first request would seem likely to provoke soul-searching capable of taking much longer. It must be remembered, however, that the Athens guidelines call for consultation if "time and circumstances" permit and that the NATO chains of command are paralleled by the national chains of the nuclear members. In particular SACEUR is also C, in C.U.S. Forces, Europe and it would doubtless be in his latter capacity that he would receive permission to use nuclear weapons from his President. Moreover as the use of nuclear weapons would serve such a crucial symbolic function in the management of the war and its escalation, it is very possible that the initiative, if it ever came, would be from the top down, rather than be taken to allow some local commander to try to solve his immediate problem in such a drastic way.

Once some nuclear weapons had been used and released, it must be uncertain how well control could continue to be exercised. To the dangers arising from the political emotions and tensions the use of nuclear weapons would cause, must be added the strain on command and communications imposed by destruction, by the dispersal of nuclear weapons and by the fact that it is not possible to retain control of individual nuclear weapons, one by one, at head of government level. Thus while there is no prior delegation of authority to use nuclear weapons, if release once begins and follow-on uses are contemplated, some kind of *de facto* delegation must almost certainly occur, even if military discipline and self-restraint prevent this resulting in imprudent use. No one has any experience of such an "environment" and it is to be hoped this in itself would constitute a powerful force for restraint.

'STARWARS' and NATO: Ballistic Missile Defence in Europe

As so many aspects of the NATO-Warsaw Pact confrontation demonstrate over the years, strategic assumptions and plans can be over-turned by technological change. Nowhere perhaps is such an upset more possible than in the impact of emerging defensive technology on the role of ballistic missiles. One of the relatively fixed points in the difficult debate over the control of nuclear weapons has hitherto been the assumption that a ballistic missile, once launched, will arrive at its target. The calculability of this and the freedom from compulsion to launch several strike vehicles, as with aircraft, with consequent uncertainty about the weight of the attack the enemy will experience, has often been cited as a positive factor in keeping a nuclear "exchange" under control. The advent of effective defences against ballistic missiles could destroy these certainties. 'Starwars' technology could also, of course, alter some of the assumptions about the overall American nuclear guarantee to Europe that under-pins NATO.

The much used term "Starwars" has come to be confusingly used to designate both measures for attacking space-satellites and intercepting ballistic missiles. This confusion has arisen partly because some of the most effective but also most technologically difficult ways of intercepting missiles might be based on satellites and because satellites could also play an important part in the surveillance associated with any ballistic missile defence (BMD) system.

The main attraction of satellite based systems is that they could attack missiles in their 'boost phase' when they are slow and vulnerable and when all their multiple warheads, if any, still offer only one target. Interception in the early phase also leaves time for another try when the warheads re-enter the atmosphere. Satellite interception systems might use small missiles but more excitement has been aroused by the prospect of using lasers or other directed energy beams. This technology will almost certainly only be available for full deployment in the next century and the more immediate future for BMD is likely to involve "terminal" defence at the re-entry stage, using high acceleration interceptor missiles which, unlike the proposed systems of the 'sixties, could now achieve such accurate interceptions that conventional or "non-nuclear kill" mechanisms could be used, with consequent relaxation of control require-ments, alleviation of many practical anxieties and removal of at least one source of political opposition.

These possibilities have direct relevance to NATO's defensive problems in Europe. In the past BMD has chiefly been associated with the interception of the long range strategic missiles that constitute the mainstay of national "deterrents". This association has arisen partly because this is the task that would create the biggest strategic revolution and partly for the practical reason that intercontinental ranges give more time to conduct the interception exercise. The proposals made by President Reagan in 1983, which set off the most recent "Starwars" debate, were chiefly directed toward the goal of an ultimately "leak-proof" defence of American cities. This proposal aroused considerable alarm in Europe, where members of NATO feared that it would undermine the existing strategic arms control regime, centred round the ABM Treaty, threaten the efficacy of the small British and French nuclear deterrents, and tempt the United States to retire at least psychologically into a "Fortress America" leaving the Europeans outside. This argument seems paradoxical, for a defended United States ought to be able to take greater risks for its allies, but there can be no doubt substantial sections of West European opinion do have serious misgivings on this score. A somewhat contradictory fear also expressed is that a defended United States might behave provocatively and that the Soviet Union might feel obliged to launch a pre-emptive war before American defences were in place.

Partly to assuage such fears and deflect such criticism, the United States has proposed that BMD should be provided for NATO Europe. If the city-protecting, leak-proof form of BMD became available it could be extended to Europe; indeed the boost phase interception to protect the United States would provide a certain amount of inherent protection for Europe too. But scepticism as to whether a really effective leak-proof defence can be provided for cities against a major and determined nuclear power has particular weight in Europe, because one of the sources of doubt is the possibility of even an impermeable BMD being outflanked by other, airbreathing delivery systems such as manned bombers and cruise missiles. Clearly the ranges involved and the vast theatre nuclear arsenal already at the Soviet Union's disposal make this problem much worse for NATO Europe than for the United States.

The other objection sometimes raised against BMD for Europe, namely that the shorter ranges involved reduce the flight time available for interception, appears to be offset by the slower re-entry speed of the shorter range ballistic missiles. Indeed the new U.S. anti-aircraft missile, *Patriot* and the Soviet SA 10 and newer SAX 12 missiles are said to have already an interception capability against such missiles as the NATO Lance and possibly the Pershing II.

BMD for Europe thus seems technically feasible within limitations. The question is whether there is a strategic use for such a capability. There are strong arguments that there is. Quite clearly ballistic missiles are about to acquire an enhanced role in a potential European war. The Soviet Union began its missile effort focussed on Europe and maintains and is refurbishing a large arsenal containing such old and new vehicles as the SS 4, 12, 20, 21, 22 and 23, together with the Frogs and Scuds. NATO has Lance and Pershing, the French Pluton and Hades, and is contemplating the much wider use of ballistic missiles, conventional as well as nuclear armed, in the interdiction and counter air roles.

It can therefore be argued that Anti-Tactical Missiles (ATM) systems are a necessary and natural follow-on and concomitant to air defence. While European cities may be indefensible against an effort simply to destroy them, the fear of escalation to mutual destruction makes it much more likely that the task of Soviet missiles, nuclear or conventional, would be to launch early strikes on NATO reinforcement ports and routes, air bases and nuclear facilities. ATM could seriously degrade such an effort and, in contrast to the task of defending cities, even partial successes could be regarded as very worthwhile. Moreover the considerable NATO air defence system creates a quite different situation from that in the continental United States, where virtually no air defence exists. The free "end-run" around BMD by air breathing systems in not available against ATM; indeed it is the problem of penetrating air defences that is giving rise to interest on both sides of the Warsaw Pact — NATO confrontation in missiles.

Many political as well as technological difficulties persist. The cost of ATM would be high and there would be European fears of being expected to pay for systems chiefly benefitting U.S. defence industry. Although ATM would not technically be a breach of the ABM Treaty — which deals with defence against *strategic* missiles — many would see ATM as merely a forerunner for BMD for all purposes and therefore a blow to existing arms control measures. Moreover even ATM would pose problems for the limited French and British forces and, indeed, for the limited theatre strike plans of SACEUR. Advocates of ATM argue that it would have a generally stabilizing effect by creating uncertainty in the Soviet mind as to the outcome of one of the most important preparatory strikes in their campaign. The characteristic of the ballistic missile, especially with a nuclear warhead, is relative certainty that once launched it will fulfil its mission. ATM could destroy that assumption and therefore, it is argued, undermine Soviet confidence in resorting to war in Europe at all.

British and French Nuclear Forces in NATO

The possible effect of even limited Soviet BMD capability on the small British and French nuclear forces poses serious questions about the efficacy of those forces as national deterrents. These forces have always had important implications for NATO as a whole and for the place of nuclear weapons within its strategy. The other European allies have to consider whether the French and British forces offer any extended deterrent protection for them; all must wonder whether these independent forces might drag them, including the United States, into nuclear war against their will.

Great Britain first acquired nuclear weapons on the assumption that as a great power it needed the full range of available weaponry which might also serve as a lever to re-establish the co-operation on nuclear matters it had enjoyed with the United States during World War II. In the latter effort Britain was at least partially successful, and has received a great deal of technical assistance, as well as the right to purchase first Polaris and now Trident II missiles. Britain justifies its force as a "contribution" to the nuclear power of NATO as a whole and as a national deterrent of last resort. In order not to suggest that they have doubts about the reliability of the American nuclear guarantee to its allies. British spokesmen normally put the case for independence in terms of possible Soviet miscalculation: that is, to insure against the danger that in some circumstances the *Soviet Union* might doubt whether the United States would use nuclear weapons on behalf of its allies. Targetting of the British forces is co-ordinated with the United States and Britain participates fully in the NATO processes of consultation about nuclear operational doctrine and, should the need arise, about actual use as part of the flexible response.

In the earlier stages of the French nuclear effort occasional explorations were also made of possible American collaboration. These were rebuffed by the United States, in part because of fears about French security and scepticism about the technological level of the French effort and any possible contributions from it to American programmes. For many years now the French nuclear force has been based upon a vehement assertion of technological, operational and political independence. While the French claim their force renders a general service to the North Atlantic Alliance by complicating Soviet calculations, the explicit role of the force is to fend off attacks on France itself by threatening retaliation against Soviet cities if aggression persists after an initial warning use of French tactical nuclear weapons as part of initial defence of French frontiers. French tactical weapons have therefore not been considered part of a "war fighting" strategy but as an element in strategic deterrence. France does not participate in joint targetting or doctrinal discussions but there may be some exchange of information about broad principles.

The attitude of the other allies to the British and French forces has varied. In the Federal Republic of Germany, for instance, earlier disapproval based on dislike of division in alliance decision-making processes and perhaps resentment of implicit discrimination against West Germany — which has formally undertaken by treaty not to manufacture nuclear weapons — seems to have mellowed and been replaced by approval as a strengthening of deterrence and insurance against the possibility of ultimate American withdrawal from defence arrangements in Europe.

The crucial ally is the United States and its attitude has been ambivalent. Early restrictiveness about nuclear matters was greatly relaxed in favour of the United Kingdom but this remains exceptional. Ironically the important decision to sell Britain Polaris came in 1962, the same year that Secretary of Defense Robert McNamara's secret speech to the North Atlantic Council in May 1962 and a later public version the next month, issued a severe warning against the dangers of divided nuclear control and the uselessness of small nuclear forces. By 1974, however, whether from acceptance of the inevitable or genuine change of heart, the United States was willing to endorse a declaration at the Ottawa meeting of the North Atlantic Council testifying to the constructive role of the French and British forces in Western security.

The main fear of allies who criticise the French and British forces, apart from diversion of resources from other defence purposes, is that these independent nuclear centres of decision might turn nuclear a war that might otherwise remain conventional. This is, of course, the obverse of another argument put forward in favour of the national forces, that multiple centres of decision increase Soviet uncertainty and therefore deterrence. A major factor in this scenario is the possibility that American nuclear forces would be drawn into the battle so that the Soviet Union would be all the more deterred; if such a process actually occurred, of course, the United States would almost certainly pay the price of Soviet retaliation. Some French and British theorists have suggested that this possibility of "catalytic" war is a deliberate purpose of the national forces.

Such a theory is, however, incompatible with the French belief that nuclear forces are only used for and credible as defences of national territory. Moreover, rather than be drawn into a strategic nuclear war, the United States could either abstain, making a deal with the Soviet Union, or at least confine its action to the European battlefield, thereby realizing exactly the danger the French force in particular is designed to avoid.

Naturally for political reasons neither the French nor British governments would openly claim a catalytic role for their deterrents, but it really does not seem likely that the idea plays a significant part in the rationale for their nuclear forces. That is not to say, however, that the existence of independent national forces might not accelerate the process of escalation by degrading command, control and communications, complicating targetting and generally causing confusion. The whole trend of nuclear thinking at least outside France, has recently been moving toward greater efforts to limit nuclear war if it breaks out. Such efforts can never be foolproof, however, and the remaining uncertainty must have a powerful deterrent effect. It remains a matter for debate whether the national forces do more to reinforce this stabilizing phenomenon than to increase the danger of escalation if deterrence fails.

Below: French and British nuclear forces are far from negligible, even though their submarine forces are limited in number and therefore possibly vulnerable to Soviet ASW. The number of aircraft available for delivery of theatre and tactical weapons is only an estimate. Both countries have programmes in hand that could greatly increase the number of re-entry vehicles and warheads on SLBMs.

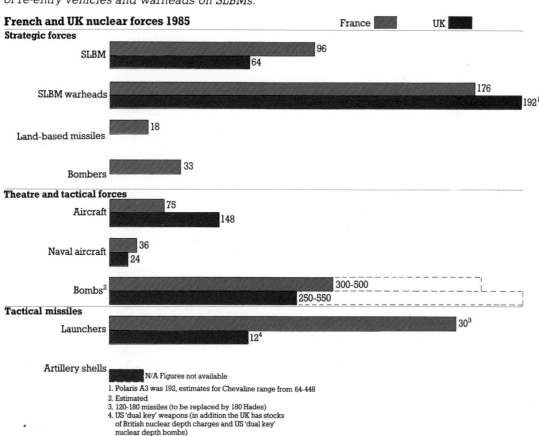

French and UK nuclear forces 1985

France ▨ UK ■

Strategic forces

SLBM	France 96 / UK 64
SLBM warheads	France 176 / UK 192[1]
Land-based missiles	France 18
Bombers	France 33

Theatre and tactical forces

Aircraft	France 75 / UK 148
Naval aircraft	France 36 / UK 24
Bombs[2]	France 300-500 / UK 250-550

Tactical missiles

Launchers	France 30[3] / UK 12[4]
Artillery shells	N/A Figures not available

1. Polaris A3 was 192, estimates for Chevaline range from 64-448
2. Estimated
3. 120-180 missiles (to be replaced by 180 Hades)
4. US 'dual key' weapons (in addition the UK has stocks of British nuclear depth charges and US 'dual key' nuclear depth bombs)

The Ambiguous Role of France

Nuclear weapons have for so long been the dominant motif of French contributions to the European strategic scene that it is in this context one can best digress to more detailed if brief consideration of the anomalous role of France at once within the North Atlantic Alliance and without the integrated framework of NATO.

Occupying a pivotal place in the strategic geography of Western Europe, a founder of the North Atlantic Alliance and still a member, France withdrew in 1966 from the integrated machinery for planning and does not undertake to make any forces available to NATO commanders in war. The disposition of French forces is regarded as entirely a matter for decision by French national authorities. Yet as a member of the Alliance France is still under an obligation to assist the other members of the alliance by means which may involve the use of armed force. France also retains obligations under the Western Union Brussels Treaty of 1948.

From the earliest days of the Alliance the French attitude to European security has been individualistic. For historical reasons France has a special concern for the place of Germany in European affairs and French initial bitter opposition to the rearmament of West Germany led it in 1950 to propose the establishment of a European Defence Community in which German forces would be merged without a national identity. The EDC venture also had overtures of asserting European rather than American priorities in security policy. This concern for independence from the United States, often pursued by way of relations with

Below: Once modest, the French nuclear force has rapidly become extremely formidable so far as the number of warheads is concerned. While many of these could perhaps not be delivered, falling victim either to pre-emptive attack or interception, such potential destructive power cannot be ignored.

West Germany, persists to the present day. Thus in 1973, after many European allies were irritated by United States policy during the Middle East war of that year, the French Foreign Minister began a French effort to resuscitate WEU and more recently that organization has been promoted as a framework for European collaboration in the production of arms. Also recently regular bilateral Franco-German consultations on defence matters, launched at the 1982 France-German summit meeting between Giscard d'Estaing and Helmut Schmidt, have taken on a partly institutionalised form, though the practical results, if any, have not been publicized.

Nuclear questions exacerbated French sus-

French strategic nuclear weapons 1963-1996

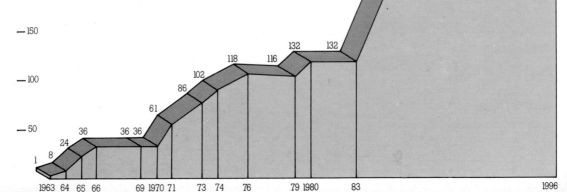

picion of the United States and American policy during the Suez crisis of 1956 reinforced French fears of divergence between French and American interests outside Europe. Upon his accession to power in 1958 President de Gaulle proposed a three-power directorate of France, Britain and the United States, within the alliance, which would co-ordinate policy on a global scale. This proposal was rebuffed by the United States which could not accept such a restriction on its role as a Superpower or exclusion of West Germany and which incidentally also wanted no complicity in the still unresolved French problem of Algeria.

The sense of undue dependence on the United States continued to cause restiveness in France well exemplified in the pronouncements of President de Gaulle. As American strategic policy moved away from Massive Retaliation and towards Flexible Response, the French President began to articulate his fear that the two Superpowers might conduct a nuclear war in Europe while sparing each other's

Below: The map shows the range of various French tactical nuclear weapon delivery systems. Despite claims that Hades will end the embarrassment that the present French tactical nuclear delivery missile Pluton must be targetted on West Germany if based on French soil, it can be seen that the problem is not really solved. It must be doubtful how many Mirage IV could penetrate Pact defences to the depth shown.

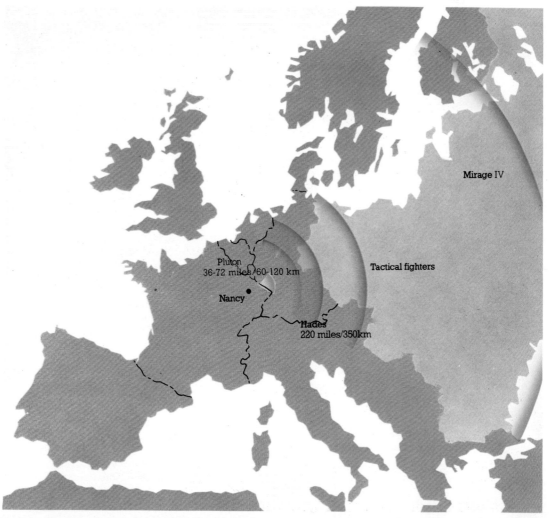

territory. When the United Kingdom abandoned Franco-British talks, in 1961 and 1962, directed toward possible nuclear collaboration, and based the future of the British nuclear force on Polaris, acquired at the price of ever closer commitment to the Americans, President de Gaulle vetoed British membership of the European Economic Community. Equally offended by the efforts of the new American Secretary of Defense, Robert McNamara, notably at the Athens meeting of the North Atlantic Council in May, 1962, to discourage small national deterrents and co-ordinate all nuclear policy under the control of the United States, President de Gaulle moved toward French secession from the integrated military structure of NATO in 1966 and the expulsion of all NATO headquarters and forces from France.

From that time to the present, French military policy has been based on the idea of national independence, preserving for France a freedom of choice ranging from full neutrality in a future war to participation on the side of NATO but on French terms. The loss of French territory in itself imposes severe handicaps on NATO as a result of losing airfields, room for dispersal and deployment, and many of the best logistical routes from Atlantic ports to the German front.

The French hope of preserving independence and even neutrality is based on the French national nuclear force. Decisions leading to the creation of this force antedate the rise of President de Gaulle. The Suez debacle prompted the government of the day to accelerate the programme and in April 1958 the first test was authorized, to be carried out in 1960.

Over the years the French have provided themselves with a "triad" of strategic nuclear forces based on aircraft, intermediate range ballistic missiles (IRBM) and submarine launched ballistic missiles (SLBM). Although some components of this triad are of questionable quality and "survivability", the French authorities believe the number and variety of systems provide both a degree of invulnerability and an insurance against technological surprize. The force is in constant transition but currently consists essentially of: some thirty obsolescent Mirage IV aircraft the usefulness of which it is hoped to extend to the mid-'nineties with a 100 km range stand-off missile with a 1-300 KT warhead; some new Mirage 2000N aircraft with a mixed tactical-strategic role; eighteen S3 IRBMs based in silos on the Plateau d'Albion, with a range of some 3500 km, a 1 MT warhead and some penetration aids; and five, soon to be six, SSBN, most with 16 M20 SLBM with 1 MT warhead, but the sixth to have and others to be retrofitted with a MIRVed M4 missile of some 4000 km range with six re-entry vehicles of some 150 KT and a reported CEP of 2-400 metres.

The philosophy of the French force de dis-suasion begins with the assumption that, in the words of the French Defence White Paper of 1972, "deterrence is exclusively national . . . nuclear risk cannot be shared". A modest national force can be an effective deterrent if the damage it can threaten is disproportionately large compared to the value defeating the nation concerned would have for an aggressor. From this perspective the doctrine of flexible response is both dangerously weak in appearance, sapping the credibility of the ultimate threat, and also wasteful in requiring preparation to fight two battles, a preparatory forward one before the nuclear one that counts and is therefore the real deterrent.

At one period in the 'sixties French nuclear policy seemed to be moving to a true neutralism as expressed by the French Chief of Staff, General Ailleret who suggested France should be ready to repel an enemy from any direction and therefore needed a deterrent for tous azimuths. But President de Gaulle never clearly endorsed this view and just before his fall his then Chief of Staff General Fourquet issued a modified description of French defence policy in which the still unnamed enemy came "from the East".

At this time, doubtless encouraged by the coming diversification of French nuclear forces by the addition of tactical weapons and perhaps influenced reluctantly by theoretical criticisms of complete inflexibility in deterrence, General Fourquet also acknowledged that the French First Army and Tactical Air Force might play some part in the bataille d'avant or forward battle, perhaps in co-operation with NATO, perhaps alone if NATO showed reluctance to introduce nuclear weapons.

A second battle would begin if the foe threatened French borders. At that time the French would execute their national "deterrent manoeuvre", that is, a fairly nominal resistance by conventional forces would lead quickly to brief use of tactical nuclear weapons to issue a warning shot that the moment for the force de dissuasion was approaching. As in NATO policy the exact circumstances when the nuclear forces would be used are deliberately left vague. Also as in NATO the initial tactical use is intended to be not a mere demonstration but a serious blow at enemy forces: what a French Defence Minister has described as a "militarily significant tactical nuclear stopping blow". This requirement has been interpreted as demanding a relatively large scale use of tactical nuclear weapons, concentrated in time and space, ruling out any prolonged, "war-fighting" introduction of tactical nuclear weapons as an adjunct to a sustained convetional campaign, a possibility proponents of this French view fear may be implied by NATO's flexible response. French tactical weapons sometimes significantly called "prestrategical" are intended to test enemy intentions and signal French resolve.

Consequently a relatively small force is based on aircraft — a role now carried by Mirage 2000N and Super-Etendards — and on a force of solid fuel *Pluton* ballistic missiles with a warhead of either 10 or 25 KT yield and a range between 20 and 120 km, now being supplemented by the *Hades,* with a range of 350 km, greater mobility and a warhead up to 60 KT. There has been discussion of a French "neutron" or enhanced radiation warhead for its tactical nuclear weapons.

Nuclear strategy, weapons and expenditure

Below: The diagram summarizes the French capability to support NATO. Relatively small though the conventional forces are, they would loom large to SACEUR, short as he is of uncommitted reserves, provided he had sufficient notice of their availability. By contrast, the French nuclear forces though they may or may not reinforce deterrence of war in Europe, would be something of an embarrassment as an uncertain element in a nuclear confrontation that NATO would be highly anxious to keep under control.

France's possible contribution to the central front battle

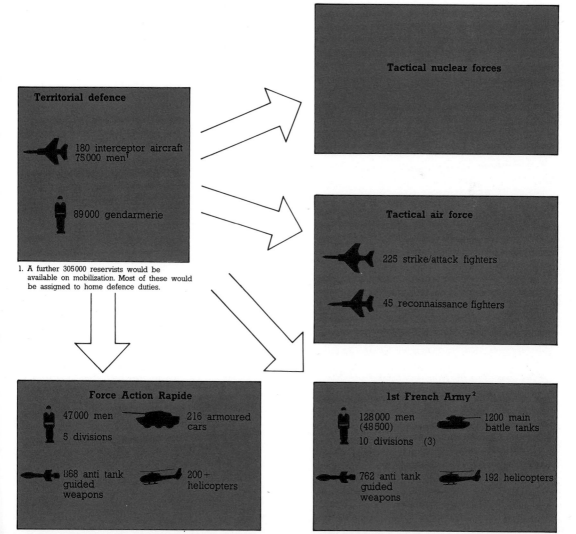

Territorial defence

180 interceptor aircraft
75000 men[1]

89000 gendarmerie

1. A further 305000 reservists would be available on mobilization. Most of these would be assigned to home defence duties.

Tactical nuclear forces

Tactical air force

225 strike/attack fighters

45 reconnaissance fighters

Force Action Rapide

47000 men   216 armoured
                   cars
5 divisions

868 anti tank   200+
guided   helicopters
weapons

1st French Army[2]

128000 men   1200 main
(48500)   battle tanks
10 divisions   (3)

762 anti tank   192 helicopters
guided
weapons

2. Figures in brackets refer to forces deployed in Germany in peacetime.

have dominated French defence policy since 1960. Under Giscard d'Estaing however, from about 1976 to the early 'eighties, there was a refurbishment of French conventional forces and a rather more sympathetic approach to their role. In particular it was more freely admitted that France might play a greater part in the forward battle. A very significant pronouncement of the French Chief of Staff, General Méry, in 1976, much disputed by more orthodox "gaullists", declared that "it would be extremely dangerous for our country to deliberately hold herself aloof from this first battle, in the course of which our security would in fact already be at stake". Thus General Méry envisaged France as having "a second-echelon participation in the first battle". This would, of course, be a very important factor in NATO and Soviet calculations, for the French First Army represents one of the few true "reserves" on which the Western command could call.

As a result of this thinking French conventional forces have undergone substantial reorganisation and some re-equipment, though they are still relatively starved of resources. By the mid-'eighties the French Army was being restructured to provide six small armoured divisions and a number of motorized (i.e. wheeled rather than tracked) infantry divisions. Two light armoured divisions were created from the resources of military schools. As a result the Army would be deployed as three Corps: the First, at Metz with 2 Armoured, 1 Light Armoured and 1 Infantry divisions; the Second at Baden-Baden with 3 Armoured divisions, and the Third at Lille with 1 Armoured, 1 Light Armoured and 1 Infantry division. Placing this Third Corps at Lille represented a shift to the North in emphasis and a further move toward supplementing NATO resources by falling in behind the weaker NATO NORTHAG rather than solely CENTAG as hitherto.

In addition the forces once chiefly dedicated to the overseas intervention role were reshaped to provide a reinforcement capability in Europe also. A Force d'Action Rapide (FAR) was created out of a light armoured division, a new Airmobile division with some 200 helicopters, and Alpine, Naval Infantry and Parachute elements.

As a result of all this the French Army was reduced by some 40,000 men, allegedly compensated for by streamlining headquarters and administration. Serious criticisms continued to be levelled at the scale of equipment, particularly in tanks, artillery and anti-aircraft weapons. Similar anxieties were expressed about the French Tactical Airforce (FATAC) which had only about 300 aircraft at its disposal, organized in 21 squadrons of which 5 were chiefly dedicated to a nuclear role. Few aircraft were ordered in the early 'eighties and French aircraft were alleged to be technologically well behind those of many other European powers in electronic sophistication, as a result, it was alleged, not merely of shortage of funds but of undue attention to Third World export markets.

These rearrangements of French conventional forces were carried out by the Socialist governments under President Mitterand as well as their predecessors under Giscard d'Estaing. A move toward greater potential co-operation with NATO thus continued, though it was not politically acceptable to express it in that way. Such a move accorded with French efforts to develop a closer relation with West Germany. The French armed forces had always continued to be more co-operative with NATO than political rhetoric suggested, especially in the naval area, and this pattern continued. French defence policy could be regarded as having three or four circles: the force de dissuasion, the forces conventional and nuclear for a battle both on and beyond the national frontier in Europe, territorial forces for defence of the interior, and a capacity for overseas intervention on a small scale.

On the other hand nationalism, economy, and doctrinal considerations saw to it that the retreat from a national form of "massive retaliation" as the basis of French strategy, which might have been thought to be under way in the time of Giscard d'Estaing, was clearly arrested; as the socialist defence minister declared at one point: "to reduce our conventional forces too far would give rise to charges of neutralism; to develop them in an exaggerated fashion would be to behave as if nuclear weapons did not exist" and reduce the credibility of France using them.

Whether this credibility is sufficiently high remains a subject for debate. The most plausible occasion for French use, a Soviet attack on French cities, is not one of the more likely contingencies. France, however, like the United Kingdom, enjoys the luxury of lying behind German territory, at least so far as a land campaign is involved. Some of the more difficult problems of escalation are thus not likely to be faced first by France unless French doubts about NATO firmness of purpose are all too true. Despite logical inconsistencies French defence policy seems to retain the confidence of most sectors of French opinion.

NATO's Options: (2) Conventional Improvements

The tentative moves toward a more robust conventional element in French strategy respond, of course, to the misgivings about thorough-going reliance on nuclear weapons which led the other members of the North Atlantic Alliance to espouse the flexible response in 1967 and which still inhibit a return to primary reliance on nuclear weapons even though the burdens of conventional defence are rendered progressively heavier by the enhancement of the forces of the Warsaw Pact and the refinement of its strategy. Political support and economic provision may not be forthcoming for conventional forces strong enough to permit the elimination of deliberate nuclear escalation as the key element in the flexible response, but equally public anxiety about nuclear weapons in the 'eighties and tensions between allies in vastly different geopolitical circumstances, compel NATO at least to make conspicuous efforts to improve its conventional capabilities. Despite the theoretical logic and economic temptations of a more nuclear approach to deterring war in Europe, the main NATO response to the rising challenge from both the Soviet Union and advancing conventional military technology is to seek ways of harnessing the latter to deter or defeat the former.

Not the least difficult problem is to choose between the almost numberless areas in which improvement of NATO's capabilities could be sought. In particular, choices have to be made between increasing the size and capability of NATO's existing forces and harnessing revolutionary new technology to the service of both established and possibly quite new strategic concepts.

The Long Term Defence Improvement Plan of 1978 identified nine major programme areas in the conventional field, the tenth being nuclear. A later study made by the US Congress in 1983 named ten "critical persistent deficiencies" in NATO: (1) early available ground forces; (2) reinforcement support structure; (3) offensive "counter-air" capability; (4) capacity for "sustainability" — i.e. supplies etc.: (5) reconnaissance (6) capability to attack rear areas; (7) command and control; (8) counter-measures to (sea)mines; (10) defence against chemical weapons.

With the possible exception of the problem of attacking rear areas, this list concentrates on deficiencies in NATO's capability to fight the war in orthodox terms, and the demands might be characterized as "more of the same". Such an effort calls chiefly for making good the largely quantitative shortages from which NATO has chronically suffered. These shortages affect both the forces available at the outset of hostilities, to counter the Warsaw Pact's initial thrust, and those for sustaining the resistance as the defences are worn down, containing penetrations and launching counter-attacks. NATO not only lacks resources to sustain the formations bearing the initial brunt of the fighting but is grievously short of forces that can be held back from the battle as an operational reserve to plug gaps and counter-attack. This lack deprives NATO of the vital element in a modern mobile defence and relieves the Warsaw Pact of what would otherwise be a major anxiety inculcating a more cautious offensive strategy.

It would be a considerable contribution to solving this problem if SACEUR could rely more confidently on the participation of the French First Army. Other suggestions have concentrated upon organizational reforms in NATO forces. Some of these have involved efforts to improve the "teeth to tail" ratio of NATO forces. Here a distinction must be drawn between simple criticisms of excessive headquarters staffs and other "frills" and more radical sacrifices of support functions to initial combat power on the grounds that "sustainability" is not much good if the war is lost in the first few days. Clearly, however, such remedies, though perhaps a reasonable ordering of priorities, simply shift the problem from one place to another. Other organizational solutions suggest a greater reliance on German reserve forces — in the sense of part-time or former soldiers, not to be confused with the concept of an operational reserve — to fight the early stages of the defensive battle, strengthened by modern light anti-tank weapons, releasing the high quality German and perhaps other armoured units to form a mobile reserve for counter-attacks.

NATO's overall capacity to resist is vitally dependent on the rate of reinforcement by British, Canadian and, above all, American units. In recent years we have seen considerable efforts have been made to speed up this process, acceleration of which could serve several purposes, not merely increasing forces in place in Europe and reducing Soviet opportunities to interfere, but also providing a useful deterrent signal for crisis management. The process is, however, an expensive one. A modern armoured division is immensely heavy and the task of bringing it across the Atlantic can only be economically — and in the case of some weapons, physically — managed by ships over a period of weeks. By the mid-'eighties the programme for prepositioning equipment had rendered the United States capable of moving four divisions to Europe in ten days, with the intention to increase the number of divisions to six to achieve a goal of "ten divisions in Europe in ten days".

There are, however, severe problems. Exercises show that "marrying up" troops to equipment is not always an easy process. Until this is complete and the division deploys, it and its equipment offer an ideal and easily identified target for enemy air attacks, saboteurs or airborne forces. Equipment must be duplicated in the United States so that units can train — though this can be used by less ready reinforcements later — and men must be diverted to guarding and maintaining the stockpiles in Europe — a function largely fulfilled by German units. Somewhat similar problems affect the deployment of aircraft. While the aircraft themselves can rapidly be moved, subject to facilities for refuelling, there need to be airfields to receive them — preferably equipped with active defences and hardened "hangarettes" — and they will not be operational without munitions, spares and until joined by ground crews. As the United States has hundreds of aircraft to redeploy, this again is no small requirement. French withdrawal from the integrated military planning of the alliance has compounded this problem by severely reducing the number of airfields reliably available.

As always in military affairs, money spent on the mechanics of reinforcement is money diverted from other supplies to increase "sustainability".

Shortage of weapons and ammunition to maintain resistance over time, even if it is initially successful, remains one of NATO's main problems. This limitation is obviously directly related to the role of conventional resistance in deferring the moment of nuclear escalation. NATO has long had the modest goal of enough supplies to permit fighting for thirty days, but hardly any ally has achieved this across the board. There are also major discrepancies between national forces. Quite clearly disaster will befall even a well-equipped NATO division if the friendly forces on its flank are overrun for want of supplies and this problem is compounded by the widespread incompatibility of equipment and even ammunition between many allied armies and airforces. Often even nominally identical aircraft, like the F4 Phantom, in different national ownership cannot make use of one another's facilities, by reason of different fittings and specifications.

It must also be admitted that while NATO's lack of sustainability is serious, the remedies can conflict with other goals. The resources needed for reinforcement, such as air and sea lift and the ready forces themselves, compete for funds with the additional equipment and ammunition needed by each unit to bolster its staying power. Nor is it obvious where extra quantities should be applied if available. While

it is true that a gun that runs out of ammunition in the second week of war is henceforth useless, it becomes so even earlier if the whole battle is lost in the first week for lack of a second gun. Similar considerations apply to the trade-off between numbers and quality. An ironical Israeli military man is quoted to the effect that nothing is more important in weapons than quality, provided you have enough of them.

The day has passed when NATO could assume such qualitative advantages as to justify some complacency about numbers. For many years NATO, or at least its leading members, could console itself with the higher quality and effectiveness of its weapons but this is less and less clearly so. In the first place, the Soviet Union has dramatically closed the gap in quality. This is true even when Soviet weapons are evaluated by Western standards and preferences. There is considerable reason to believe, however, that some of these Western standards are misplaced, and that superficially cruder, simpler, Soviet systems may actually have high military effectiveness under combat conditions which frequently render some of the theoretically impressive capabilities of weapons irrelevant — long range, for instance, when targets cannot actually be seen or, "acquired — at such distances. Recent operational research in NATO, especially with regard to air warfare, suggests that in many situations numbers rather than quality — within the reasonable limits exemplified by current types of equipment — carry the day. Moreover, quality is by no means always on the NATO side. There are types of weapon in which the Soviet Union has led in innovation and where NATO has only recently followed — armoured fighting vehicles for infantry, for example, or multiple launch rocket systems (MLRS).

The situation should not be exaggerated. Experience in the Middle East has demonstrated impressive successes for American equipment over Soviet systems, though allowance must be made for the skill of those operating the weapons. If the Soviet Union led with Multiple Rocket Launchers, the United States probably leads in applying them to the delivery of cluster weapons so effective as to be proclaimed an effective substitute for the smaller battlefield nuclear weapons. The West and above all the United States undoubtedly enjoys great advantages wherever electronics are critical. But certainly the combination of NATO's quantitative disadvantages with the relative rise in quality of Soviet weapons is cause for serious concern. While it is true that thanks to the Soviet tendency to retain old weapons, justified by a rather lavish use of conscripts to man them, much of the quantity in Warsaw Pact inventories is less than the latest, it must also be realized that the quantities of Pact weapons are

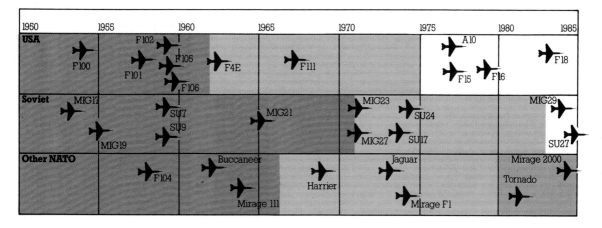

1950	1955	1960	1965	1970	1975	1980	1985

USA
F100, F102, F101, F105, F106, F4E, F111, A10, F15, F16, F18

Soviet
MIG17, MIG19, SU7, SU9, MIG21, MIG23, MIG27, SU24, SU17, MIG29, SU27

Other NATO
F104, Buccaneer, Mirage III, Harrier, Jaguar, Mirage F1, Mirage 2000, Tornado

Above: The chart gives a rough idea of the Soviet lag behind the West and particularly the United States in aircraft design. Aircraft capability is a compound of performance of airframe, power plant and electronics or avionics. Estimates of the efficacy of various combinations vary but the chart shows that the United States was introducing the F4, still a "current" aircraft in the early 'sixties, Britain's Harrier came in the mid-'sixties, while the equivalent Mig 23 did not enter service until the early 'seventies. Similarly the F15, introduced by the United States about 1975, was matched by the Mig 29 and SU27 only in the mid-'eighties. There thus still seems to be about a ten year lag from United States to Soviet progress with Western Europe somewhere between. It should be noted that the avionics position of the package increasingly seems to be the dominant one and this should help the United States retain its lead.

so large that the modern component within the force is frequently larger than the total NATO force; this is true, for example, of the so-called "fourth-generation" tanks (those with at least several of the following characteristics: large calibre, high velocity, smooth bore gun, laser range finding, shaped-charge defeating armour, automatic loading, and high power, high speed cross-country capability). The whole French tank force represents six weeks current Soviet production.

For all these reasons there are plentiful opportunities for NATO to make greater investments in making its established posture more robust. There are, however, more radical proposals to reshape NATO's operational plans.

Below: The generation gap exists within the Pact also. The top chart shows the small proportion of "current" aircraft such as the Mig 23 in non-Soviet Pact inventories and the large number of obsolescent aircraft like the Mig 21. At the bottom is displayed the small number of new generation aircraft like the Mig 29 and SU27 in even the Soviet inventory and the substantial 35% of old aircraft of the Mig 21 vintage. In interpreting these figures the large overall numbers should be borne in mind.

Aircraft
Warsaw Pact

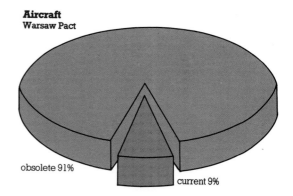

obsolete 91% current 9%

Soviet Union
obsolete 35%

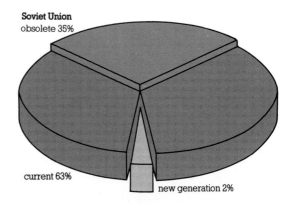

current 63% new generation 2%

111

most promising of weapons to impede and advance by men or vehicles. Laborious mine-laying of the past can now be replaced by a variety of methods for rapidly dispensing mines, though with some penalty in the degree of concealment attainable. Heavy mines can be laid quickly by the towed mechanical layer (Barmine) shown. Lighter mines can be dispensed by aircraft, by helicopters, MLRS and conventional artillery. Such methods permit minelaying well behind enemy lines to damage and inhibit his rear area activities and reinforcements. Similarly rapidly laid mines could help contain forces, like OMG, that have penetrated to friendly rear areas.

Below: Mines of various kinds, given much greater efficacy than in the past by shaped charges and a variety of sensors to activate them, are currently regarded as one of the

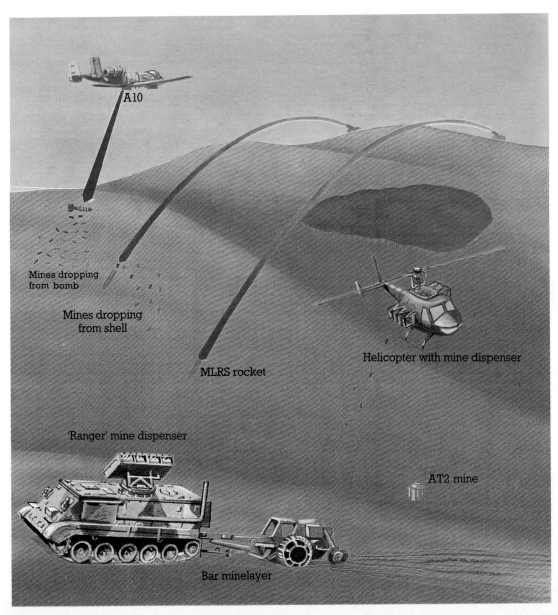

A10

Mines dropping from bomb

Mines dropping from shell

MLRS rocket

Helicopter with mine dispenser

'Ranger' mine dispenser

AT2 mine

Bar minelayer

NATO'S Options: (3) New Defensive Concepts

Most of the more far-reaching proposals to make NATO's defences more effective take the form of yet another effort to redress the military balance by exploiting supposed technological advantages enjoyed by NATO. This is not entirely so; there are those who advocate much greater reliance on a very long-established mode of defence: field fortifications. Quite modest investment in prepared barriers and firing positions would, it is argued, greatly impede the advance of the Warsaw Pact, channel its offensive forces into "killing grounds", thereby rendering them much more vulnerable to relatively static, lightly armed, perhaps reserve forces, and releasing NATO's more costly armoured mobile forces for counter attack. At first sight such an idea flies in the face of the notions of mobile defence that have become something of a fetish in some armies. More troublesome, however, has been persistent German resistance on political grounds. In part this stems from reluctance to see Germany's role as a battlefield so clearly illustrated by defensive preparations. Perhaps even more serious has been the belief that to fortify the "inner-German frontier" would symbolize and possibly even reinforce the division of Germany.

The probable military rewards for better preparation of the battlefield, are so great, however, that in the mid-'eighties renewed efforts were being made to win acceptance for the idea. Technology may indeed be able to help this rather old-fashioned strategic concept, for modern earth moving equipment makes the emergency construction of obstacles much more practicable, especially when used in conjunction with the new rapidly dispersible mines. Properly exploited, static defences could enhance the capability of NATO's other forces for mobile operations.

Nevertheless, the greatest attention has been directed at strategic innovations depending on very high, so called emerging technology. In the broadest sense, this embraces all the ways of using modern methods of surveillance and target acquisition — sophisticated radar, both land-based and airborne, the latter perhaps carried by remotely piloted vehicles (RPV), combined with new techniques for accurate delivery to enhance conventional firepower and place Warsaw Pact armoured formations at something approaching the same degree of risk as was once obtainable only with nuclear weapons.

This possibility rests chiefly on the improvements in the ability to design much more effective conventional munitions, "tailored" to specific types of target, and then to deliver them accurately and with certainty. Accuracy and destructive power of warheads interact to determine effectiveness. Until recently NATO's only hope of effectively engaging many important targets both in front and rear areas, seemed to be by using nuclear weapons. In the 'eighties the emerging technologies already briefly described offer increasing prospect of dealing economically with these targets with conventional munitions.

Although nuclear weapons possess some characteristics that cannot be duplicated by other means, characteristics such as really immense radii of destruction or residual radiation, or though some chemical weapons might go some way to replicate the latter, in many cases plans to use nuclear warheads merely sought to compensate for inaccuracy of target location and weapons delivery. The much greater accuracies now made possible by electronics not merely permit the use of smaller nuclear warheads — in itself a significant advantage given the inhibition against large nuclear weapons arising from collateral damage and danger to friendly forces — but in many instances permits the employment of conventional weapons to carry out missions previously assigned to nuclear weapons. Even if the conventional option may in some cases be more expensive, it relieves the political and military commands of immense anxieties. The consequently much greater freedom of initiative permitted military commanders is thus itself one of the major enhancements of effectiveness.

At long ranges the kind of terrain-following guidance employed in many modern NATO aircraft and in the US cruise missiles, whereby a vehicle updates its inertial navigation system by radar matching of the terrain below with digitally prestored data, already permits accuracies of some 100 metres at unlimited ranges. The US Global Positioning System of stationary satellites now being installed, permits accuracy of 10 metres. Thus, as with all good guidance systems, accuracy ceases to be a function of range.

At shorter ranges the now familiar techniques of "precision guidance" permit direct hits on small targets in more than 50% of the cases. Many of these systems, such as those dependent on infra-red sensors or lasers, are subject to degradation by smoke and atmospheric conditions but nevertheless a radical revolution in accuracy has taken place.

Interdiction missions at long range, however accurately they may be carried out, still face problems of target identification and location. For known positions, such as bridges and airfields, this is not so, and the main difficulty is to penetrate defences over a long distance. Pending the arrival of effective anti-ballistic

Left: A stylized impression of an ET battlefield; aircraft drop cluster weapon dispensers which distribute target seeking shaped charges over tank formations while escort fighters and electronic surveillance aircraft patrol overhead; at the same time dispensers fired from cannon and the MLRS and carried in missiles like the proposed JCTAMS and MRASM also arrive over the target before deploying parachutes to descend to dispersal altitude.

Right: Cluster sub-munition detonates shaped charge upon sensing heat of tank engine.

missile systems, the penetration problem can be solved by ballistic missiles, provided they can carry the appropriate payload and so long as it is not thought that long range missiles are so associated with nuclear missions as to have escalatory implications.

Finding mobile targets at long range remains a largely unsolved challenge very relevant to NATO's task of attacking the Soviet rear echelons. One solution is to assume that such targets inevitably build-up behind choke points, some of which will have been created by NATO's destruction of bridges and other communication bottlenecks. Alternatively, mobile targets must be attacked by manned aircraft, possibly gaining some security from damage already wrought by the cruise and ballistic missile strikes on the Warsaw Pact air defence system.

At shorter ranges target location is not such a problem and the challenge becomes delivering sufficient effective warheads to the target. Munitions developed for such purposes can, of course, be utilized by long range systems if appropriate targets can be located.

The simplest precision system in concept is the single anti-tank or other missile guided onto an individual target by an operator. To deal with larger numbers of targets and at rather longer range calls for a different approach, ideally one that will replace the nuclear weapon's ability to blanket a considerable area with destructive

effect. One such device is the fuel-air explosive (FAE), whereby an aerosol cloud of combustible material is dispersed and then ignited, producing an explosion of evenly distributed effect — unlike the attenuating effect radiating from an explosion at a single point — and one of great efficiency in proportion to weapon weight because the explosion utilizes oxygen in the atmosphere. FAE can have great utility in forests, for instance, where targets may be known to exist without knowledge of the precise location of individual elements. Yet in forests and in many other environments — uneven terrain, windy areas — the even dispersal and ignition of FAE may be very difficult. For this and other reasons FAE are no longer so confidently hailed as the conventional equivalent of small nuclear weapons as was once the case.

Knowledge of where the enemy is, what he is doing and in what strength, has been a vital ingredient of military success throughout the history of warfare. This has never been more so than in the age of nuclear weapons and precision guidance, which greatly raise the probability that a target once seen will be destroyed. The mobility of modern armed forces also increases both the difficulty of knowing what is where, and also the capacity to take rapid advantage of strategic and tactical opportunities. It is only natural, therefore, that modern technology and particularly electronics have been pressed into the service of intelligence. The diagram provides a checklist of some of the more important systems, ranging from stay-behind parties of troops in radio contact with friendly forces, through reconnaissance aircraft and drones to such extremely high technology instruments as AWACS aircraft and satellites. The mass of information revealed by such devices, all subject to enemy efforts to deceive and obscure, must be processed, sifted and assimilated if it is to prove useful rather than confusing. While computers can contribute to this task too, there remain serious concerns as to whether the flood of intelligence will be manageable rather than give rise to entirely new ways to become confused and make mistakes.

Intelligence systems

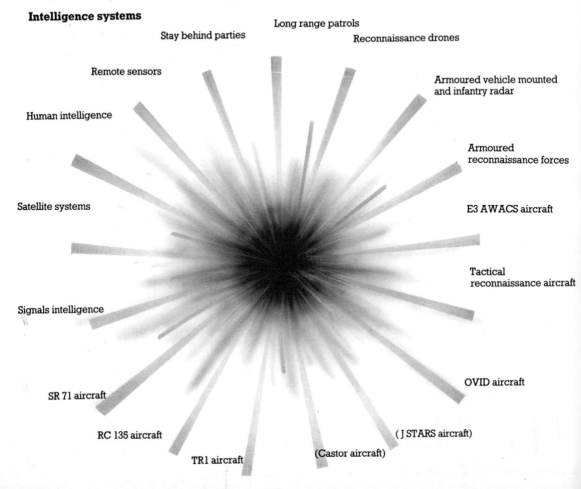

Stay behind parties

Long range patrols

Reconnaissance drones

Remote sensors

Armoured vehicle mounted and infantry radar

Human intelligence

Armoured reconnaissance forces

Satellite systems

E3 AWACS aircraft

Tactical reconnaissance aircraft

Signals intelligence

OVID aircraft

SR 71 aircraft

RC 135 aircraft

(J STARS aircraft)

TR1 aircraft

(Castor aircraft)

Most popular in contemporary thinking are "sub-munitions": small multiple warheads delivered as a distributed package to act either directly as active weapons or as "target-activated" weapons or mines. As with the small precision guided anti-tank missiles, the effectiveness of such small warheads is achieved by exploiting the axial-shaped hollow charge principle, whereby the penetrating energy is derived not from the kinetic force of the vehicle but from a directed jet of hot gases usually propelling a molten mass formed from a shaped liner of metal. Such warheads are much less sensitive to the angle of incidence — achieved on the target than kinetic projectiles — which are commonly ineffective at an angle of greater than 30° — but do require detonation at an optimal distance from the target surface. Such anti-tank missiles as the American TOW or Soviet Sagger, carry a warhead of some 3-4 kg and can drill a conical hole four or five times the diameter of the charge in length in mild steel and ten to twelve diameters in reinforced concrete. A large charge of 800 kg with a diameter of 90 cm can drive through 10 metres of concrete. Against the inmates of tanks and pillboxes much of the damage is done by fragments of the wall "spalled" off the interior. Modern types of "spaced" armours using composite materials can, however, considerably degrade the penetrating performance.

Clusters of submunitions can be delivered in various ways. The West German MW1 consists of a 10,000 lb dispenser designed for the Tornado and can scatter munitions over a 400 m wide pathway. MLRS can deliver patterns at shorter range as can conventional artillery pieces of larger calibers. Simpler cluster weapons rely on random statistical distribution to cover the target area and secure hits on specific objects within it.

A tank constitutes a target area of some 20 sq. metres from above. More sophisticated and more expensive designs under development build a degree of "smartness" or intelligence into the submunition so that it will home in on an appropriate sub-target. Thus once dispersed in a square search pattern the US Skeet uses a two-colour infra-red sensor and an altimeter to home in on the heat of vehicles. If the sub-munition fails to locate a hot target before hitting the ground, it detonates as an anti-personnel weapon. It is claimed that an MLRS salvo delivering Skeet could secure as effective a tank kill as a .1 kiloton enhanced radiation or 1 kt normal radiation nuclear weapon, although it would not provide the nuclear weapon's assured kill of the crews.

A major benefit of the modern munitions is greatly reduced logistical and delivery system requirements. Thus it is estimated that to destroy 60% of the 2,500 vehicles in a Soviet Motor Rifle Division would require 2,200 aircraft sorties with unguided conventional bombs, 300 sorties with "dumb", unguided sub-munitions and only 50-60 with systems of the Skeet type. So far as aircraft are concerned all these systems require hazardous direct overflight of the usually well-defended targets. Stand-off systems could eliminate this hazard.

While all this technology clearly has multiple conceivable applications, recent efforts to identify vulnerabilities in Soviet operations has focused particular attention on the possibility of undertaking relatively deep strikes on Warsaw Pact forces, to interdict their advancing rear echelons and destroy their airfields in ways which again were only conceivable in earlier years by employing the widespread and consequently undiscriminating effects of nuclear weapons. By attacking likely logistical "choke points" for advancing forces it can be hoped to produce traffic jams that would afford further targets.

Attacking such targets has long been the aim of NATO airforces but modern air defences threaten to make the price of such efforts unacceptably high. The new accuracy of cruise and ballistic missiles, whether ground launched or used as stand-off weapons by aircraft, combined with new conventional munitions, offers new possibilities of conducting such operations in a cost-effective way. Moreover once Soviet forces are damaged and disorganized by such operations, a less hostile environment might ensue in which manned aircraft could resume their traditional role. A particularly clear example of such a possibility is represented by airfields, for if the "main operating bases", which are heavily defended, can be rendered unoperational, surviving Warsaw Pact aircraft will have to fly from much more vulnerable diversionary fields.

By the mid-'eighties, the United States had sponsored two variants of a strategy exploiting such ideas and technology. One, espoused by the U.S. Army and Air Force, but not NATO doctrine, was the "Air-Land Battle", which involves striking enemy forces as far as 150 kilometres back from the main battle line, which would involve bringing enemy formations under surveillance about 96 hours before they would join the battle and under attack about 72 hours before that moment. This doctrine aroused anxiety in some NATO quarters because as enunciated for the U.S. Army it is not a strategy necessarily confined to conventional weapons.

In some ways an even more ambitious proposal favoured by SACEUR is "Follow-on Force Attack" (FOFA). This envisages purely conventional strikes on rear echelons up to some 400 km behind the battle. As compared to the Air-Land battle, such a concept would not only permit an attack on a greater proportion of Warsaw Pact forces, but would not violate NATO's established preference for centralizing the control of airpower so as to concentrate and maximize its effect. The Air-Land concept, by applying the bulk of its effort close to the line of ground combat, would require much closer co-ordination with much greater numbers of lower army commanders, thereby posing a task for command and control that may exceed present day capabilities. As it is, with fixed wing manned aircraft, RPV, helicopters and missiles both friendly and hostile all operating in relative constrained areas, the air over the battlefield is already immensely complicated and congested.

A considerable number of doubts do indeed beset the various versions of "deep strike". The most fundamental, perhaps, questions the basic priority suggested by such proposals. While advocates of deep strike claim remarkable degrees of efficiency for the strategy and the technology becoming available to execute it, no one pretends the cost is negligible. Perhaps the most widely noted public study calls for 1000 short-range MLRS systems, 5000 stand-off cruise missile submunition carriers and 900 conventionally armed ballistic missiles at a cost of $10-$30 billion over the decade — a soberingly imprecise as well as high estimate. Given the general shortage of resources, it can therefore be argued that the first priority must be to improve NATO's capacity to fight the initial main battle at the front line, for if that is lost, Soviet reinforcements become irrelevant. More tanks, it is said, are more urgently needed than new missiles.

This criticism can be sharpened by pointing out that some of the tasks posed for the new strategies require technical capabilities that have not yet been proved however promising the theoretical possibilities may seem. In particular there is doubt about target acquisition; airfields and bridges are certainly in known positions but the problem of locating mobile forces at any great distance from the front remains largely unsolved. For that role, conventional weapons may not yet be an effective substitute for nuclear warheads.

Even more disconcerting is the possibility raised by trends in Soviet strategy. If the Soviet Union is bringing its combat power forward, and becoming more able to fight a major battle without relying on a deeply deployed second echelon, then the targets for deep strike may not exist in such profusion or be an essential component of early Soviet success. If such were the case, then the argument that it is the first line of defence and not deep strike that deserves any spare resources would be greatly strengthened.

Other grounds for scepticism concern the delivery technology required. There can be no doubt cruise and ballistic missiles can be built — indeed some exist — to reach their targets with high accuracy, if the location is known. Modern conventional munitions offer good prospects of destroying some targets, but others still represent an unresolved challenge. Until the terminally guided submunition is perfected, reasonably dispersed armoured vehicles are not easy to destroy cost effectively. Airfield runways also present a difficult problem; whereas a nuclear strike would finish off an airfield for good, attacks with even the best conventional systems would have to be repeated perhaps every few hours, given the hardness of runways, the effectiveness of modern runway repair, and the increasing capability of aircraft to make do with imperfect surfaces.

Furthermore, the supposed advantage of missiles over aircraft is their lower cost and greater capacity to penetrate defences. Many members of NATO, however, such as Britain and West Germany, have recently spent a high proportion of their available defence funds on new ground-attack aircraft, such as the Tornado. They are unlikely to be early clients for a whole new expensive delivery system. This is all the more so as both cruise and ballistic missiles owe their advantage in part to the absence of effective counter-measures. Cruise missiles, however, are clearly vulnerable to rapidly improving air defence systems now being increasingly tailored to deal with that problem. Soviet AWACS aircraft and "look-down" interceptor systems are a case in point.

By 1985 it was clear that even the ballistic missile might not for ever enjoy immunity from interception. For decades the most important characteristic of the ballistic missile, subject to rapidly reducing limits of accuracy, was the certainty that once launched, it would arrive. This is not only effective, but greatly simplifies planning. We have already seen that the technology of ballistic missile defence, though chiefly publicized at the "strategic" level of the "Star Wars" debate, may also be applicable to shorter range missiles used in theatre warfare. Indeed the slower re-entry speed of such missiles is said to more than compensate for the probably shorter warning time. Some air defence missiles that came into service in the mid-'eighties, such as the American *Patriot* and the Soviet SA12, already had a limited anti-missile capability. With ballistic missiles long known to be part of a possible nuclear war in Europe and with new ideas such as "deep-strike" foretelling a conventional role for them, it is only to be expected that anti-ballistic missile defence will become part of the offence-defence dialectic. Moreover, the task set for such defences in a theatre war is in several respects inherently easier than in the strategic balance; for if we assume the targets of the ballistic missile are military installations rather than cities, then not only are the targets probably "harder", but also a less than perfect defence may be militarily very worthwhile.

Finally, it should be noted that the evident analogy that can be drawn between the role of the missile in both nuclear and conventional war, accounts for yet another objection raised to the deep-strike concept. Such a strategy would, it is said, dangerously blur the line between nuclear and conventional war, an impending conventional missile attack being easily mis-perceived as the opening of the nuclear phase and provoking prompt, perhaps pre-emptive retaliation "in kind".

Such fears can naturally cause political contro-versy in the West. Like those who advocate that NATO should adopt a more offensive strategy on the ground, geared not merely to tactical counter-attack but to driving into Warsaw Pact territory, so as both to compel diversion of Warsaw Pact forces and to seize bargaining cards for negotiating termination of the war, so the proponents of deep-strike have been accused of espousing an "aggressive" strategy alien to the nature of NATO as a defensive alliance and consequently damaging to its underlying political consensus. Certainly one can expect Soviet propaganda to encourage such misgivings and the earlier campaigns against the "neutron bomb" and the INF deployment showed how inhibiting such controversies can be to innovation in NATO strategy.

The history of NATO suggests that the outcome of these controversies will be ambiguous and that NATO strategy will evolve not by radical change but by gradual modifi-cation. In any case, the money for prompt radical changes does not exist. If war comes in Europe in the remaining years of this century, virtually all of the weaponry that will be used has already been designed and a great deal of it already deployed.

On the other hand the new technology cannot be ignored. Even those who press the claims of the front line see the need for some attacks on the enemy rear, and those who are fascinated by novel methods of deep strike see the need to hold the front. The whole history of NATO warns, however, that new technology is never a panacea and that those who seek to apply it incrementally to repair deficiencies and rectify shortages in existing strategy are usually more constructive than those who suggest that novel-ties can render those shortcomings irrelevant. What matters is an effective balance of effort: money spent on deep strike can prevent enemy forces reaching the front; money spent on the front line forces and reserves can strengthen the resistance encountered by the enemy units that do get through. The task of the force planners is not to opt for one or the other but to strike the best compromise, a compromise with which the extreme advocates of either approach are bound to be dissatisfied.

The Economic Basis of Strategy

The debate about "deep-strike" and other ways of harnessing new technology to NATO strategy, illustrates very clearly that underlying the whole structure of defence is a constant balancing of priorities for scarce resources. Strategic insight and skilled leadership in actual combat are vital intangible elements but more than ever in the modern era, a sound defence depends on money. The cost of today's armed forces is extremely high, conventional forces being much more expensive than nuclear weapons, in no small part because of their much greater demand for manpower, one of the most expensive resources in modern society and one soon destined to become much scarcer in both East and West as a result of demographic trends. Moreover the cost of weapons, embodying as they do increasing amounts of high technology, much of it "state of the art", has been steadily rising faster than the general rate of inflation: a very modest estimate suggests some 30% faster.

Sophisticated contemporary weapons are, of course, much more effective than older equipment, but they face opposition which is also more effective. It is not always the case, therefore, that the latest weapon can do more tactically for its owner than could its predecessor in the environment it then faced. In some cases the number of weapons that is needed cannot be simply measured solely against the number of enemy forces but must be related to geographical factors and the length of front to be covered. Consequently the inexorable process whereby increasing costs drive down the number of weapons that can be procured is a serious problem, especially as the very effectiveness of weapons drives consumption in combat to high levels. In the 1973 Middle Eastern War, a second rate military power like Egypt lost more tanks than the entire inventory of the British Army. Over the next few years NATO plans to buy no less than 600,000 rockets for MLRS.

These problems obviously face the Soviet Union also, which must sustain the competition from a less productive economy, but one which can apparently bear higher rates of sacrifice for military purposes. Just how much the Soviet Union spends on defence and what it gets for its money is a source of great contention, the secrecy of the Soviet Union and Western ignorance of its price structure rendering all answers debatable. There seems little doubt, however, that the result is to give the Soviet Union a considerable advantage in ready forces.

So far as NATO itself is concerned, there are difficulties affecting both the overall level of expenditure and the balance between allies.

Annual increases in NATO defence spending, 1971–83 Changes in constant dollar by percent

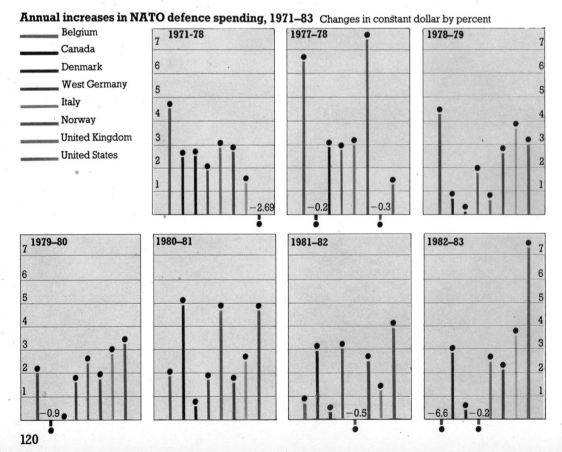

Belgium
Canada
Denmark
West Germany
Italy
Norway
United Kingdom
United States

Having by far the greatest absolute defence budget, the United States is typically inclined to suggest its allies do not pull their weight. In the late 'sixties and early 'seventies, European investment in NATO relatively outstripped that of a United States embroiled in Vietnam. Once that war was over, the United States turned to reviving its investment in NATO; one fruit of this was the LTDP with its target of 3% more per annum in real terms. By the early to mid-'eighties most Europeans had begun to fall behind this goal, largely as a result of economic recession, while a combination of the Reagan Administration's enthusiasm for military spending with pressures on the United States budget and Congressional desire to reduce the cost of defence, sharpened the long-running debate over "burden-sharing". By 1985 President Reagan had to accept a much lower rate of finance in U.S. defence expenditure, perhaps scarcely keeping pace with the general rate of inflation.

Being concerned as it is with defence expenditure, the bulk of which goes on costly conventional weapons, it is not surprizing that the burden-sharing debate should become entangled with that over a shift from nuclear to a conventional emphasis in NATO strategy. Americans who felt that Europeans (and Canadians) were not contributing enough in financial terms, could also argue that by not supporting the build up of NATO's conventional power, Europeans were refusing to help reduce the danger of ultimate nuclear devastation to which the flexible response exposes the United States. Thus, in 1984, the Nunn-Roth amendment to the U.S. defence budget, though rejected by the Senate, called for a reduction in American forces in Europe unless the Europeans met criteria all geared to the shift from a nuclear to a conventional emphasis. These criteria were attainment of the 3% real increase target for defence expenditure, or all or some of: moving 20% of the way from existing stocks of munitions to the goal of thirty days supply; providing 20% of the missing airfield facilities for reinforcing U.S. aircraft; or enabling SACEUR to certify a significant increase in conventional capacity.

Some of these criteria do have the merit of shifting the scrutiny from input to output. It is not, after all, the money that matters but the defence capability it will buy. In fact in terms of output, the balance between the United States and the Europeans is not nearly so unfavourable to the latter as often supposed. In the European theatre and surrounding oceans European members of NATO provide 90% of the ground forces, 90% of the armoured division, 80% of the tanks, 80% of combat aircraft and 70% of combat naval vessels. Europe's military manpower numbers some 3 million active forces and 3 million reservists; the corresponding figure for the United States is 2 million active and 1 million reserve.

Even in financial input the equation is not too bad for Europe if the American contribution is limited to that dedicated to NATO rather than the other global concerns of the United States. A U.S. General Accounting Office study of 1982 estimated the NATO share of the U.S. defence budget to be 56%. In 1984 the U.S. Department of Defense put the proportion at 58%. On that basis the United States was devoting some 3.7% of its Gross National Product (GNP) to NATO; equivalent figures for other allies were: United Kingdom 5.1%, France 4.2%, Federal Republic of Germany, 3.4%, Norway 3%, Canada 2.1%. The cost of the U.S. forces stationed in Europe was put at 3.7%.

Such figures are, of course, open to much

Left: The charts compare real defence expenditure by eight members of NATO, especially during years of the agreed long term plan to increase investment in defence by at least 3% per annum. Such comparisons must be treated with some caution, for while comparisons are much more predictable than with the secretive, administered price Soviet economy, they still do not provide a wholly reliable way of comparing effective defence effort. Spending is an input to defence, not an output.

Right: The chart shows the heavier sacrifice imposed on the Soviet economy than on the American by the military competition, the relatively parallel course of this expenditure, and the tendency to rise in recent years.

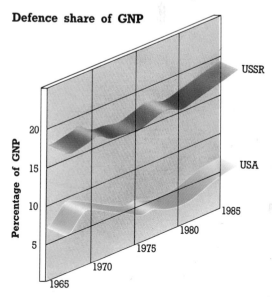

Defence share of GNP

121

Collaborative Procurement of Arms

International comparisons of defence expenditure are notoriously difficult to establish but it can be argued that the members of NATO, enjoying two and a half times the Gross Domestic Product and having one and a half times the population of the Warsaw Pact, spend more on defence than the Pact and get less for it. There are many variables contributing to this disputable statement, but the fragmentation of NATO arms industry with consequent inefficiencies of production and diversification of product is universally acknowledged to be one of the most important. There has therefore long been a drive to rationalize NATO arms production.

Militarily the rewards for such rationalization would be increased effectiveness deriving from standardization or at least greater interoperability of weapons and other equipment. Economically, rationalisation ought to cut costs by eliminating duplication of research and development (R and D) and gaining the economies of longer production runs.

Unfortunately arms industries form an important part of many NATO national economies, so that any rationalization that required, as it would, the suppression of particular parts of a national design or manufacturing capacity would threaten employment, destroy export possibilities, and kill a sector of industry often regarded as a necessary contributor to technological innovation. To compound the problem, the nation in question would face the need to import weapons in the category concerned. As a result the military desire for rationalization encounters powerful political obstacles. Nor indeed is the military voice always on the side of rationalization. National military establishments have preferred operational doctrines and practices with implications for the design of weapons. Moreover when a nation is capable of manufacturing weapons, its military establishment may be reluctant to become dependent for weapons and spares on a possibly unreliable foreign supplier. The U.S. military in particular take such a view, which is understandable not merely because of the scale of U.S. manufacturing capability but by reason of the wartime vulnerability of the United States' European partners. This reluctance to "buy foreign" is one reason for a dominance of U.S. military industry that arouses considerable resentment in Europe. In 1983 alone Europeans spent $6 billion more on arms in the United States than U.S. purchases in Europe.

As usual U.S. interests in this situation are mixed; indeed, as so often, the overall voices coming from the jostling multiple interests within American industry and government are contradictory. While it would suit the United States to make NATO procurement more effective, the health of the U.S. arms industry is also important. While the United States has often encouraged the consolidation of European

Below: The cost of modern military equipment with its high technology content has risen much more rapidly than the general rate of inflation in the civil economy. The chart shows the multiplication of cost in real terms for several types of system, almost all of which have escalated at a pace above the commonly set target of an increase in NATO defence expenditure of 3% per annum in real terms.

Increasing costs of weapons

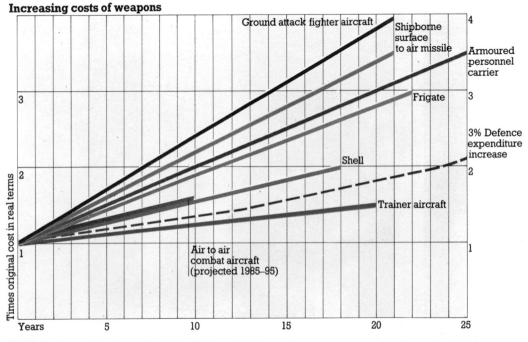

defence industry as a more powerful partner for American industry, there are political as well as economic sources of potential conflict between American and European interests. One source of friction is policy with regard to exports to third countries. Such sales can involve doubts about the security of technological secrets, diplomatic sensitivity with regard to the quarrels in which the third party may be involved, and resentment that an export market that might have lain open to U.S. industry is being pre-empted by Europeans.

Over the past few years the approaches to these problems have taken the form of trans-Atlantic deals on the one hand and of efforts to create European collaborative programmes and institutions on the other. Since 1966 a Conference of National Armaments Directors, under the North Atlantic Council, supervises groups concerned either with air, land and sea weapons or functionally with such matters as air defence or electronics. This network is supposed not merely to encourage collaborative projects but also exchange information on operational concepts and national procurement programmes. The latter rather obvious procedure can be of great value, for the prospect of important collaboration and co-ordination can only arise when two or more members are considering major programmes of re-equipment.

In 1970 the so-called Eurogroup of ten European members of NATO, not including France, established a European Defence Improvement Group. Later, in 1976, an Independent European Programme Group was established which did embrace France, the adjective "independent" being largely a concession to French insistence on remaining untrammelled by any U.S. domination within NATO proper.

These organizations have sponsored a series of collaborative development and procurement ventures among which perhaps the most impressive has been the Anglo-German-Italian Tornado. In 1982 a U.S. suggestion that the allies study collaboration on "emerging technologies" (ET) led to a further flurry of studies. In the mid-'eighties there were underway some twenty four defence procurement projects involving two or more European members of NATO, including a third generation anti-tank weapon, and a tripartite mine-hunting vessel. A most ambitious programme making troubled initial progress was that concerned with a European fighter to replace the F4 and Jaguar in the 'nineties. This project demonstrated all the difficulties arising from industrial rivalry, operational idiosyncracies and political jealousy.

All collaborative ventures require off-setting deals to ensure that the participants feel they are getting economic as well as military benefit. Some such offsets take the form of shares in the venture itself, often proportional to the national share in the overall alliance "buy"; others may

Below: Non-American members of NATO possess a wide variety of aircraft from many disparate sources. Although there are clear political and economic reasons for this, it is not a pattern that tends to reduce costs or facilitate effective operational co-operation.

	F100	Lightning	Buccaneer	G91R/Y	F104G	Saab 35	F5	Mirage III/V	A7	F4	F104S	Jaguar	Harrier	Mirage F1	Alpha jet	F16	Mirage 2000	Tornado	F18
Belgium								72								72			
UK		24	24							84		84	54					80	
Canada					54														*
Denmark					16	32										48			
France								135				120		120			15		
Germany					126					180					126			96	
Greece					54		68		54					36					
Italy				72	30						108							36	
Netherlands					18		54									72			
Norway																72			
Turkey	40				108		72			87	36					*			
Portugal				36					18										
Spain								30	24	36						48			

*on order

Below: Some problems and trends in technological co-operation and procurement within NATO are shown in this illustration of some types of NATO aircraft. The F4 and F104 shown are examples of US designs licence built by Europeans in the sixties and early seventies often with major and expensive national modifications. The F16 built in Europe under licence by a consortium of Danish, Norwegian, Dutch, and Belgian companies takes this trend further into the eighties with far less modification of the original design and greater benefit to the Europeans. The US meanwhile, has developed its own Air-to-Air fighter the F15 to fill the upper end of the capability range — a field where the Europeans have relied on the US to provide the capability. Meanwhile Italy, Germany and Britain have collaborated on the Tornado — a jointly designed and produced strike aircraft of considerable sophistication. In contrast France has gone its own way with indigenous designed fighters with the Mirage family developing through the Mirage III and F1 to the Mirage 2000. These difficult choices between a national, a collaborative European or a licence built US design are currently coming to a head again as European airforces try to agree on a future combat fighter for the 1990s.

F104S Starfighter (Italian)

F4 Phantom (UK)

F16 (Netherlands)

Mirage III

Tornado (West Germany)

F15 (USA)

Defence expenditure

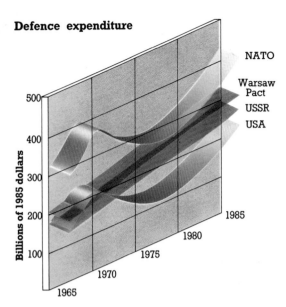

NATO
Warsaw Pact
USSR
USA

Billions of 1985 dollars

500
400
300
200
100

1965 1970 1975 1980 1985

Above: While the chart compares NATO, Pact, Soviet and U.S. defence expenditure, the result must, as explained elsewhere, be viewed cautiously as Soviet and Pact expenditure has to be estimated from a study of defence activity and of the Soviet economy. What matters militarily is the armed forces provided; a measure of expenditure may, however, give an idea of the burden defence places on societies.

The relatively small contribution of the East European states to the Warsaw Pact also contrasts with the larger share of NATO resources provided by states other than the U.S.

Below: The diagram depicts total defence expenditure of several NATO members in 1984 American predominance is dramatically apparent.

Total defence expenditure (in millions of US $)

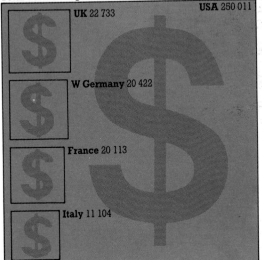

UK 22 733
USA 250 011
W Germany 20 422
France 20 113
Italy 11 104

interpretation. Americans may well argue that much of the defence effort they make outside the NATO area still benefits their allies, as in the Middle East. Such a point becomes much sharper when the United States suggests its allies should be making direct military contributions in such areas or at least be more ready to pick up the burden of U.S. forces diverted to "out of area" roles.

What is beyond doubt is that the financial pressures on NATO's defence effort will continue and that there seems little prospect, short of a major East-West crisis, of substantial real increases in expenditure. If force improvement is to continue, therefore, it will have to arise from better strategic concepts and more efficient procurement and use of the armed forces. The imbalance between American and European defence industries and the duplication of effort resulting from national economic as distinct from military considerations represents a burden largely escaped by the Soviet Union and only partly compensated for by the innovative effects of competition. Horrendous and sometimes alarmist statistics are often put about but it does seem militarily inefficient that there are said to be 11 firms in 7 NATO countries producing different anti-tank weapons, 18 firms in 7 countries making ground to air weapons, 16 firms in 7 countries producing air to ground missiles and 8 firms in 6 countries engaged upon air-to-air weapons. Such proliferation also, of course, leads to a lack of standardization or even compatability of weapons to facilitate flexibility in the field.

The problem is, however, one long

Defence expenditure as % of GNP 1983

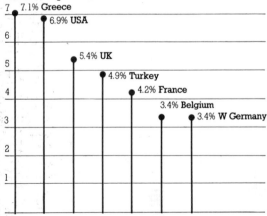

7 — 7.1% Greece
6.9% USA
6
5.4% UK
5
4.9% Turkey
4 — 4.2% France
3.4% Belgium
3 — 3.4% W Germany
2
1

Above: Defence expenditure of NATO members as percentage of GNP shows the heavy commitment a wealthy country like the U.S. can make if it chooses, but also the strain on a poorer country with security problems like Greece. The U.K. percentage remains typically high.

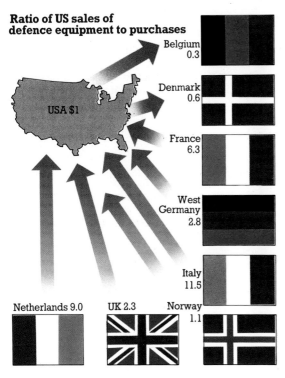

Ratio of US sales of defence equipment to purchases

USA $1

Belgium 0.3

Denmark 0.6

France 6.3

West Germany 2.8

Italy 11.5

Netherlands 9.0

UK 2.3

Norway 1.1

recognized, and the international rivalries at work, with a particular tension between the leading Americans, the vigorous and nationalistic French, and the rest, suggest that progress in rationalizing the process will be slow. Driven too hard, solutions to this problem could undermine the more general political support for NATO and its defensive effort in the member countries affected. The potential rewards for rationalization are, however, too huge to ignore.

Left: The diagram demonstrates the predominance of U.S. defence industry and the failure as yet of efforts to develop a more "two-way street" in inter-allied trade in armaments.

Below: Fears aroused by Soviet military activity in Africa and the Middle East, combined with the fall of the Shah and Soviet invasion of Afghanistan have prompted the United States to create a Rapid Deployment Force which relies in part on drawing forces if necessary from those assigned to NATO. This has aroused some European fears that American support will be distracted from NATO; equally, the United States has shown some impatience at European reluctance to offer facilities for such deployments and to show willingness to pick up the roles of any U.S. forces that might be diverted from NATO.

Below: The burden of defence can also be related to expenditure per capita.

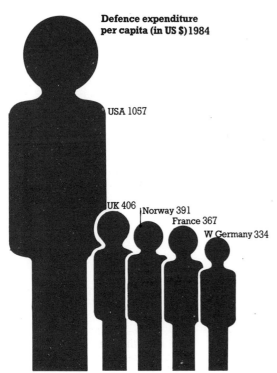

Defence expenditure per capita (in US $) 1984

USA 1057

UK 406

Norway 391

France 367

W Germany 334

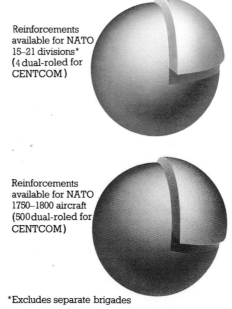

Reinforcements available for NATO 15–21 divisions* (4 dual-roled for CENTCOM)

Reinforcements available for NATO 1750–1800 aircraft (500 dual-roled for CENTCOM)

*Excludes separate brigades

involve other defence projects or even civil trade. Increasingly such deals are set up by the commercial companies as well as the governments concerned.

One of the largest ventures for the 'eighties, launched in 1979, is an American, French, German, British, Italian project to develop a new MLRS, coupled with new scatterable anti-tank mines and a later "smart", terminally guided sub-munition.

600,000 rockets are to be made, 60% by the United States and 40% by Europeans. A feature of the programme to develop a smart sub-munition is competition for the work between three consortia combining European and U.S. firms. This ensures that every country will get some of the benefits whichever consortium wins, while obtaining some degree of competitive bidding.

Another recent innovation in collaborative procurement is a feature of arrangements for the United States to buy British Rapier anti-aircraft missiles to defend its airfields in the United Kingdom. Here part of the *quid pro quo* is British agreement to man the missiles for the United States. Somewhat similar arrangements have been made between the United States and Germany and the Netherlands in procuring Patriot to replace the old Nike-Hercules systems. Both European countries are compensating the United States for favourable deals on the missiles by providing manning and, in the

German case, undertaking to maintain Roland short range air defence missiles at U.S. bases in Germany.

Below: As with aircraft, national arms industries have supplied NATO members with a wide range of main battle tanks, while several generations are now in service.

	M47	M48	Centurion	AMX30	Leopard	Chieftain	M60	AMX30 B2	Challenger	Leopard II	MI
					330						
UK						900			70		
Canada					60						
Denmark			90		120						
France				940				165			
Germany		990			2440					800	
Greece	350	1120		260	110						
Italy	550				920		300				
Netherlands			320		470					135	
Norway		30			70						
Turkey	500	2980			80						
USA							4200				800
Portugal	25	25									
Spain	350	110		300							
	Pre 1960 tanks			1960s tanks				Current production models			

Salvation Through Arms Control?

The burden of the East-West confrontation in Europe and the grave danger of war, whether local or escalating to a global conflict, naturally inspires the hope that arms control might defuse the conflict and stabilize the balance at lower and safer levels of military preparation. European security affairs are therefore caught up both directly and indirectly in arms control negotiations. Progress has, however, been notoriously slow.

At one time, in the 'fifties, thinking about arms control measures specifically directed toward Europe was dominated by the idea of "disengagement"; that NATO and Warsaw Pact forces might withdraw, leaving a neutral buffer zone. This notion foundered for various reasons, not least the question of Germany's future in such a Europe and the anxiety of the West Germans not to be left outside the pale of NATO. A vestige of the idea lingers on in proposals for "nuclear-free zones" of various dimensions. These proposals have not made much headway. In addition to the usual obstacle of mutual mistrust, the nuclear-free zone idea is vulnerable to criticism as not being easily amenable to verification, as possibly seeming if not in reality to remove the zone from the nuclear umbrella that is the essence of NATO's deterrent strategy or, alternatively, being meaningless in that there is little relationship in an age of flexible delivery systems between where nuclear weapons are kept and where they are used. Nevertheless the problems of controlling the shorter-range nuclear weapons and ensuring that they are not overrun in the early stages of a war has produced a substantial move at least on the NATO side to unilateral reductions. The longer-range theatre nuclear weapons, for their part, have been caught up in the propaganda battle over Ground Launched Cruise Missiles (GLCM) and the Pershing II, before ultimately coming under negotiation in the more or less unified Arms Reduction Talks that began at Geneva in 1984.

Right: The chart shows Soviet holdings of shorter range or tactical theatre nuclear weapons chiefly geared to the battlefield and its immediate rear. The total of Soviet tactical aircraft is shown but relatively few are likely to operate in a nuclear role and their radius of activity offers most of them a capability well beyond the battlefield area.

Soviet tactical/theatre nuclear weapons[1]

Scud/SS23	SS12/SS22	Frog/SS21	Nuclear capable artillery	Nuclear capable aircraft[2]
400+ (590)	60+ (120)	375+ (750)	1150 (2000-6000)	3000-3800 (9000+)

(Global total)
1. Excludes weapons opposite East Turkey
2. Only a small percentage of these are likely to operate in a nuclear role

The walk in the woods proposal

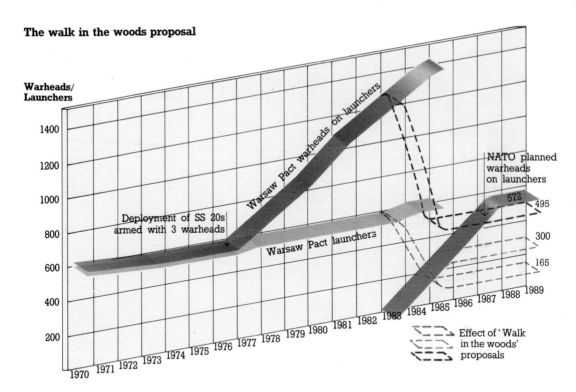

Warheads/Launchers

Deployment of SS 20s armed with 3 warheads

Warsaw Pact warheads on launchers

Warsaw Pact launchers

NATO planned warheads on launchers

572
495
300
165

Effect of 'Walk in the woods' proposals

Above: During the mid-'seventies the Soviet Union began to deploy a new, mobile, solid fuelled triple MIRVed IRBM, the SS20 in the Western Soviet Union and on the Chinese border, apparently a replacement for long established SS4 and SS5 (though once arms control negotiations began the rate of dismantling SS4 and SS5 fell, probably to protect a bargaining position). This deployment, with a much more precise capability for targeting Western Europe, especially NATO nuclear systems, aroused considerable anxiety in NATO both on military grounds and because of feared political consequences of a major asymmetry in favour of the Soviet Union. The German Chancellor Helmut Schmidt gave a particularly noted expression of anxiety in September 1977. By December 1979 NATO reached its famous "dual-track" decision to deploy Ground Launched Cruise Missiles (GLCM) and Pershing II, terminally guided, highly accurate missiles by December 1983 while entering into arms control negotiations to avert such a competition.

The initial U.S. negotiating position was the "zero-option"; that is to say, the U.S. would abort its deployment totally if the Soviet Union would destroy its SS4, SS5 and SS20 missiles. The Soviet position was that the SS20 were not an increase in forces but a modernization and that no part of the U.S. deployment was acceptable. As enunciated by President Brezhnev in February 1982 the Soviet Union

proposed a ban on all new Intermediate Nuclear Forces (INF), a freeze on existing systems and later phased reductions which should take into account nuclear capable aircraft and the French and British nuclear forces. The Soviet Union alleged that the relevant arsenals on each side were roughly equal; by U.S. count the Soviet Union enjoyed a more than 5:1 advantage.

The negotiating positions of both sides moved slightly in subsequent months but remained far apart; in particular the Soviet Union never overtly accepted any new U.S. deployment. The closest approach to an agreement was embodied in an informal agreement reached in a private conversation — later disavowed by both sides — between the U.S. negotiator Paul Nitze and the Soviet negotiator, Oleg Kvitinsky. This deal, discussed in July 1983, would have permitted 75 SS20 (225 warheads) and 75 GLCM (300 warheads). The U.S. would have cancelled the deployment of Pershing II, allegedly much feared because of its swift trajectory. Each side would have been permitted 150 medium range nuclear capable aircraft. In this deal the Soviet Union would have accepted a global ceiling on SS20 (165); at other times the Soviet Union had conceded no ceiling for Asia and no obligation to destroy missiles removed from the European theatre.

After the disavowal, the closest approach, if it ever had any sincere substance, to a deal at low levels, each side made some

Labels on map: Kopu, Tapa, Yedrovo, Yurya, Riga, Ural Mountains, Omsk, Novosibirsk, Kiev, Penvomaysk, Aleysk, Barnaul, Uzhu, China, Zhangiz-Tobe

concessions. The Soviet Union agreed to destroy removed missiles and to count warheads as well as missiles and reduced the number of missiles it would retain to some 120 but still demanded cancellation of the U.S. programme and hence a monopoly in the categories the U.S. and NATO regarded as relevant to the negotiation. The United States agreed that if the Soviet Union accepted a global ceiling, the United States would not fully match it: i.e. there would be a balance for the Soviet Union to deploy against China. In addition the United States offered to reduce the Pershing element in its programme disproportionately.

In the end, however, the negotiations, which were staged throughout against a background of Soviet propaganda against the U.S. deployment, were overtaken by the beginning of that deployment on time in December 1983. The Soviet Union broke off negotiations and the issue had to await the renewal of arms control negotiations in Geneva in 1984. By that time at least a large part of the U.S. deployment was probably beyond reversal.

Above: The map shows supposed major locations of SS20 deployments, indicating the concentrations against Western Europe and China and the bases which could engage either set of targets, thus illustrating the difficulty of designing a NATO related arms control package in isolation. While the Soviet Union has long possessed long-range-theatre or in terms of global strategy, intermediate range nuclear missile capability — against Western Europe (and other Soviet neighbours), the introduction of the mobile, solid fuelled, MIRVed SS20 in the mid-'seventies aroused great anxiety in NATO and became the focus of a major debate about the theatre nuclear balance. By the mid-'eighties several hundred SS20 had been deployed in Western Russia and along the Chinese border, and a counter-vailing U.S. deployment of Ground Launched Cruise missiles and Pershing II was well under way.

Chemical Weapons and their Control

While chemical weapons could prove a decisive factor in a future European war, for political reasons NATO has preferred to play them down and virtually its only agreed policy is to seek to outlaw them by negotiation. Most nations have already adherred to the Geneva Protocal of 1925 by which they undertake to refrain from the use — but not the manufacture or possession — of suffocating or noxious gases, liquids and solids, but many signatories have reserved a right of retaliatory use against a belligerent who himself uses such weapons. Energetic efforts to negotiate a comprehensive ban on the possession as well as use of chemical weapons have so far foundered chiefly on the very difficult problem of verification, although there is room for doubt as to whether all the negotiating states would really welcome a total ban.

Most current concern about chemical weapons centres upon modern versions of the nerve gases developed during World War II. These lend themselves to effective dispersal, are very rapidly acting, and can be prepared in a "binary" form whereby the ingredients are separated within the munition until the moment of use, thereby increasing safety and ease of handling. Alone among the members of NATO the United States has a significant stockpile of nerve gases but this is aging to the point of becoming unsafe. Congress has, however, only recently shown signs of acceding to proposals to manufacture binary replacements.

While the Soviet Union makes no official acknowledgment of chemical capability, it is known to have a large stockpile of chemical weapons, elaborate anti-chemical defences, and large numbers of chemical and counter-chemical troops. Indeed some students of Soviet strategy and manoeuvres believe the Soviet Union regards chemical weapons as "conventional".

Chemical weapons are chiefly useful for fairly localized action. Very favourable weather conditions would be required for widespread use and the outcome would be uncertain. Used locally, however, chemical weapons can cause heavy casualties. It the enemy is equipped with defensive measures, mainly masks and suits, which have considerably improved in design, he can do a great deal to minimize casualties and the chief effect will be to inconvenience him by forcing him to operate "closed down". For a long time most NATO nations seriously neglected defensive measures, preferring to rely on deterrence derived at least implicitly from nuclear weapons. The West Germans, in particular, whose civilian population could suffer grievous harm from the introduction of chemical weapons to the battlefield, have preferred to contemplate the deterrence of this as indeed of all forms of warfare by the threat of escalation to nuclear weapons. In recent years, however, the increasing scepticism about the usability of nuclear weapons and NATO's move within flexible response if not to a doctrine of "No First Use" then at least to one of no early use of nuclear weapons, has increased anxiety that the Warsaw Pact may enjoy a usable unilateral advantage at the chemical level. This in turn has led advocates of deterrence rather than defence against chemical weapons to urge the replenishment of NATO's offensive chemical capability. Successful deterrence would obviate the inconvenience of operating in defensive clothing.

Offensively it may be that the best uses of chemical weapons would not be against troops in the front-line, who might be expected to enjoy high levels of protection and where residual effects, which need not be large or persistent as in the case of nuclear weapons, might nevertheless hamper friendly forces. Used against rear areas, particularly airfields, nuclear sites, and logistical facilities, chemical weapons could greatly reduce efficiency, while the provision of widespread protective measures would impose considerable expense. This, again, may be a powerful argument for maintaining a deterrent retaliatory capability.

The most intractable aspect of arms control for chemical and biological weapons is verification. Neither chemical nor biological agents are conspicuous, though the organization for using them might be, and the facilities required for manufacture are virtually identical to those used for peaceful purposes such as the making of pesticides. The convention on biological weapons has no provision for verification, relying chiefly on the supposed lack of military demand for such weapons. Even so, episodes such as an unexplained outbreak of anthrax in the Soviet Union has given rise to suspicion of violations.

Chemical weapons present more difficult problems because of their undeniable military utility in some circumstances and the knowledge that they have been widely used, recently almost certainly in South East Asia.

The present forum for negotiation is the U.N. Committee on Disarmament which meets in Geneva. Western proposals suggest a ban on possession and manufacture, and on-site inspection to verify destruction of stocks and the cessation of manufacture. The latter might be achieved by inspection as of right "on challenge" when suspicious circumstances arise. As so often where verification is concerned, the Soviet Union is reluctant to accept intrusive methods. It has conceded the principle of continuous as distinct from spot checks of destruction of stocks but only inspection on a voluntary basis to ensure that underclared stocks do not exist or that manufacture is not continuing.

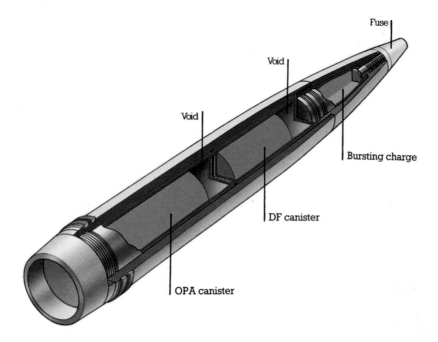

Fuse

Void

Void

Bursting charge

DF canister

OPA canister

Above: The concept of binary chemical munitions is illustrated in this cutaway picture of a chemical artillery shell; the lethal gas is created by the actual explosion of the weapon mixing two chemicals which would be harmless if either escaped separately. A new generation of chemical weapons would also be safer simply by reason of more recent and sophisticated construction.

Below: The chart suggests the degree to which the Soviet Union is better prepared for chemical defence than the United States and its allies. This is one area in which the United States is not pre-eminent even within NATO.

Verification thus remains the chief ostensible bar to an agreement on abolition of chemical weapons. So prominent is the place of chemical weapons in Soviet doctrine and military preparation that it must be wondered whether the Soviet Union really wants an agreement. Similarly, doubt about the reliability of verification and enforcement of an agreement is so great in some Western circles that it may well be that they too would rather rely on the deterrent effect of an improved NATO retaliatory capability.

Preparation for chemical warfare

	USSR	USA	NATO
Number of dedicated personnel	👤 85 000	👤 7 000	👤 few
Individual protection	✔ yes	✔ yes	✔ yes
Collective protection vehicles, ships	✔ yes	✔ few	✔ some
key facilities	✔ yes	✔ few	✔ some
Detection and warning automatic alarms and detection kits	✔ yes	✔ yes	✔ yes
reconnaissance vehicles	✔ yes	✘ no	✔ few

Left: Relatively good protection can be provided to individual soldiers against chemical weapons provided adequate warning is received. As can be seen, however, the protective clothing and masks are cumbersome, impeding both movement and vision. They are also extremely uncomfortable and exhausting to wear, so that military efficiency is greatly reduced. If one side to a contest had to adopt such clothing and the related measures to protect vehicles, aircraft and command posts, without having a capability to impose a similar handicap on the enemy, it would be at a probably decisive disadvantage.

Mutual Balanced Force Reduction Negotiations

Despite the importance of the negotiations over nuclear forces which resumed tentatively between the Soviet Union and the United States in 1984, and those on chemical weapons, the arms control talks which could in theory have the greatest impact on the NATO-Warsaw Pact confrontation is the Mutual Balanced Force Reduction conference which has been meeting in Vienna since 1973.

The start of these negotiations followed a long series of proposals for disarmament and arms control in Europe, such as the several Polish Rapacki and Gomulka plans and the more general notion of "disengagement". Most of these concepts were essentially political, intended to register the territorial division of Europe or to improve the diplomatic climate. Soviet motives in launching proposals for a conference on security in Europe, which led ultimately to the Helsinki agreements of 1975, were also widely believed to be aimed only at consolidating Soviet control over Eastern Europe. The Western powers consequently insisted on a parallel negotiation on the strictly military aspects of security and from this arose the MBFR talks at Vienna.

The Helsinki agreements included modest confidence building measures such as a strictly limited process of mutual notification of military exercises. A French proposal in 1978 for negotiations to achieve "mutually complementary confidence and security building measures to reduce the risk of military confrontation in Europe" led to the Conference on Confidence and Security Building Measures and Disarmament which began in Stockholm in January 1984.

Unlike the Stockholm conference, MBFR concerns only a limited area of Central Europe, comprising the two Germanies, Belgium, Luxembourg, the Netherlands, Poland and Czechoslovakia. Hungary is excluded despite the considerable Soviet as well as local forces stationed there, partly as compensation for French refusal to participate in the discussions. The United States, Soviet Union, United Kingdom and the countries in the area are primary participants in the negotiations; other NATO and Warsaw Pact members are "special" participants. Each side negotiates as a bloc.

Below: The diagram indicates the discrepancy between NATO and Warsaw Pact estimates of existing manpower in the area under negotiation and the possible consequence of applying suggested formulae for reductions to them. While the resultant difference may not seem large it could permit the maintenance of significant additional combat formations, especially of Soviet Troops.

Mutual Balanced Force Reduction (MBFR)

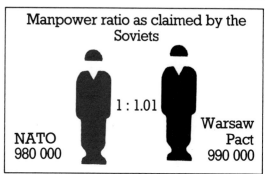

Manpower ratio as claimed by the Soviets

1 : 1.01

NATO 980 000 — Warsaw Pact 990 000

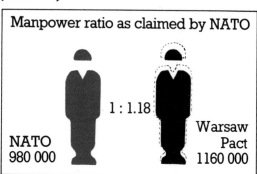

Manpower ratio as claimed by NATO

1 : 1.18

NATO 980 000 — Warsaw Pact 1160 000

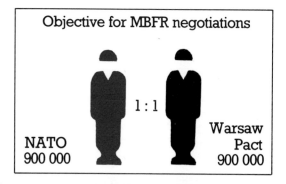

Objective for MBFR negotiations

1 : 1

NATO 900 000 — Warsaw Pact 900 000

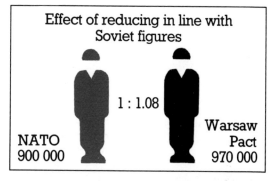

Effect of reducing in line with Soviet figures

1 : 1.08

NATO 900 000 — Warsaw Pact 970 000

The original NATO aspiration was to use the negotiations to reduce the military preponderance of the Warsaw Pact and permit a reduction in the burden of defence. These complementary motives can also conflict; thus while NATO as such wishes to keep up its strength relative to the Pact, individual countries are quite eager to find excuses to reduce their own contributions. A particularly complex set of national interests affects the Federal Republic of Germany, for Soviet negotiating strategy has constantly sought to find ways of imposing especially restrictive constraints on West German forces within general formulae. The requirement for countries in the area under negotiation to disband forces affected by reduction — whereas "stationing" powers need only withdraw them, perhaps subject to restrictions on redeployment — means that ceilings negotiated with the Soviet Union would be imposed on German armed forces unless the Western preference for "collective ceilings" was adopted. As a variant of such single national ceilings, the Soviet Union has in recent years suggested a rule whereby no ally could compensate for more than 50% of any other ally's fall below its established contribution to its coalition's force levels.

As always in arms control negotiations, which are by definition between adversaries, each side seeks to obtain advantages both in the ultimate agreement and in the prior political sparring. The task of designing limitations on conventional armaments in Europe is, however, also a genuinely difficult intellectual problem. Tortuous though the negotiations on strategic arms have been, the great variety of conventional weapons, their complex interaction, the influence of terrain, distance, doctrine and the precise circumstances in which war arises, with varying degrees of warning, makes striking a conventional balance infinitely more difficult, especially as the negotiation involves a large number of countries.

These complexities affect not merely the substantive nature of an agreement but the task of verifying it — hence the variety of monitoring and inspection measures advocated by the Western powers. A foretaste of the difficulties that might arise was provided when in 1979, for obscure reasons, President Brezhnev announced the unilateral withdrawal of 20,000 Soviet troops and 1,000 tanks from East Germany, including the 6th Soviet Tank Division. The Division certainly disappeared with its 10-11000 men and about 350 tanks. But NATO was quite unable to assure itself that the division had left East Germany; rather than being redeployed locally in fragments, and was equally unable to satisfy itself that the balance of the 20,000 men and 1,000 tanks had also left other units.

The basic yardstick adapted to cut through the problem of comparability has been man-power. Each side has, however, accompanied proposals leading to equal residual levels of manpower with additional provisos to suit its interests. Thus in its initial demand that the Soviet Union withdraw 68,000 men, to 29,000 Americans, NATO required that the withdrawal include a complete tank army with 1,700 tanks, thereby attempting to redress NATO's inferiority in the combat element most relevant to the success of a Soviet offensive. In later stages of negotiations it has been the Warsaw Pact that has been most eager that reductions should be by units complete with equipment, so as to complicate NATO's task of bringing in reinforcements or mobilizing reservists.

This example illustrates the basic Western problem: being inferior in combat formations, NATO lacks bargaining power and can ill afford any reduction in its forces. Being absolutely short of weapons, NATO has had to move away from formulae requiring removal of equipment from the area of reductions, because of its reliance on prepositioning supplies for air transported reinforcements. Moveover the increase in the margin of Soviet superiority in most categories of weapon since MBFR talks began, means that the original formulae would leave NATO, if better off than it would otherwise be, considerably worse off than the originally intended result. Thus in 1973 a Soviet withdrawal of 1700 tanks would have left the balance in tanks about 15,500 to 6,500 in favour of the Warsaw Pact. By 1980 the result would have been 19,000 to 8,000. Another way in which erosion of NATO advantages has deprived NATO of bargaining power involves theatre nuclear weapons. Believing itself superior in these, NATO was initially able to offer one negotiating package known as Option III, in which removal of 1,000 tactical nuclear weapons was offered in return for large Soviet withdrawal of tanks. By the mid-'eighties NATO was almost as concerned about the nuclear balalnce as that in armour.

A fundamental difficulty in the negotiations has been the absence of agreed data on existing force levels. Until 1976 the Warsaw Pact refused to supply figures on its forces. When it did offer some, they set Warsaw Pact ground force levels about 150,000 less than those confidently estimated by NATO intelligence, a discrepancy including some 68,000 Soviet troops.

This discrepancy greatly increased anxiety about the verification problems that would attend an agreement. Perhaps more fundamentally, it cast doubt on whether the Soviet Union really accepted the ostensibly agreed goal of parity in ground forces, for if initial levels were allegedly equal, the Soviet concession of disproportionate cuts in Warsaw Pact manpower would effectively be withdrawn. The dispute over data on force levels thus came to be the essence of the negotiation.

By the mid-'eighties agreement between the two sides could be summarized as:

a common ceiling of 700,000 men in ground forces;

collective rather than national ceilings; nuclear weapons excluded from MBFR; two phases of reduction, with the first involving only U.S. and Soviet forces which would accept, for these two alone, national ceilings before a guaranteed phase two affecting other nations was implemented.

The chief remaining difficulties concerned the baseline data from which the reductions should begin and the subsequent system of verification. These difficulties are so large and the shifts in negotiating positions have been so great in the past that it may well be the negotiations are not in fact any nearer reaching agreement than when they began. Nevertheless the economic pressures on both sides and the coming demographic constraints on manpower of military age, coupled with the propaganda costs of seeming to abandon the search for agreement, seem likely to keep the negotiations alive indefinitely.

In more recent years, hope has risen that a way forward may lie in so-called Confidence Building Measures (CBM), which have been widely debated at the Conference on Disarmament in Europe. The idea is to provide reassurance that neither side is about to attack by such devices as notification of manoeuvres and troop movements, observation posts and other supplements to unilateral intelligence measures. In theory such devices should reduce tensions, permit lower force levels and curb escalation in crisis.

Many difficulties lie in the way of a successful agreement on the reduction of force levels in Europe. Not the least is geography. An agreement that reduced Nato European force levels would require these units to be disbanded whilst the Soviet Union would only be required to move its forces outside the treaty area. Any agreement that entailed withdrawing US forces would also give the Warsaw Pact an advantage as the withdrawn or other Soviet forces would find it far easier to return to Central Europe over short road and rail distances than US forces would facing a transatlantic journey. Though US forces could return quickly if given additional airlift and prepositioned equipment this might make the cost of the exercise prohibitive.

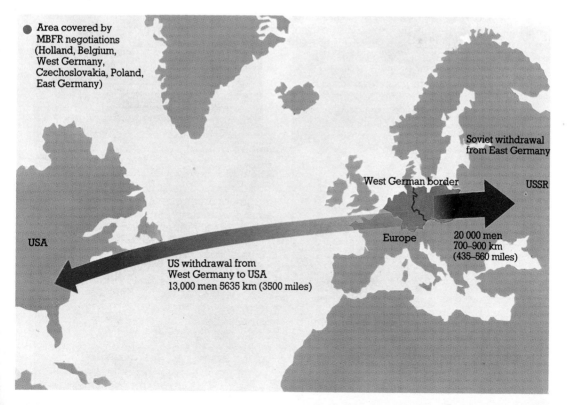

Area covered by MBFR negotiations (Holland, Belgium, West Germany, Czechoslovakia, Poland, East Germany)

Soviet withdrawal from East Germany

West German border

USSR

USA

Europe

20 000 men 700–900 km (435–560 miles)

US withdrawal from West Germany to USA 13,000 men 5635 km (3500 miles)

Conclusion

Perhaps the most fundamental problem of all is whether the Soviet Union can afford to let NATO have the reassurance it seeks from arms control. For most of the postwar era the Soviet Union has sought to maintain and has profited politically from a degree of military superiority in Europe. Its conception of security seems to require a clear capability to deal with any military threat that might arise from Western Europe, particularly Germany, and its strategy for dealing with such a threat is offensive, and therefore requires attainable superiority.

In theory it is possible that such schemes could enable the Soviet Union to retain some of the margin of superiority it seems to find so reassuring while NATO could be confident that the Soviet Union was not about to use its advantage. In practice it is obviously not easy to reconcile a far-reaching system with the Soviet Union's aversion to intrusive verification. Even in theory it is not axiomatic that CBM would be stabilizing. Much would depend on the "indicators" chosen and even more on how the parties to the system reacted to its messages. All of the cautionary observations about intelligence, warning and surprize apply as much to the operation of agreed measures as those that are taken unilaterally and it would be as possible to be complacent or dilatory with such a negotiated framework as without it. Moreover such a system could actually become a source of friction rather than an answer to it. Nevertheless, the possibility of error or misuse does not mean that it must occur and CBM may well offer a more flexible and practicable arms control contribution to European security than the elusive agreements on force levels. It must at least be admitted that it is virtually the only area in which even a modest agreement has actually been reached in the restricted provision for notification of exercises contained in the accords of the Conference on Security in Central Europe (CSCE), forerunner in this respect of the CDE.

Many of the strategic issues and technological trends that would affect the outcome of a war between NATO and the Warsaw Pact have been discussed briefly in the preceding text or outlined in the charts and pictorial material. The overwhelming impression is one of complexity. A land, air and sea war in Europe and the surrounding oceans would turn upon the performance of an immense variety of weapons, equipment and men, upon the influence of terrain and weather, and upon the quality of leadership, strategy and tactics. The equation is much more complicated and the answer correspondingly uncertain than in the more widely studied strategic nuclear balance.

The important questions are whether NATO is adequate to deter aggression by the Soviet led Warsaw Pact and whether, if that deterrence did fail, the consequent conflict could be contained and terminated short of a global nuclear holocaust. To the first question the answer is "probably" and to the second "perhaps"; neither answer is sufficiently firm to be wholly reassuring.

By most quantitive measures the Warsaw Pact, more particularly the Soviet Union, is in the lead. In a number of areas NATO is ahead to a helpful degree, but to a lesser extent than was once the case. It must be increasingly uncertain that the degree of technological advantage, where it exists, can compensate for the numerical deficiency. It may be, however, that the current electronic revolution is opening up NATO's technological lead again, at least for the time being, in several important respects.

Nevertheless, a study of the quantities and qualities involved in the balance suggests that if war came, the Warsaw Pact would probably prevail. A number of considerations affecting the factors of warning, surprize and response tend to support that conclusion. Earnest though its efforts are, NATO remains a far from wholly integrated coalition, of unmilitary temperament, committed to defend a vulnerable and narrow strip of territory against a massive, offensively oriented enemy.

The question remains, however, as to whether the Soviet Union actually would launch an attack against the defence NATO can mount. The answer is very dependent on the intensity of the political motive to attack. So far as the purely military equation is concerned, the deterrent effect of even NATO's present posture is probably considerable. Favourable though many elements in the equation are to the Warsaw Pact, they are not so favourable that victory is certain; still less is it certain that victory would be quick and easy. As we have seen, technological and strategic developments have led the Pact to a revision of its strategy and force posture that is not yet complete. Until it is, uncertainty is enhanced and uncertainty about a speedy, favourable outcome must be particularly deterrent against a foe whose recipe for defence includes the possibility of escalation to the use of nuclear weapons.

What would be the effect of such escalation and is the NATO threat to do it wise or credible? Here NATO is in grave difficulty. Recourse to nuclear weapons in the last resort was adopted as a strategy in a period of virtual monopoly and later at least marked superiority at both tactical and strategic levels. It was therefore possible if short-sighted to assume that NATO could use short range nuclear weapons against Warsaw Pact conventional forces without much fear of effective retaliation, because the Soviet Union lacked both suitable weapons to use on the battlefield and a sufficient power to threaten escalation to the strategic level; indeed its strategic inferiority meant it would have to be careful the use of any tactical nuclear capability it might possess did not provoke the United States to escalate.

Today all that has changed. Parity in the strategic balance makes NATO threats to escalate to that level sound hollow. Meanwhile the Soviet Union has developed a very powerful tactical and theatre arsenal. Its theatre arsenal, unlike that of NATO, is targeted chiefly not against NATO's conventional forces, with which the Soviet army and airforce can deal without nuclear weapons, though they have them to use if they choose, but against the theatre of tactical nuclear component of the NATO forces. That is, Soviet TNF exist chiefly to remove the TNF element from NATO's answer to the Pact's conventional superiority.

For NATO to have recourse to nuclear action to repel a successful Soviet advance without accepting the probability of wider nuclear strikes in Europe would require great confidence in Soviet willingness to observe the firebreak between battlefield and deeper strikes, presumably for fear of the retaliatory power of NATO's intermediate range nuclear forces (INF). Given the emphasis in Soviet doctrine on neutralizing NATO nuclear weapons, if necessary by pre-emption, such confidence would probably be excessive. At the first sign that NATO was about to use nuclear weapons, it is all too probable that the Soviet Union would launch heavy and widespread nuclear attacks of its own on NATO nuclear weapons and bases. Presumably the Soviet Union would hope that its strategic forces would deter NATO INF from striking Soviet territory, just as NATO would have — vainly, on this hypothesis — hoped its INF would deter the use of Soviet theatre nuclear weapons. Should the Soviet hope prove misplaced and nuclear war on Superpower homelands begin, then war in Europe might indeed prove to have been the eve of the nuclear holocaust.

Even when strategic weapons are used, there need not necessarily be an all-out nuclear war. The theories as to how states might employ "limited strategic options" belong to a wider study of global nuclear strategy. The very real possibility of rapid and extensive escalation from the use of tactical nuclear weapons suggests, however, that such a use should perhaps be regarded more as a possible limited option within the general nuclear deterrent balance than as simply a component in the theatre war.

There is still strong reason to believe that the presence of the tactical nuclear option within NATO's flexible response extends and continues to extend a powerful deterrent aura. If war did nevertheless break out, however, the possibility of disastrous escalation is obviously all too real. Serious doubt must therefore exist as to whether NATO would actually cross the nuclear line.

Would the Soviet Union rely on this doubt and launch an attack? It seems unlikely. The risks are too high and the incentives seem too low. Certainly it would take a very reckless leadership to go to war for the positive gains that would accrue from a conquest of Western Europe. It is possible to write scenarios arising from Soviet efforts to reverse a collapse of its position in Eastern Europe, even from national unrest in the Soviet Union itself. But the evidence so far suggests there would be safer measures with which to meet such emergencies.

Nevertheless, political situations are unpredictable. The situation in Eastern Europe could take an unexpectedly grave turn; crises could break out on NATO's flanks or in "out of area" conflicts related to Superpower relations and feed back into hostilities within the NATO area. Risks and the estimation of risks can change. Such estimations are the product of political imperatives on the one side and the likely costs and outcome of armed action on the other.

Soviet development of a military strategy to win in Europe before nuclear weapons are used, while perhaps reassuring so far as fear of Soviet first use of nuclear weapons is concerned, actually increases the chance of war by reducing the risks to the Soviet Union. Such a conventional answer to the nuclear element in NATO's flexible response keeps alive the Soviet Union's politically useful offensive threat against Western Europe and exposes yet further the agonizing nature of the escalatory decision NATO's strategy of flexible response may require.

These dilemmas suggest the rising value of the capacity to mount a staunch conventional resistance to Pact aggression. There can be little doubt, however, that to proceed in that direction testifies to misgivings about the nuclear element in deterrence and may reduce Soviet inhibitions about resorting to force in the first place. In other words, efforts to avoid or at least greatly postpone the escalatory decision NATO would have to take if a war went badly, can probably only be pursued at the price of alleviating Soviet dilemmas at the moment it decides to go to war.

One way to reconcile oneself in pragmatic if not pure theoretical terms to this conflict of interest is to assume that sufficient residual fear of escalation will survive in Soviet minds so long as nuclear weapons have any part in NATO's arsenal and strategy, while a stiffer conventional resistance will raise the price of an attack, and, by making rapid success less certain and a prolonged and messy war more likely, increase the danger of escalation in the older sense of the word as a process that occurs without anyone actually willing it.

Of course, if NATO could realize a conventional defensive capacity so obviously powerful as to deprive the Warsaw Pact of any reasonable hope of victory even in prolonged conventional war, deterrence would be established on the firm and traditional basis familiar in prenuclear times, by displaying a capability to deny the enemy success rather than to punish him for it buy nuclear retaliation. The history of prenuclear deterrence makes it clear, however, that it has never achieved the universal success that nuclear deterrence has hitherto in its short experience achieved by setting a clearly unacceptable price for challenging it. This has been so partly because it is difficult to erect an unquestionably adequate defence against major adversaries and partly because conventional balances are hard to evaluate.

In any case the record suggests that NATO will not make the effort to build an overwhelmingly adequate conventional defence, both because of reluctance to devote the resources of the feeling that nuclear deterrence makes it unnecessary. Nevertheless it may be that we are entering a technological era, dominated by electronics, in which NATO may enjoy a reasonably prolonged advantage and which may make it possible to erect a defence which, if not impervious, sows such substantial doubt in Soviet military leaders' minds that aggression seems and unattractive option. Other devices such as fortification could strengthen these inhibitions. Because the most important concern must be to reinforce the deterrent against the Soviet Union taking the initial decision to go to war, it would also seem wise to give priority to the capacity for initial resistance over measures to improve ability to prolong resistance. This may fly in the face of the fashionable concern for sustainability and should clearly not be taken to extremes. But where, for instance, there is a choice to be made between such measures as pre-positioning and enhancement of airlift and increasing the capacity to fight the maritime battle in the Atlantic, the former should perhaps take precedence.

There can be no perfect answer to the security problem of Western Europe, bordered as it is by a Superpower which makes armed strength its primary claim to international status, avows an expansionist ideology and presides over an uneasy empire. Faced with this problem the realistic goal must be to ensure that today is never the day when aggression looks a reasonable option for Soviet leaders even if political circumstances prompt them, as normally they almost certainly do not, to consider the question actively. It is encouraging that in recent years NATO seems to have developed a much more coherent analytical approach to its problems, assessing Soviet motives, doctrines and capabilities and designing NATO's own strategy and defensive preparations much more specifically to meet the threat and deter its implementation. In all this the overarching role of the United States is essential. However far incipient moves for a greater European identity within NATO may go, the solidarity of all including the United States constitutes the single most important element in averting the outbreak of the war that of all wars could most readily envelop the whole globe.

Glossary

A

AAFCE	Allied Airforces Central Europe.
ABM	Anti-Ballistic Missile.
ACE	Allied Command Europe.
ACEMF	Allied Command Europe Mobile Force — multinational NATO land and airforce available to deploy to any threatened area to demonstrate NATO capability, unity and resolve.
Active	Emitting radiation to detect and/or home on the target as in active sonar which sends out a sound wave which bounces back from its target and active radar homing where a radar signal bounced back from the target shows its location. Active systems are generally more precise and are the only system available against targets which give out little radiation of their own (eg a "quiet" submarine). Their disadvantage is that they give away their location when they themselves radiate.
Active Defence	Defence strategy adopted by the US in the seventies and later influential with other NATO armies. Active defence seeks to use a series of defence positions to draw in an attacker. At each position the defence will destroy as much of the attacking force as possible before if necessary withdrawing to the next position. The strategy was critized as being too defensive (though counterattacks were envisaged) and based too much on a linear static defence which relied on firepower to destroy the enemy.
ADM	Atomic Demolition Munition — atomic mine.
AF	Allied Forces eg AF Cent = Allied Forces Central Europe; AFSOUTH = Allied Forces Southern Europe; AFNORTH = Allied Forces Northern Europe.
Air-Land Battle	Criticism of active defence and fresh US thinking led to greater emphasis on manoeuvre warfare. This envisaged a more fluid battlefield with NATO forces attempting to destroy an enemy attacks cohesion by aggressive as well as defensive action. Such thinking also reflected the new capability afforded by new equipment such as the M1 tank and the political problem that even if "active defence" worked Warsaw Pact forces would still be halted well inside West Germany with no prospect of their being pushed back to the border.
Anti-Radar	Weapons designed to suppress radar installations.
AS-	NATO designation of Soviet Air to Surface missiles as in AS4, AS6, AS9.
Assault Breaker	US proposal in the late seventies for a system designed to rapidly destroy Soviet armour using new emerging technology. Assault breaker missiles, 2000 under one proposal, would each carry 20-24 submunitions into the Soviet rear echelons perhaps killing as many as ten tanks per missile. Programme led to current CTAMS programme which has similar objectives.
ASW	Anti-submarine Warfare.
ATGW	Anti-Tank Guided Weapon.
ATM	Anti Tactical Missile missile — US proposal for missile system for defence against Soviet Surface to Surface missiles targetted on Europe.
AWACS	Airborne Warning and Control System.

B

BALTAP Baltic Approaches — Joint German and Danish Command covering Denmark and Schleswig Hostein.

BAOR British Army of the Rhine.

Binary In two parts — the US is currently proposing to deploy the 'Bigeye' chemical bomb and artillery shells based on the binary principle where, when the weapon is armed, two non-lethal chemicals combine to produce a lethal nerve agent. In peacetime storage the weapons would be far safer than existing aging stocks of chemical weapons which contain already lethal material. US officials see these as necessary weapons to maintain a deterrent against Soviet chemical weapons.

C

C3 (C Cubed) Command, Control and Communications.

C31 Command, Control, Communications and Intelligence.

Captor Encapsulated Torpedo: anti-submarine mine equipped with MK46 Torpedo.

CBM Confidence Building Measures.

CBW Chemical, Biological Warfare.

CENTAG Central Army Group.

CEP Circular Error Probable, a measure of the accuracy attributable to ballistic missiles. It is the radius of circle into which fifty per cent of the warheads aimed at the centre of the circle are predicted to fall.

CG Cruiser — Guided Missile armed.

Chaff Radar reflective material sometimes comprised of fine wire pieces cut to fractions of the wavelength of the radars to be jammed. Chaff operates by obscuring the target from the detecting radar by creating a much larger radar signature due to the reflectivity of the chaff material.

C in C Commander-in-Chief.

CINCHAN Commander-in-Chief Channel.

Close Air Support Direct support of ground forces by airforces — often using specialized aircraft like the US A10 and Soviet Su 25. The Soviets are increasingly using armed helicopters in this role.

COB Colocated Operating Base — Airforce base used in peacetime by NATO airforce: earmarked in wartime to receive reinforcing US or other NATO air units.

Counter air Missions aimed at the destruction of the enemy airforce. Offensive operations would include attacks on airbases and attempts to gain air superiority over enemy air space.

CRAF Civil Reserve Air Fleet — civilian airliners and crews ear-marked for use by the military — some aircraft are being especially modified for this role.

CV Aircraft Carrier.

CVN Nuclear Powered Aircraft Carrier.

CVS Anti-submarine Aircraft Carrier.

D

Damage Radius   The radius of a circle from the centre of which the destructive effects over distance are measured for specific weapons.

DD   Destroyer.

Defence suppression   Operations designed to destroy or dislocate enemy anti-aircraft forces either by destroying, jamming or deceiving the defences.

DoD   Department of Defence.

Dual Key Systems   The method by which more than one country is included in the final decision to use nuclear weapons during time of war. This allows for consultation among allies as to the decision to resort to a nuclear attack.

E

ECM   Electronic Countermeasures. A range of electronic and other measures (eg chaff) used to retard the effectiveness of enemy electronic systems, primarily radars, missile guidance systems and communications and surveillance systems.

EECM   Electronic Counter Countermeasures. A range of measures that can be implemented to counteract or reduce the effectiveness of ECM by improving the resistance of radars to jamming for example.

ELINT   Electronic Intelligence.

EMP   Electromagnetic Pulse. The pulse of intense electromagnetic radiation emitted by a nuclear explosion.

Enhanced Radiation   A nuclear weapon whose design maximised the generation of radiation effects over those of blast and heat.

ERAM   Extended Range Anti-Armour Munition.

ERW   Enhanced Radiation Weapon — the so-called neutron bomb — a weapon designed to increase the radiation effect of a given yield at the expense of other effects. In practice ERWs developed for the US Lance missile and 8″ shell have been lower yield weapons than the weapons they have replaced allowing similar results to be achieved against armour using the radiation effect whilst the reduced yield presents less of a threat to nearby connurbations and civilians.

ET   Emerging Technology.

EUCOM   United States European Command.

Eurogroup   Acronym used for informal group of NATO European Defence Ministers.

F

FAR Force Action Rapide — French mobile reserve for overseas or European contingencies.

FASCAM Family of Scatterable Mines.

FEBA Forward Edge of Battle Area.

FOFA Follow On Forces Attack. A modification of US strategic thinking on how to fight a European war now accepted by NATO. FOFA takes some ideas from Air Land Battle and stresses the importance of Soviet follow-on forces to Soviet success. It argues that if those forces can be delayed or disrupted the NATO defences will not be faced with overwhelming odds.

Force de Frappe The French independant nuclear deterrent. Now usually referred to as The Force Nucleaire Strategique.

FRG Federal Republic of Germany.

FROG Free Flight Rocket Over Ground. A rocket without specialised guidance whose ballistic trajectory is determined by its pre-launch elevation and azimuth. Used by NATO to refer to earlier generations of Soviet short range SSM as in Frog 7.

G

GLCM Ground Launched Cruise Missile.

GIUK Greenland-Iceland-UK Gap.

GMPB Guided Missile Patrol Boat.

GSFG Group of South Forces Germany.

H

HAS Hardened Aircraft Shelter — steel and concrete hangarette designed to protect aircraft from all but a direct hit with a conventional weapon.

HNS Host Nation Support — scheme by which European states provide men and equipment to support reinforcing US forces. Assistance ranges from security guards to truck drivers.

HUMINT Human Intelligence — derived from agents in the opposing state or from specially trained individuals and teams inserted into enemy territory or left behind the enemy's advancing forces to gain intelligence.

I

IGB Inter German Border.

INF Intermediate Range Nuclear Forces.

Interdiction Missions intended to penetrate into the enemy's territory and attack his lines of communication. Targets may include vehicles, choke points like bridges, or supply dumps. Operations near the battlefield are termed 'Battlefield Interdiction'.

J

Jamming — The effect of disrupting or confusing an enemy's communications radars and allied equipment. This can be done by electronic means or by the use of such material as chaff.

JCTAMS — Joint Conventional Tactical Missile System — proposal for a 250 km range missile to carry skeet type submunitions.

JSTARS — Joint Surveillance and Targetting Radar System — system to detect, track and provide targetting information to ground and air launched missiles intended to attack mobile and static Warsaw Pact targets.

K

Kt — Kiloton. An explosive yield equal to 1,000 tons of TNT.

L

LAMPS — Light Airborne Multi-Purpose System. Anti-submarine helicopter which operates search radar, sonar buoy and MAD equipment, plus eletronic support equipment.

LAW — Light Anti-Tank Weapon.

LCC — Launch Control Centre. The supporting vehicle for a Cruise Missile TEL, providing launch capability for the missile.

LGB — Lazer Guided Bomb.

LOC — Lines of Communication.

Look-down-radar — Aircraft radar with the ability to distinguish from above airborne targets from the ground clutter produced by the Earth's surface. Cruise Missiles are capable of detection in this way.

LTDP — Long Term Defence Programme.

M

MAC	Military Airlift Command.
MAD	Mutually Assured Destruction.
Main Operating Base	The normal location of a GLCM, such as Greenham Common in England, from which the weapon would be moved to its operational deployment area in time of conflict.
MBFR	Mutual Balanced Force Reductions.
MBT	Main Battle Tank.
MCM	Mine Countermeasures.
MICV	Mechanized Infantry Combat Vehicle — a personnel carrier designed to operate alongside armour on the battlefield instead of just conveying troops to the battle as the armoured personnel carrier. It is heavily armed with cannon and often with ATGW as well.
MLF	Multi-Lateral Force. A scheme for collective NATO nuclear forces.
MLRS	Multiple Launch Rocket System.
MRASM	Medium Range Air to Surface Missile — proposed 400KM range missile for launch from aircraft including the B52 bomber to destroy Warsaw Pact airfields and other targets.
MRL	Multiple Rocket Launcher.
MSC	Military Sealift Command.
Mt	Megaton. The yield of nuclear weapon, equivalent to 1,000,000 tons of TNT.
MSBS	Mer-Sol-Ballistique. Strategique. French term for an SLBM.

N

NADGE	NATO Air Defence Ground Environment — NATO's Air Defence network of radars and command sites.
NAEWF	NATO Airborne Early Warning Force — force of 18 US built E3 AWACS aircraft — jointly manned with command rotating between countries based in Gelenkitchen and operates out of Norway, Turkey and Italy.
NATO	North Atlantic Treaty Organization. A body created by treaty comprising fourteen countries in Europe and North America, guaranteeing mutual assistance and military co-operation.
Navocformed	Naval-On-Call Force, Mediterranean. A multi-national naval force similar to STANAVFORLANT but only called together for particular exercises or missions.
NBC	Nuclear, Biological and Chemical. A NBC suit is available for issue to infantry and other fighting men, in the event of the use of any of these three weapon types on the battlefield.

O

OMG
Operational Manouver Group — Soviet unit designed to penetrate deep into NATO's rear threatening SAM, supplies, airbases, headquarters and key industrial/urban complexes. The intention is to destroy an enemy's will, morale, cohesion and lines of communications. The OMG will enjoy massive artillery, missile, helicopter and air-support and may consist of a division if used to aid an army or an army if designed to achieve a decisive breakthrough for a front. US intelligence reports two new corp sized units being formed in the USSR each with 450MBT which may be intended to act as OMGs.

OTAXI
Organization du Trité de l'Atlantique Nord — French name for NATO.

P

Passive
A detection system that performs its function without emitting radiation — which relies on natural radiation or that emitted by its target as in passive night sight, passive sonar and passive homing.

PGM
Precision Guided Munition.

POMCUS
Prepositional Overseas Material Configured in United States.

Prepositioning
Prepositioning equipment in Europe for use by US and other allied reinforcing forces offers several advantages — it means that heavy equipment can now be left in the country required and does not have to be sent there by sea. All that is now required is to fly the men to the equipment which takes far less time and limits the problem of the very short warning time possible in an European war. The disadvantages of prepositioning are primarily that a duplicate set of equipment costs a great deal for each unit involved, some equipment cannot be stored and the vulnerability of the equipment of the war starts while it is still in store.

PSI
Pounds per square inch overpressure — measure of the pressure above that already imposed by the atmosphere produced by the blast wave of an explosion. 5 PSI would destroy most residential homes.

Q
R

QRA	Quick Reaction Alert.
Radius of Action	Distance which a combat aircraft can fly to perform a mission and return — calculated to allow for flight profile, combat return flight and reserves. As this distance differs with aircraft payload, weather, fuel carried and all of the above factors not to mention the availability of inflight refuelling such figures need to be treated with caution.
RDF	Rapid Deployment Force. US force, 200,000 rising to 440,000 strong by 1990s, designed to give the US a balanced capable force for intervention beyond Europe. In 1983 was orientated towards South West Asia and redesignated as *Centcom?*
Real Time	Something instantaneous, like communications with or between military forces, or instantaneous reconnaissance for example by spy satellites.
Reforger	Return of Forces to Germany — exercise return of forces stationed in the USA to Germany.
REM	Roentegen Equivalent Man — Measure of radiation dose received. A dose of 350-550 rem would kill roughly 50% of those exposed to it if received in a short period of time. This would only be the case in the open — normal buildings would give considerable protection from a 500 rem dose. Longer doses only slightly nearer to the bomb's explosion would however, prove lethal to those indoors as well.
RPU	Remotely Piloted Vehicle.

S

SACEUR	Supreme Allied Commander Europe.
SACLANT	Supreme Allied Commander Atlantic.
SACT	Strategic Arms Limitation Talks.
SADARM	Search and Destroy Armour — shell dispensing anti-tank skeet munitions.
SA	NATO designation for Soviet Surface to Air Missiles as in SA3, SA6, SA10.
SAC	Strategic Air Command.
SAM	Surface to Air Missile.
SDI	Strategic Defense Initiative — President Reagan's.
SFW	Sensor Fused Weapon — bomb containing skeet submunitions — likely to be the first of the ET weapons to enter service in the late 1980s.
SIGINT	Signals Intelligence — intelligence derived from the study of the enemy's signals, traffic, its scope and content.
SLBM	Submarine/Sea Launched Ballistic Missile.
SLCM	Sea Launched Cruise Missiles. Currently being fielded by both superpowers in long-range versions. US weapons come in a variety of antiship (450mls range), land target attack (700ml range) and nuclear strike (1500ml range).
SLOC	Sea Line of Communication.
SNLE	Sous -marine Nucleaire Lance-Engins. French nuclear missile submarines able to carry the MSBS.
Sonar Buoy	A buoy equipped with sonar equipment designed to detect submerged submarines. A passive Sonar Buoy listens for sounds from the submarine whilst an active buoy sends out signals that bounce back from the submarine.
SPG	Self Propelled Gun.
SS	Submarine.
SSB	Submarine armed with Ballistic missiles — main role providing a strategic or threatre deterrent force.
SSC	Coastal submarine.
SSG	Submarine armed with guided cruise missiles — anti ship role.
SSN	Nuclear powered submarine.
SSBN	Nuclear powered submarine armed with ballistic missiles — role strategic deterrence.
SSGN	Nuclear submarine armed with guided cruise missiles.
SSBS	Sol-Sol-Ballistique-Startegique. French term for IRBM.
SSM	Surface to Surface Missile.
Stand-off Weapons	Weapons designed with a range capability that allows them to be launched from outside the immediate defences of their target.
STANAVFORCHAN	Standing Naval Force Channel — standing multi-national naval force of minehunters and sweepers.
STANAVFORLANT	Standing Naval Force Atlantic — standing naval multinational force of destroyers and frigates — fulfills similar mission to ACEMF.
START	Strategic Arms Reduction Talks.
SU	Old designation of Soviet self-propelled guns. US sources now refer to these by the designation M followed by the date when first detected, eg M-1973, M-1975. In some cases Soviet designations are known and are also used, eg 2 S1, 2 S5.

T

TAC	Tactical Air Command.
Tactical Aircraft	Land and Carrier based aircraft capable of carrying out a variety of roles especially in and around the battlefield. This can include the carrying of tactical nuclear weapons.
TAS	Towed Army Sonar. Long-range passive sonar trailed behind ships or submarines.
Teeth-to-tail ratio	The ratio of fighting men (Teeth) to the logistical support personnel and hence non-fighting men (Tail) or armies especially when deployed in an operational area.
TEL	Transporter Erector Launcher — Launcher for GLCM.
TNF	Theatre Nuclear Forces.
TNW	Tactical Nuclear Weapon.
TOW	Tube launched optically Guided Weapon — US long-range ATGW.

U

UKADR	United Kingdom Air Defence Region.
US	United States.
USAFE	United States Airforce Europe.
USAREUR	United States Army Europe.
USSR	Union of Soviet Socialists Republics.

V

VSTOL	Vertical Short Take-Off and Landing.

W

Warsaw Pact	Military Alliance of Eastern Europe comprising some seven countries, which arose in response to the creation of NATO and the re-militarization of West Germany in the 1950's.

Z

Zero Option	A proposal for limiting the deployment of nuclear weapons in Europe, put forward by US President Reagan. Proposal envisaged cancelling US INF deployment in return for dismantling of Soviet forces.

Index

A

B

C

N

O

P

Introduction to illustration sources and credits

All of the material used in this work was obtained from unclassified sources. Some of the material is adapted from standard sources like the *Military Balance*, *Soviet Military Power*, the *NATO-Warsaw Pact Force Comparison* and has been amended to reflect different assumptions or to deal with conflicting evidence between these sources. In these cases and where other material has been adapted the figures here should not be taken as being approved by the original source.

p.9 *Military Balance 1984/5* (IISS, 1984). **p.10** Calculated from *Military Balance 1984/5*. **p.15** NATO Information Service. **p.20** top — *NATO and the Warsaw Pact Force Comparisons* (NATO 1984) Figures for long range missiles show the worldwide total. **p.20** bottom — *NATO-Warsaw Pact Force Comparison* Figures exclude French and Spanish forces. **p.21** top — *NATO-Warsaw Pact Force Comparison* Figures exclude French and Spanish forces and Soviet forces in the Western military districts. **p.22** Estimated from *Military Balance 1984/5, Soviet Military Power 1981 (USGPO 1981), ibid, 1985*; M Urban, *Soviet Land Forces* (Ian Allen 1985). **p.23** Department of Defence (D o D) figures. **p.24-25** Extrapolated from *Military Balance 1984/5*; *NATO-Warsaw Pact Force Comparison*; *Armed Forces Journal July 1983*; M Urban, *Soviet Land Forces*. **p.28-29** Estimated from *Military Balance 1984/5*; *Soviet Military Power 1985*; M Urban *Soviet Land Forces*; and various articles on *South East Air Review* and *Aviation News*. Aircraft figures includes OCU aircraft likely to be committed for action over the Central Front and forces based in Denmark. Excludes British, French and Soviet air defence forces which are assumed to be held back for the defence of their own airspace. **p.30** Based upon *Military Balance 1984/5*; *Military Technology*, No. 11 1984, *Soviet Military Power 1985*. **p.31** *Military Balance 1984/5*; Aircraft estimates from *South East Air Review* and other data. **p.32** top — *Military Balance 1984/5*; *Military Technology* No. 11 1984; Tornado radius is illustrative only. **p.32** bottom — as for chart on p.31. **p.34** top — Figures from *Military Balance 1984/5*; *Soviet Military Power 1985*. **p.34** bottom — *Military Balance 1984/5*. **p.35** *Military Balance 1984/5* Air figures estimated. **p.40** Adapted from *Armed Forces Journal* May 1984. **p.42** *German Defence White Paper 1983*; *Michelin Guide to Germany 1984*. **p.43** US D o D. **p.43** Adapted from SM Meyer "*Soviet Theatre Nuclear Forces* — Part 1"; *Adelphi Paper* No. 187. **p.45** *Statement on the Defence Estimates 1976, ibid 1977*; *Military Balance 1973/4, 1984/5*; *Statement on the Defence Estimates 1974-1985*. **p.46** Estimated from *US D o D Annual Report 1985*; *Military Balance 1984/5*; *Soviet Military Power 1985*. **p.52** based on '*Armed Forces Journal*' April 1985; *D o D Annual Report FY 1985*; ibid 1986. Arrival times are estimates based on announced readiness, speed of ships and distance to be covered with an allowance for loading and unloading. Times might be substantially longer if shipping had to adopt countermeasures against Soviet

Naval activity or if delays occured at departures or arrival ports. **p.53** *Soviet Military Power 1985*; US D o D data. **p.54** Estimated from a variety of sources including *The Military Balance 1984/5*. **p.55** US reinforcements estimated. Figures reflect aircraft assigned to Combat units. They exclude 30 Dutch, 30 French, and 70 British OCU aircraft. This follows the *Military Balance 1984/5* which does not distinguish between Belgian or German OCU and Combat units. The *Trinational* ? Tornado Training Establishment in the UK has 50 Tornados that might be available as might a number of armed advanced trainer aircraft. **p.57** *German Defence White Paper 1983*; West German figures include French but exclude Spanish force. Spain's possible contribution is indicated on p.34 & 58. **p.58** estimated from the *Military Balance 1984/5* and other data. Figures exclude 14 German and 6 Spanish ASW aircraft that might be available for Atlantic operations. **p.60-61** Figures from J R Hull, *Anti-submarine Warfare* (Ian Allan 1984). **p.60** US D o D figures. **p.79** Adapted from *The Illustrated Encyclopedia of Aircraft* part 146; M Skinner, *USAFE, A primer of Modern Combat in Europe*; *Armed Forces Journal* June 1985. **p.85** top — *Armed Forces Journal*, March 1985; J M Epstein *Measuring Military Power*; *The Soviet Air threat to Europe* (Taylor and Francis, 1984). **p.89** US D o D estimates; *Soviet Military Power 1985*. **p.92** *Janes Defence Weekly*, 9.6.84. **p.93** *Nuclear Bomb Effects Computer*; *The Nuclear War File*, Professor Laurence Martin (Ebury Press 1983) 5PSI and 500 Rem circles shown for a variety of weapons — 1kt is typical of artillery shells, 20kt might be the yield of a tactical nuclear bomb, 150kt is the estimated yield of one Soviet SS20 warhead. **p.94** *Soviet Military Power 1985*; assumes that 5PSI would be adequate to disable a Cruise missile launcher. **p.95** top US D o D. **p.103** *Military Balance 1984/5*: estimates based on M Simpson, *The Independent Nuclear State* (MacMillan 1983); *Army, Naval and Air Statistical Record*. **p.104** *Military Balance 1962/3, 1984/5*. **p.105** The shield range for Hades reflects ambiguity about whether the missile could be fired from the border to obtain maximum range or from a tactically less vulnerable position back in France. **p.107** *Armées d'Ajourdhui*, February, March 1985; *Military Balance 1984/5*. **p.111** Calculated from *Military Balance 1984/5*. **p.120** J R Golden et al, *Conventional Deterrence* Lexington Books, 1984). **p.121** US D o D figures. **p.122** based upon *Statement on the Defence Estimates 1980*. **p.123** *Military Balance 1984/5*. **p.126** top US D o D. **p.126** bottom left — *Statement on the Defence Estimates 1985* **p.126** bottom right — *Statement on the Defence Estimates 1984*. **p.127** top — *Armed Forces Journal*, July 1984. New accounting measure which attempts to include total expenditure by US forces in Europe in the balance. **p.127** bottom left — *Statement on the Defence Estimates 1985*. **p.128** *Military Balance 1984/5*. **p.129** *Soviet Military Power 1985*; *NATO-Warsaw Pact Force comparison*. **p.130** S Talbot, *Deadly Gambits* (Picador 1984); NATO-Warsaw Pact Force comparison. **p.131** SS20 locations from *Military Balance 1984/5*.